SEX EDUCATION FOR THE HEALTH PROFESSIONAL:
A CURRICULUM GUIDE

SEMINARS IN PSYCHIATRY

Series Editor
Milton Greenblatt, M.D.

Assistant Dean, School of Medicine
Professor of Psychiatry, and
Director of Social and Community Psychiatry
University of California at Los Angeles

Chief of Staff, Veterans Administration Hospital
Brentwood, Los Angeles

Other Books in Series:

SEX EDUCATION FOR
THE HEALTH PROFESSIONAL:
A CURRICULUM GUIDE

Edited by

Norman Rosenzweig, M.D.
Chairman, Department of Psychiatry
Sinai Hospital of Detroit

F. Paul Pearsall, Ph.D.
Chief, Problems of Daily Living Clinic
Sinai Hospital of Detroit

GRUNE & STRATTON
A Subsidiary of Harcourt Brace Jovanovich, Publishers
New York   San Francisco   London

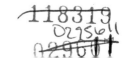

Grune & Stratton, Inc.
111 Fifth Avenue
New York, New York 10003

Distributed in the United Kingdom by
Academic Press, Inc. (London) Ltd.
24/28 Oval Road, London NW 1

Library of Congress Catalog Number 78-69565
International Standard Book Number 0-8089-1100-7
Printed in the United States of America

Contents

Foreword

Freud, Havelock-Ellis, Kinsey, Masters and Johnson, and other pioneers have given society a new impetus to examine its instinctive repressions, to liberate its sexual attitudes, and to experiment more actively and openly with new social forms of pairing and mating. As a result, in recent decades a veritable revolution has followed. Many in society have come to appreciate how great our ignorance regarding sex practices and attitudes has been, and how crippling the effect of this ignorance has been on the lives of many thousands of individuals. This realization has been accompanied by a proliferation of so-called specialists, counselors, and consultants; the mushrooming of curricula; and a veritable forest of clinics—many of them half-baked—for the treatment of sexual inadequacies. The spawning of clinics has run ahead of the current capacity of reputable training establishments to produce quality personnel. Indeed, many reputable training establishments have only recently seriously accepted responsibility to supply the field with trained manpower. Only recently, for example, have medical schools begun to cope with the appalling ignorance of students in matters sexual, although the data supporting that ignorance have been around for a long time.

In one state, California, the legislature has been aroused to the point of *prescribing* special sex education for professional groups practicing in this area, and has made specific recommendations to the profession of medicine to organize proper instruction for medical students before bestowing the graduate degree. The goal of this instruction would be not only to make medical students more aware of the body of knowledge and new techniques, but to make them more comfortable with their own sexuality and, therefore, more objective with their future clients.

This excellent compendium of presentations, *Sex Education for the Health Professional,* is directed to all professionals who claim some degree of domain in the area of sex inadequacies, sex pathology, and the treatment thereof. The need for education through sophisticated instruction is very great. Although their training in human relationships may have been extensive, these professionals, psychiatrists included, do not necessarily possess the background and technology to be truly effective sex therapists. Some practicing professionals got their orientations before the Masters and Johnson era. In addition, a whole zone of mystery is beginning to be explored—namely, the sex disturbances and pathologies associated with physical disease that, to an important degree, demand experience in liaison medicine. The sex lives of the brain damaged, the paraplegics, the quadriplegics, prostatectomy cases, neuropathies, patients receiving antihypertensive drugs, cases of postmyocardial infarction, mastectomies and hysterectomies, and the debilitations of terminal illness are being actively probed. The relationship of physical pathology to sex adaptation, and the social implications, including particularly the reactions of sexual partners, more and more are coming in for study and treatment.

Rosenzweig and Pearsall have wisely perceived a clear and present danger if the expansion of sex therapy is left in the hands of ill-trained persons, charlatans, or exploiters. They have, therefore, developed this collation, based on the work of the most reputable minds in the field, whose presentations, as far as possible, are founded on definitive research or on vast personal commitment and experience.

Milton Greenblatt, M.D.
Editor in Chief
Seminars in Psychiatry

Preface

The pioneering work of William Masters and Virginia Johnson in outlining their successful and widely accepted treatment program for sexual distress has resulted in a proliferation of "sex therapists." Considering the sexual health of persons not only became respectable, but came to be viewed as an essential consideration in all attempts to help persons function well in their daily lives. Unfortunately, educational programs in human sexuality have developed at a slower rate than sex therapy or counseling programs, resulting in some instances in attempts by persons in the helping professions to counsel others toward sexual health with little or no training in the several dimensions of human sexual functioning. Help became a primary motive, and a more important issue of educated help was neglected.

We believe this book is the first attempt to bring together in a systematic fashion the various pedagogical approaches of our contemporary leaders in sex education as they relate to the training and work of health care professionals. It is intended to facilitate discussion and examination of the several dimensions of sexuality curriculum design and as a medium for sharing ideas and orientations toward such curricula. It is hoped that the work of the contributors will be viewed as "assessment in progress," promoting evaluation of educational efforts in a field of study that is growing rapidly, at times in unclear directions.

As will be seen in the contents of the volume, many successful human sexuality educational programs have reflected the leadership and charismatic qualities of the teachers. It has been our intent to preserve these qualities in the contributions to this volume, in a matrix which addresses such pedagogical issues as problems of deciding curriculum content, choosing appropriate teaching methods and materials, striking the proper balance between attitudinal change and imparting of information, and between attention to general subject matter vis a vis specialized subject matter. Some of our contributors give a highly personal presentation, relating their own experiences, while others pursue an academic approach and rely heavily on research data. Some follow a middle course. We regard all as equally valuable in presenting to the reader the variety of approaches which true experts in the field have adopted. We believe the readers can profit most by exposure to the various viewpoints and techniques presented here, and by forming their own conclusions regarding what will work best in their own unique setting. We are not immune to value judgments, but given the many individual differences in approach and concept of our authors, it has been our intent that our own values should not constrain the expressions of our contributors; we hope we have been successful in achieving this aim.

For the most part, this volume has been a collaborative venture, each contributor being aware not only of the scope of one's own contribution, but how it would relate to the contributions of others. Nevertheless, in the interest of the volume as a whole, it has sometimes been necessary to revise or condense a particular contribution to conform to space requirements, to avoid excessive duplication, or to facilitate coordination of the contributions within the topical framework. Although we have attempted to obtain a certain logical continuity, we have striven to avoid tampering with the substance of the contributions. Similarly, we have sought to preserve the individual style of expression, because we believe that the pedagogical style is as integral to the lesson as the formal content. All of our contributors are outstanding educators in a field in which there are so few experts. We apologize to any of our authors who may feel that our editorial revision has distorted their literary intent.

If effective dealing with people's sexual health involves reducing myths and presenting documented knowledge about sexual behavior and function in a sensitive nonjudgmental manner, then who teaches the teachers and what and how the teachers are taught become central concerns. This book is intended for a reader who holds these concerns.

We wish to express our appreciation and thanks to Dr. Milton Greenblatt; to Ms. Nancy K. Mundt for her invaluable, generous, and intensive editorial assistance; to Mrs. Lucy Lee for researching the references; and to Mrs. Betty Taylor and Ms. Billie Jewell for their expert secretarial contributions. Above all, we wish to acknowledge our indebtedness to the greatest assemblage of sexperts to be found between the covers of a single volume.

Norman Rosenzweig, M.D.
F. Paul Pearsall, Ph.D.

Contributors

Francois E. Alouf, M.D.
Associate Professor
Director of Education;
Director, Human Sexuality Program
Northwestern University Medical School
Chicago, Illinois

Michael S. Aronoff, M.D.
University Physician
Indiana University Student Health Center
Bloomington, Indiana

Ronald Bantis
Media Technician
Department of Psychiatry
Sinai Hospital of Detroit
Detroit, Michigan

Ruth Beasley
Training Seminar Coordinator
Institute for Sex Research;
Ph.D. Student, Graduate Library School
Indiana University
Bloomington, Indiana

Oliver Bjorksten, M.D.
Assistant Professor of Psychiatry
Medical University of South Carolina
Charleston, South Carolina

Mary M. Briggs, D.A.
Sexual Health Consultant
Program in Human Sexuality
University of Minnesota Medical School
Minneapolis, Minnesota

Mary S. Calderone, M.D., M.P.H.
Co-Founder and President
Sex Information and Educational Council of the United States
Hempstead, New York

Theodore M. Cole, M.D.
Professor and Chairman
Department of Physical Medicine and Rehabilitation
University of Michigan Medical Center
Ann Arbor, Michigan

Sheldon Fellman, M.D.
Clinical Assistant Professor of Surgery (Urology)
University of Michigan Medical School
Ann Arbor, Michigan

John C. Flatter, Ed.D.
Therapist
Problems of Daily Living Clinic
Department of Psychiatry
Sinai Hospital of Detroit;
Adjunct Professor, College of Education
Wayne State University
Detroit, Michigan

Paul H. Gebhard, Ph.D.
Director
Institute for Sex Research, Inc.
Professor of Anthropology
Indiana University
Bloomington, Indiana

Richard Green, M.D.
Professor
Departments of Psychiatry and Behavioral Science and Psychology
State University of New York at Stony Brook
Stony Brook, New York

E. Ingvarda Hanson, R.N., M.S.N.
Certified Sex Educator
American Association of Sex Educators, Counselors and Therapists
Associate Professor, College of Nursing
Wayne State University
Detroit, Michigan

James P. Held, B.ChE.
Research Fellow
Evaluation Coordinator
Program in Human Sexuality
University of Minnesota Medical School
Minneapolis, Minnesota

Harold I. Lief, M.D.
Professor of Psychiatry
Director, Division of Family Study
Marriage Council of Philadelphia
Center for the Study of Sex Education in Medicine
University of Pennsylvania
Philadelphia, Pennsylvania

William L. Maurice, M.D., F.R.C.P. (C)
Associate Professor
Department of Psychiatry
University of British Columbia
Director, University of British Columbia Sex Therapy Unit
Vancouver, British Columbia

Ted McIlvenna, M.Div., Ph.D.
Academic Dean
Institute for Advanced Study of Human Sexuality
Co-Director, National Sex Forum
San Francisco, California

William R. Miller, Ph.D.
Director of Research
Marriage Council of Philadelphia
Assistant Professor of Psychology in Psychiatry
University of Pennsylvania School of Medicine
Philadelphia, Pennsylvania

John Money, Ph.D.
Professor of Medical Psychology
Associate Professor of Pediatrics
The Johns Hopkins University and Hospital
Baltimore, Maryland

F. Paul Pearsall, Ph.D.
Chief
Problems of Daily Living Clinic
Department of Psychiatry
Sinai Hospital of Detroit
Detroit, Michigan

David M. Priver, M.D.
Attending Staff
Department of Obstetrics and Gynecology
Sinai Hospital of Detroit
Detroit, Michigan

Domeena Renshaw, M.D.
Director
Sexual Dysfunction Clinic
Loyola University
Maywood, Illinois

Norman Rosenzweig, M.D.
Chairman
Department of Psychiatry
Sinai Hospital of Detroit
Detroit, Michigan

William R. Stayton, Th.D.
Assistant Professor of Family Study in Psychiatry
University of Pennsylvania School Of Medicine
Bryn Mawr, Pennsylvania

George Szasz, M.D.
Associate Professor
Department of Health Care and Epidemiology
Faculty of Medicine
University of British Columbia
Vancouver, British Columbia

John Vasconcellos
Assemblyman, California Legislature
San Jose, California

Raymond W. Waggoner, M.D., ScD.
Professor and Chairman Emeritus
Department of Psychiatry
University of Michigan Medical School
Ann Arbor, Michigan

Douglas Wallace, Ph.D.
Acting Director
Human Sexuality Program
University of California Medical School
San Francisco, California

Diane B. Watson, M.D., F.R.C.P. (C)
Mental Health Services
South Burnaby
Burnaby, British Columbia

Ann Marie Williams, Ph.D.
Research Staff
Marriage Council of Philadelphia;
Instructor in Psychiatry
Department of Psychiatry
Division of Family Study
University of Pennsylvania School of Medicine
Philadelphia, Pennsylvania

PART I

Developing a Pedagogical Approach to Sex Education for the Professional

Norman Rosenzweig
F. Paul Pearsall

Introduction

The inclusion of instruction in human sexuality in the medical school curriculum has been a fairly recent phenomenon, as Dr. Lief points out in his chapter. Even today there are many differences between programs in the amount of time devoted to the subject and in the pedagogical approach. Many programs continue to experience problems in the teaching of this subject, and it is hoped that the present volume will prove helpful to those attempting to find solutions for such problems.

The reasons for the difficulties are many and complex. In her chapter, Dr. Calderone traces the historic roots of the antisexual bias that has characterized the social morality of the Western world more or less since earliest Christian times. This antisexual bias has had multiple consequences that have contributed to our present pedagogical problems, not the least of which is the fact that medical students and their teachers alike were raised in cultures that regarded the very subject of sex as unwholesome, and shrouded it with an aura of sin and guilt. To speak of the "pleasures of the flesh" was to give evidence of having a dirty mind, if not a sick one. Sexual innocence (or ignorance) was regarded as a virtue, and sexual knowledge and attempts to impart it or acquire it were regarded as unsavory. This is well demonstrated by the words of Dr. Howard Kelly, Gynecologist-in-Chief at Johns Hopkins, quoted in Dr. Calderone's chapter.

Thus, despite the widespread public belief and expectation that physicians were knowledgeable about human sexuality, doctors were plagued by the same emotional barriers to the acquisition of knowledge about sex as laymen. While great progress had been made in the physical and even in the biological sciences, Western medicine had little factual information and much misinformation about human sexual functioning.

One might wonder here, since sexual prudery was peculiar chiefly to Western Christian society, whether the cultures of the East, to which we are indebted for so much, were any better schooled in the subject. Unfortunately, while sexuality was approached much more directly and openly in the East, it was not subjected to scientific study. Although much was said and much advice given in Chinese, Japanese, and Hindu cultures, the products were a mixture of information and misinformation. Further, the context of such communications was the religious-philosophical orientation of the particular cultural group, and hence was authoritative and gnostic; therefore, there was no need to question the information nor to improve it. Knowledge of sex was often a part of folk wisdom, and a kernel of recognizable truth tended to endow the entire message with verisimilitude.

Thus the dawn of the movement for the scientific study of sex in the latter part of the Victorian era had no foundation on which to build, either from East or West. These first efforts were retarded by censorship even as they accelerated the progress of sex education. When scientists and scholars began writing about human sexuality in learned publications, such publications were likely to be banned as obscene and their authors attacked.

Another retardant was the fact that those who asked the first scientific questions about human sexuality were themselves raised in the Victorian climate of prudery and superstition. Therefore they did not always ask the right questions and often they came up with the wrong answers. For instance, with the increasing acceptance of evolutionary theory, mankind came to be viewed by "enlightened" scientists as but a high species of animal. It seemed only logical to extrapolate studies of animal sexual behavior to humans. Society considered it much more permissible to make direct observations of the mating behaviors of beasts, and since man was believed to function in similar fashion, animal studies were regarded as an appropriate yet decent way to learn about the taboo subject. In consequence, human sexual behavior was believed to be instinctive and biologically determined, as it was in horses and cattle. Unfortunately, these assumptions completely ignored the importance of human psychology to human sexuality and resulted in the dissemination of a great deal of misinformation as scientific fact. We are still struggling with the problems of unlearning "facts" about human sexuality extrapolated from animal studies.

Calderone emphasizes that even those who sought to explore human sexuality from the psychological side were so conditioned by the notion of biological determinism that they made their observations through a distorting lens. Thus Freud interpreted the stages of psychosexual development that he observed in his patients as biologically determined phenomena. He regarded human sexuality as instinctive and believed libido to consist of quantities of biological energy comparable to and subject to the same laws as energy in physics. His clinical conclusions also reflected the prevalent Victorian attitudes toward sexuality. For example, he believed that masturbation could lead to neurasthenia due to an excessive discharge of sexual energy.

As Calderone points out, Havelock Ellis, in contrast to Freud and Krafft-Ebing, was interested in the normal rather than the pathological aspects of sexuality. Unfortunately, as far as the scientific literature is concerned, he is known more by his name than by his work, which was based largely on anecdotal rather than scientific data. While he was one of the first to recognize that the prevalent social value system regarding sex was idiosyncratic to the time and culture, and while he regarded variant aspects of sexual behavior as normal that Freud would have considered sick, he had little impact on the accepted medical "knowledge" of his time.

All of which is to say that even were it not for the other impediments to the teaching of human sexuality in medical schools, there would not have been sufficient accurate information available to warrant special courses on human sexuality until the pioneering researches of Kinsey, Masters and Johnson, and others. Indeed, much of what was taught in courses in physiology and psychology supposedly dealing with human sexuality was replete with inaccuracies, misinformation, and myths.

Nevertheless, as Lief emphasizes, even following the information explosion produced by 20th century research on human sexuality, the medical schools were still not ready to teach the subject, nor were the students prepared to learn it.

Traditional medical education begins with the medical student's confrontation with a cadaver. The months spent in the anatomy laboratory serve to allow the student to develop an emotional armor that will insulate him or her from the shocks of subsequent exposure to death and disease. This emotional insulation makes it possible for the student to intellectually and impersonally learn facts and procedures that otherwise might provoke intense anxiety. Although well suited to the objective acquisition of abstract information, this walling off of the student's emotional reactions is antithetical to the teaching of human sexuality and leads to the kinds of difficulties in relation to the sexuality of patients described by Lief.

Human sexuality cannot be taught as another set of compartmentalized facts. If students are truly to learn about human sexuality they must somehow become aware of, confront, examine, and come to terms with their own sexual feelings. Therefore, an approach very different from the traditional is needed. Later in this book a variety of such approaches, developed in various centers, are reviewed; but Lief's chapter admirably summarizes the problems of pedagogical philosophy and practice which must be faced in developing a sexuality curriculum.

Nontraditional approaches to the teaching of human sexuality would have been impossible in earlier social climates, since they would have run headlong into the prevailing social taboos and would thereby have aroused further resistance.

Fortunately for all of us, the 20th century has witnessed a significant change in the social climate. Many of the factors contributing to this change are well described in Dr. Calderone's chapter, and she herself has made significant contributions. In the United States a very important factor was the changing attitudes of the courts toward so-called pornography. These court decisions were instrumental in breaking down the legal enforcement of public prudery and censorship in this country from the early 1920s onward.

We will return to the subject of censorship in the introduction to the section on methodology. For now, we can take some comfort in the great distance the law has come, at least in the State of California, as illustrated by the pioneering legislation described by Vasconcellos and Wallace. This chapter brings us full circle from the primitive attitudes described in the first section of Calderone's chapter. Rather than endorsing ignorance, the farsighted legislators of California have recognized the need for accurate information and proper education in human sexuality for professionals entrusted with the responsibility of counseling others about their sexual problems.

Mary S. Calderone

1

Historical Perspectives on the Human Sexuality Movement: Hindsights, Insights, Foresights

INTRODUCTION

For any professional moving actively into the field of human sexuality or simply expanding knowledge or raising consciousness about it, it is useful, indeed imperative, to begin with a brief historical overview. We need not examine minute details, but we can identify intersecting cycles and repetitions of patterns in sex attitudes and behavior over the centuries that help to place contemporary developments in context.

HINDSIGHTS*

Ancient Times. Sex has always been of intense interest to every human being of no matter what age, gender, culture, or century. Such interest has usually taken one or more of several directions, relating to the prevention or fostering of reproduction, the status of women, or the pursuit of pleasure. The relation of sex to religion has almost always been extremely critical, with special importance often attached to the loss of virginity in a ritualistic manner such as a sacrifice to the gods. An offshoot of such ritualism was prostitution as a sacred aspect of worship, as in ancient Egypt and elsewhere.

In Judaic tradition, procreation was considered the dominant reason for sexual functioning. Marriage was vital for survival of the Jewish

*See Acknowledgement, page 20.

7

people, and failure to marry could result in exclusion from the religious and social community. Homosexuality and bestiality were forbidden because of their nonprocreativeness rather than for moral reasons. Although sexual pleasure was not of primary importance, it was nevertheless approved for both husbands and wives. In fact, a wife who did not receive sexual satisfaction from her husband was entitled to divorce him! But sex itself was not looked upon as sacred, nor did it assume the importance that it achieved among the ancient Greeks, particularly in Athens where classic art forms portrayed all kinds of sexual activities as highly regarded aspects of daily life. Thus Greek idealism accepted homosexual relationships in which older men became the sexual mentors of younger males who had passed puberty.

The Roman view was quite different. Sexuality was pragmatically accepted as a physical activity. Toward the close of the Roman Empire, sex in daily life assumed more and more the characteristics of hedonism and license that eventually brought it into conflict with Christianity, thereby setting the stage for the recurring Puritanism of later centuries.

The Middle Ages. From the fall of the western part of the Roman Empire to the beginning of the Renaissance, western Europe's attitudes regarding the nature and role of human sexuality were formulated by leaders of the early Christian church. The theology that set moral standards stressed two ideals: sex for procreation only, and total celibacy. Even though the act that might lead to procreation was acceptable for married couples, the absolute asceticism of the times frowned on sexual pleasure in either husband or wife. Nevertheless, sexual pleasure continued to be valued and sought. Even the enforcement of official celibacy within the Church was remarkably ineffectual, and problems relating to prostitution, licentiousness, and pregnancy among priests and nuns continued to plague the Roman Catholic Church. In spite of the Biblically based strictures against homosexuality, it was well known that much same-sex behavior occurred among the so-called celibate. One minor way in which the church was able to exert its power during the Middle Ages was in its successful advocacy of the man-above–woman-below coital position as the only proper one. This is now generally known as the "missionary" position.

The attempts by Christianity to control the sexuality of each human being, whether layman or clergy, suffered constant setbacks, partly because of the stubborn insistence of human nature, and partly because of the influence of external events. Crusaders, for example, became aware of different sexual practices and attitudes in the lands through which they traveled and fought, and those who survived brought these home to western Europe.

During medieval times, just as during the much later era of

Puritanism, harsh punishment, such as self-flagellation to bleeding for any sin of illicit sex, or even for desire for it, or the more powerful obsession with witchcraft and its rituals, took over literally with a vengeance. Sexual desire was itself considered to be an infernal bewitchment. Because women provoked the desire, they were seen as instruments of the devil. These beliefs in possession by Satan were to result in the extraordinary trials of the Spanish Inquisition.

Whether as reaction to, or as logical outcome of, the violence being done to the sexual component of human life, a phenomenon known as the Age of Chivalry appeared in France in the 11th and 12th centuries. Upper class women, who previously had been regarded as chattels, were placed on a pedestal and accorded a position of distant unattainability. Men fought for a lady's favors; noblemen sang under her window; young page boys swooned for love of her; but everyone in the game knew that, except for her husband, she was unreachable. This was the age of iron chastity belts, some of which protected anus as well as vulva. (In a way, this phase presages the artificiality of 17th and 18th century France under Louis XIV and Louis XVI, when lords and ladies of the court just as unrealistically played games of rustic courtship with shepherds and shepherdesses.) The rules of chivalrous courtship were complex and based on the concept of "pure" love. In its highest form, consummation of that love was forever (at least officially) denied. At the same time, there was obsession or at least great preoccupation with sex, and the social standards of sexual morality were clearly and unrealistically in conflict with human sexual desires and actual behavior.

The Renaissance. During this period, the intellectual or artistic man (and to some extent, woman) came into ascendancy as an individual, and sexual expression in art, literature, and life itself was more simply and realistically accepted. As the northern Italian urban centers grew in wealth and power, people's minds stretched to encompass the known world and to imagine an even greater world. The basic unit of measurement of secular glory became the human being and his achievements. Sex, being human, was not so much a point of conflict between men and women and their religious beliefs as an expression of their expanded horizons. There was a return to values of Greek idealism, and labeling some expressions, such as homosexuality, as vices stemmed more from tradition than from religious reasons. Eventually these freer expressions came to border on the casual and were reflected in overt sexual behavior at the very highest secular and religious levels. The concurrent appearance and pandemic spread of syphilis in the 16th century highlighted a licentiousness reminiscent of the state of affairs in the same land 1500 years previously.

Once again, in 1517, the pendulum swung with scythe-like effect when Martin Luther nailed his views to a church door. He challenged official Christian doctrines as unrealistic in relation to sexual and other forms of human behavior, and postulated that so-called sexual evils resulted from the inability of people to live up to overly rigid church standards. He recognized clearly that to be alive was to be sexual, and he stated that chastity and celibacy were not necessarily virtues simply because they were church-imposed.

Calvin, on the other hand, believed the rules of the Roman Church did not go far enough. He advocated an ultra-rigid view that classed singing, dancing, gluttony, and other pleasurable activities with adultery and promiscuity. In fact, Calvinism provoked such a Roman Catholic over-reaction that Pope Paul IV ordered clothing painted over the nude figures of Michelangelo's Last Judgment in the Sistine Chapel!

Seventeenth and Eighteenth Centuries. The explosion of knowledge during this period led to many changes in European thinking. Previous blind dependence on literal interpretation of the scriptural word gave way to the increased rationalism associated with scientific enlightenment. A less inhibited attitude toward sex during the long reign of Elizabeth I is evident in Shakespeare's plays, with their many fearless and accepting portrayals of sexual events, coupled with his forceful use of sexual terminology.

Elizabeth, however, was succeeded by King James VI of Scotland, who became King James I of England. Having suffered a rigid Calvinistic upbringing, he could not tolerate the liberated Elizabethan attitudes. Some extreme Calvinists, calling themselves Puritans, emigrated to America via Holland, taking their rigidities with them. Under Cromwell, others who remained in England were able to reimpose strictures against such sensual delights as dancing, singing, the theatre, sex for pleasure as well as for procreation, and even such phallic rituals as dancing around a maypole. (A decade later, during the Restoration, the maypoles were re-erected to unprecedented heights.)

And so back and forth, in England and on the Continent, the struggle between sexual repression and liberalism went on, with sexual liberalism temporarily restored in England during the Restoration, and in France by the age of Louis XIV. Meanwhile the churches, as official keepers of morality, continued their efforts to persuade people to regulate, manage, negate, suppress, or completely repress the sexual side of their nature. Our Puritan heritage is reflected in the attitudes of many people of today who are unable to cope with human sensuality and who, in the face of its irrepressibility, try to deny its existence. These attempts never succeeded, for as Davies commented, "The consequence was that the Puritans, in their endeavors to compel men to be good (as they understood goodness), defeated their own ends."[1]

Pre-Victorianism and Victorianism. Ambivalence continued to mark human attitudes and behavior about sexuality. Sexual standards in late 18th century England once again became stricter, probably in response to the excesses of the French Revolution across the Channel. Then, during the first half of the 19th century, a mood of romanticism swept across England, with much interest in and agitation for socialism, free love, eugenics, birth control, equal rights for women, and marital reform. When Victoria gained her throne, a countermovement began, and in the second half of the 19th century the rigid, puritanical sexual code known as Victorianism developed. Tables and pianos did not have legs but limbs to be draped or clothed in pantalettes. There was such antipathy to any natural approach to bodily functions that euphemisms were used even for "pregnancy."

As in other repressive eras, the unpublicized part of Victorian life, as characterized by Marcus,[2] was incredibly pornographic and licentious. The self-appointed guardians of public morals were united and organized. The medical profession, especially, appears to have been obsessed by masturbation, the many ills and depravities supposedly resulting from its practice and methods for suppressing it. As a result, parents put their children, particularly their sons, through inhuman punishments and treatment to prevent masturbation. These same Victorian gentlemen, who expected their wives never to experience, or certainly never to display, any erotic pleasure, then turned to the hypersexual activities of the underworld for their own satisfaction.

During the last few years of the 19th century, Richard von Krafft-Ebing of Germany embodied the official Victorian antipathy to sex in his book *Psychopathia Sexualis,* in which he made it clear that he "viewed human sexual behavior as a collection of loathsome diseases . . . (which) probably did more to elicit a disgust with sex than any other single volume."[3] According to Krafft-Ebing, the only "normal" sexual pattern was occasional intercourse during the early years of marriage for the purpose of begetting, with only the husband experiencing orgasm. Any other sexual activity was identified as perversion. He developed a terminology for such deviations as fetishism, homosexuality, and nymphomania, which is still in common use although perceived somewhat differently today. His specialty of forensic psychiatry led him to chronicle all manner of sex crimes in lurid and overabundant detail. However, he did most damage by insisting that "masturbation is the soil out of which all sexual variations seem to grow . . ."[4] and that any sexual manifestations in children or the elderly are pathological. Because his theories were known to the medical profession throughout the western world, they reinforced the sexual fears of people, physicians included, whose backgrounds inclined them to Puritanism.

One startling example occurred at the very highest levels of American medicine. At the meeting of the American Medical Association in 1899, a Chicago gynecologist, Dr. Denslow Lewis, presented a paper, "The Gynecologic Considerations of the Sexual Act." In it, he described sexual responsiveness in women, including the role of the clitoris and multiple orgasms. He recommended strongly that girls and young women receive sexual education, and indeed was an advocate of the rights of women.

The editor of the Journal of the AMA refused to publish this paper, and Lewis then brought up the matter at the next meeting of the AMA House of Delegates in 1900. Among the arguments presented was the following:

> With all due respect to Dr. Lewis, I am strongly opposed to dwelling on these elementary physiologic facts in public audience. I am very sorry he has read the paper. I think we can sum up these matters very safely and be guided by our common sense and experience. The husband should show due respect to the wife, and the wife to the husband in the consideration of this subject, and I do not believe in the current teaching of the day . . . I should be very sorry if in this country these matters became as freely talked about as they have been on the other side of the water. I do not believe mutual pleasure in the sexual act has any particular bearing on the happiness of life; that is the lowest possible view of happiness in married life . . . I do hope we shall not have to go into details in discussing this subject. It is not necessary. Its discussion is attended with more or less filth and we besmirch ourselves by discussing it in public.[5]

These words were actually spoken by Dr. Howard Kelly, then Gynecologist-in-Chief at the Johns Hopkins School of Medicine! Our present society still has not recovered from the effects of such beliefs.

The Age of Science. After Queen Victoria's death in 1901, a series of giant figures emerged to lay the groundwork for escape from this sexual morass. They undertook to replace overcharged emotion with reason and research, to understand human sexuality and, by understanding it, to manage it responsibly and at the same time, enjoyably.

The first of these was Sigmund Freud, who viewed many "perversions" as signs of immaturity rather than of gross sexual pathology. He denied any link between masturbation and sexual deviation, but suggested instead that masturbation, which could logically be linked to nocturnal emissions, might cause neurosis. Except for homosexuality, he considered most of the so-called deviations to be illnesses, but he did not look upon them as loathsome. He also recognized the existence and importance of sexuality in earliest childhood and the critical role of parents in the child's sexual evolution. Gagnon comments ". . . the shock for adults of Freud's discoveries was not that children might be involved in sexual activity, but that this activity was not confined to a few evil children and was, in fact, an essential precursor and component of the development of the character structure of the adult."[6] Freud's eminence as a psychoanalyst helped to neutralize some of Krafft-Ebing's damaging effects, but, unfortunately, it was Freud who popularized the distinction between "clitoral" and "vaginal" orgasm, and who theorized that the former is a sign of immaturity.

Another man, almost an exact contemporary of Freud, should receive even greater recognition for formulating the theories and philosophies about human sexuality which underlie modern belief and practice. Unlike his predecessors, Havelock Ellis was primarily interested in broadening the definition of normal sexuality for all ages. He recognized that sexual activity, including masturbation, is normal in children, and he postulated that women were sexual and could have multiple orgasms. He theorized that male impotence and female frigidity stemmed for the most part from psychological rather than physiological causes. He also gave realistic but sensitive recognition to the extraordinary differences in kind and nature of sexual enjoyment among human beings, thus setting in motion attitudes that today lead to the use of the word "variation" rather than "perversion." Ellis is a beacon in the human sexuality movement because of his recognition of the devastatingly negative effects on human lives of sexual ignorance and sexual repression, and his conviction that these effects could largely be avoided if people could grow up in an atmosphere of knowledge, acceptance, and wisdom about sexuality.

In 1926 a Dutch gynecologist, Theodore Van de Velde, published *Ideal Marriage,*[7] a book which successfully reached the general public with the message that mutual sexual pleasure in marriage is both acceptable and desirable. Although dangerously compulsive in his insistence on simultaneous orgasm, he performed a valuable service by treating female sexual response as normal and accepting various sexual techniques (such as other-than-the missionary position and oral genital sex) when they bring mutual enjoyment.

Robert Latou Dickinson, presaging the work of Masters and Johnson, used his gynecological practice to observe, measure, record, and draw. His atlas, *Human Sex Anatomy,* remains in print,[8] and is a storehouse of information as well as a model for the thoroughly professional and accurate, yet warm and sometimes witty, treatment of the facts of sexual response. Marie Stopes and Helena Wright in England stood staunchly for sexual freedom for women. So did Margaret Sanger in the United States, although her overriding interest was the birth control movement.

In the early 1930s, Dr. Harry Benjamin secured funds to support the first research to isolate biologically potent male hormone from urine. This research paved the way for the development of testosterone for clinical use. He is best known, however, as the father of transsexual medicine. In *The Transsexual Phenomenon,* published in 1966, he and his associates reported a series of over 1300 cases, many followed through sex reassignment surgery.[9] His exposition of the problems of transsexualism and how they might be handled led to the development of gender identity clinics as we know them today.

In the 1940s Kinsey and his colleagues recorded the sexual histories of almost 18,000 individuals, male and female, of all ages, from all walks of life and in all kinds of situations including universities, social clubs, places of work, as well as in prisons and brothels. As people gave their histories for this epochal work, they were able to recall factors they felt had influenced their sexual attitudes, learning, and experiences. Kinsey's appearance in mid-century, 50 years after Ellis and 25 years after Van de Velde, illustrates the slow yet steady growth of the rational approach to sexuality.[10,11]

The next step was inevitable: direct observation and measurement of the actual process of sexual interaction and response, just as had already been done with all other bodily functions. The impact of Masters' and Johnson's *Human Sexual Response*[12] in 1964 was enormous and is still being felt. The completeness of their research apparently obviated the need for replication. No further significant studies of the basic functioning of sexual response in the human being have been conducted. The same is almost equally true of their second study, *Human Sexual Dysfunction,*[13] at least as far as taxonomy of sexual dysfunction is concerned. What is slowly being added are studies of various adaptations of their revolutionary male-female dual therapy techniques, and additional modalities.

Another area in which highly significant research has been conducted since 1950 relates to how sexuality develops in the human child. Here some major contributors are Gagnon,[6] Stoller,[14] Money and Ehrhardt,[15] and Green.[16] Their findings indicate that gender identity is fixed by the age of two and that gender roles, programmed by the child's own environment, are established by the time he or she reaches puberty. It is interesting to note that this research parallels evolution of the women's movement with its strong emphasis on freeing both men and women from gender-stereotyped sex roles.

The explosion of sexological knowledge based on modern research is reflected in the number of specialized journals that have appeared during recent years. *The Journal of Sex Research,* published by the Society for the Scientific Study of Sex, first came out in 1965. The Society, which was founded in 1957, is described by Money as "the first time in the U.S. that a group of sexologists banded together to defy the all but universal taboo on the study of human sexuality in its recreational—as well as purely procreational—function."[17] The five sexologists who founded this organization were Hugo Beigel, Albert Ellis, Henry Gruze, Hans Lehfeldt, and Robert Sherwin.[18]

In 1967, the journal *Medical Aspects of Human Sexuality* appeared. Initially distributed free to physicians in the United States, its rapid recognition and acceptance were evidence of its excellent quality. Currently, the Institute for Sex Research lists 12 journals which contain the word "sex" in their titles. Other publications, such as the *Journal of Marriage and the Family,* often contain articles related to sex, but they generally cover broader fields of psychology, family sociology, and anthropology. *Medical Tribune,* a highly respected and widely distributed bi-weekly newspaper, carried a special section, *Sexual Medicine Today,* once a month. This is now published independently.

Sexology is another serious publication deserving mention, especially because its nature and purpose have led to severe attacks. A monthly magazine for the general public, *Sexology* was founded in 1933 by Hugo Gernsback. Its Board of Consultants has always been drawn from the ranks of respected professionals. *Sexology* is noted for its colloquial language, the wide range of sexual topics it covers, and its deliberately sensationalized titles and illustrations, designed to draw attention to the informative articles. These articles were usually written by recognized professionals for the less educated newspaper reader for whom the magazine was their only source of sexual information. For 14 years, until his accidental death in 1970, its editor was Isadore Rubin, PhD, whose scholarliness and almost encyclopedic knowledge of the field of sexology were well known and highly respected among his colleagues. At least twice *Sexology* was brought to court on charges of pornography, and each time it was cleared.[19] The magazine is still being subjected to unwarranted attacks that confuse, perhaps deliberately, explicit but sound information with pornography.

The Sex Information and Education Council of the United States (SIECUS) was formed in 1964 for the following purpose:

To establish human sexuality as a health entity; to identify the special characteristics that distinguish it from, yet relate it to, human reproduction; to dignify it by openness of approach, study and scientific research designed to lead toward its understanding and its freedom from exploitation; to give leadership to professionals and to society, to the end that human beings may be aided toward responsible use of the sexual faculty and toward assimilation of sex into their individual life patterns as a creative and re-creative force.

To achieve this goal, an entire society must, as the Jesuit sociologist and SIECUS Board member, John L. Thomas, put it, learn to view human sexuality as "an integral part of the total personality structure."[20] SIECUS therefore set out to coalesce leadership from the health and behavioral science professions, religion, education, law, business, and the arts.

Political groups such as the John Birch Society and its offshoot Movement to Restore Decency (MOTOREDE) and ultraconservative religious groups, including the Christian Crusade, began attacking SIECUS in 1968 with distorted and defamatory accusations.[21-23] These attacks were picked up by small, privately owned right wing presses one after the other. In a three-month collection of approximately 9000 clippings from these presses, one could follow identically worded accusations as they swept eastward or westward from paper to paper.* There were two main accusations: that SIECUS constituted a communist plot to debauch the youth of the nation in order to facilitate a communist take-over; and that SIECUS was publishing pornography and profiting therefrom, by means not only of its own publications but of a nefarious linkage with *Sexology* magazine. This second accusation was apparently based on the fact that Isadore Rubin served on the SIECUS Board and generously edited the SIECUS Newsletter, as well as its Study Guides, but without compensation.[18]

It seems to me that the primary purpose of these attacks was clearly political, designed to stampede local communities to elect ultraconservative members to school boards, which would then truncate psychological services or family life education. As recently as 1975, the Superintendent of the North Dakota Department of Education, in an open meeting of the state's School Board and Superintendents' Association, attacked SIECUS by quoting ten accusations leveled against the organization by Gloria Lentz in her book *Raping Our Children*.[24]†

Despite these political pressures the very people attacked have gone on in their professions to organize and head distinguished human sexuality educational programs in most of the nation's medical schools, in theological seminaries, and in undergraduate universities. They have published scientific research, received honorary degrees, and achieved eminence in this specialized field, in other countries as well as in the United States.

---

*These clippings and many other documents of possible interest to future historians of the era are in the archives of the Schlesinger Library for Women of Radcliffe College, Cambridge, Mass.

†North Dakota is one of six states presently mandating sex education as part of school health education. See p. 18.

Perhaps one of the two most significant events in the human sexuality movement was the publication in 1975 of a World Health Organization Technical Report, *Education and Treatment in Human Sexuality: The Training of Health Professionals*. Twenty-three physicians from 14 countries who were convened for four days by WHO reached conclusions and made recommendations for implementation at the public health practice level. They define sexual health as follows:

> Sexual health is the integration of the somatic, emotional, intellectual, and social aspects of sexual being, in ways that are positively enriching and that enhance personality, communication and love. Every person has a right to receive information and to consider accepting sexual relationships for pleasure as well as for procreation.[25]

The second was in 1976, when California became the first state to mandate the WHO Report's recommendation of training in human sexuality for all health professionals licensure or renewal of licensure.

INSIGHTS

The interdependence of sexuality and health, and of sexuality and personality, voiced by a rapidly multiplying number of respected leaders in various professional fields, has acted as a refreshing open-sesame. An area of knowledge which most people had previously avoided could now be looked at, studied, and talked about. Today, especially among the more educated groups, there is a receptivity and eagerness for new knowledge about sex, based on sound motivations. As this knowledge has been disseminated in the professional media, there has been an accompanying relaxation of the tensions and fears about sex that previously had crippled or distorted people's lives.

Books about human sexuality proliferate as publishers have tried to capitalize on this universally receptive market. (Between five and ten new books come weekly to the SIECUS office for review.) There is a wide range of quality and worth, from the few that actually break new ground, to some that interpret new findings to the general public, to a good many more that are excellent repetitions or recapitulations of books already published, to a proliferation of the dull and unimaginatively repetitious, to the meretricious, sensationalized, and exploitive.

New organizations have been formed for specific purposes. The American Association of Sex Educators, Counselors and Therapists, formed in 1968 by Patricia Schiller, J.D., holds regional meetings and local workshops throughout the year for practicing professionals. It has also worked to establish mechanisms for evaluation of the training backgrounds of sex educators, counselors, and therapists, and for their accreditation.

Many universities and professional schools throughout the country also conduct special training programs. Medical schools have not only increased the teaching of human sexuality to their own students, but a number of them are affiliated with special units which study and provide therapy for human sexual dysfunction.

States are quietly decriminalizing private sexual activities between consenting adults. Among those which have already enacted such laws are Arkansas, Colorado, Connecticut, Delaware, Hawaii, Illinois, Maine, New Mexico, North Dakota, Ohio, Oregon, and Washington. Six states (Hawaii, Kentucky, Maryland, Michigan, Missouri, and North Dakota) and the District of Columbia mandate sex education as part of health education in their schools. Many other states leave the decision to local communities. Louisiana, however, absolutely prohibits sex education in any school, public or private. The federal government has generally been silently negative on the subject.

SIECUS, a very small organization indeed, continues to serve primarily as mouthpiece and transmitter, and perhaps as facilitator, of what it has helped set in motion. It has also served as a balance wheel of reason against the sensationalization about sex that emanated from the media.

At the present time, the human sexuality movement is a great movement for the humanization of sexuality, a wide fellowship for acceptance of sexuality as a natural and integral part of human life. This has been particularly striking with regard to sexuality of the handicapped and the aging, groups which had previously been subjected to desexualizing attitudes by professionals and laymen alike.

The emphasis today is on meeting needs that *exist*, rather than on telling people what needs they may *not* have while meeting needs that are often arbitrarily decided they *ought* to have. Children are beginning to be included in this group. In an outstanding study of 5000 children from kindergarten through 12th-grade conducted by the Connecticut State Department of Education in 1969, the interests, concerns, and problems of urban, suburban, and rural children and young people in many areas of health, including sexuality, were recorded and analyzed.[26] Students were given ample opportunity to make recommendations, and this report remains a uniquely valid and valuable resource for parents, educators, and health professionals alike.

Research has clearly shown that, unlike other systems of the body that develop autonomously, the sexuality of each person begins developing from the moment of birth in a long learning process subject to many influences, both positive and negative.[6,8,14,15] This learning process is impeded by such factors as lack of awareness in most parents of the sexual aspects of their young children's lives, an equal lack of awareness of their own critical role in their child's sexual learning process, and poor preparation for performing this role. Many parents resist institutionalized sex-teaching programs for their children, whether in schools or in churches, on the grounds that parents should assume this responsibility, because they believe teachers are untrained and unprepared, and because they fear that their children may learn conflicting moral values and "have ideas put into their heads." Health professionals, on the other hand, are well aware that parents often don't or won't take this responsibility, and that teachers can and are being trained.

Regarding moral values, Kohlberg has demonstrated six stages through which children move in learning to establish a moral value framework.[27] The stimulus for moving to a more mature stage is exposure to discussion with one or more persons who appear to hold differing moral values because they are at the next higher level. Gilligan has shown that, age for age, children are about two years below their own age level with regard to sexual moral values as compared with their capacity to deal with non-sex-related moral values.[28] Children, being sexual people at all ages, will normally always "have ideas" about sex. The challenge is to replace false, fearful, and guilt-ridden ideas with exact, factual, and normalizing ideas which can provide a base for the sexual decisions they will inevitably have to make.

FORESIGHTS

Although a solidly growing cadre of professionals of all disciplines who are oriented to the true nature and importance of human sexuality now exists in the United States and elsewhere, this relatively elite group has yet to disseminate these concepts widely to other sectors of the population. Education about human sexuality is no different from education about nutrition or overpopulation: academic research does not guarantee popular belief or positive action. But, as environmental and economic stringencies increase, so will the need to live one's life as fully and fruitfully as possible. I perceive today the same kind of backlash toward blind, super-conservatism that took place in previous centuries in other societies, but there is no need for us to be stampeded into such a nonproductive backlash in our sexual and family lives. Rather, in times of stringency and deprivation, people who have been properly instructed

and prepared can turn to their relational lives and find that external depri-
vations are more easily borne if their quest for fulfillment in their most
intimate relationships can be answered.

Because sexuality from earliest memory goes deep into each person's
life, those who are the least informed about it are the ones who are most
apt to resist efforts to help them comprehend it. Today there is panic in
many countries regarding the increase in adolescent fertility. Persons who
insist that we deal with this trend by returning to the sterile negatives of
puritanism and ignorance are the same persons who refuse to acknowledge the valid sexuality of early childhood, and indeed of all human life. A
generation of young parents educated to understand and accept sexuality
in their own children, who can help to socialize them without damaging
their naturally emerging eroticism, might well constitute the critical mass
that could effect much needed changes in societal knowledge and attitudes about sex. It might then be possible to achieve the World Health
Organization's definition of healthy sexuality for coming generations.

Another factor, not previously mentioned, is all-important. By and
large, the sexual histories of more complex societies have related primarily to the middle and upper classes. Heretofore, sexual patterns of the
working classes and peasantry appear to have been little influenced by the
wild swings between restrictions and excesses experienced by the gentry
and religious elite. This is no longer the case. Healthy sexuality should not
be rigidly associated with younger adults, class distinction, or marital
status, but should be available to everyone. It remains for all concerned
professional people to make it possible for those who come under their
teaching, guidance, or influence to develop healthy sexual ideas and behavior patterns.

This book, planned as it is to help health professionals to move forward in this task, comes logically out of the lessons to be learned from the
stormy, unhappy sexual history of the past. To allow the centuries-long
patterns of wild swings between ignorant license and just as ignorant
repression to continue, would be a serious disservice to the people of
today. We now know better, and we have the means and the tools to share
this knowledge with others. The humanization of sexuality into fulfilling
and responsible patterns is long overdue.

ACKNOWLEDGMENT

For the material in the Hindsight portion of this chapter I have with
appreciation drawn heavily on the excellent discussions by E. Brecher
and N. Sussman in Sadock, Kaplan, and Freedman (eds.), *The Sexual
Experience*, pp. 7–78.

REFERENCES

1. Davies G: The early Stuarts, 1603–1660, in Clark A (ed): Oxford History of England, vol. 9 Oxford, Clarendon Press, 1959
2. Marcus S: The Other Victorians. New York, Basic Books, 1966
3. Brecher E, Sussman N: History of human sexual research and study, in Sadock BJ, Kaplan HI, Freedman AM (eds): The Sexual Experience. Baltimore, William & Wilkins, 1976, p 71
4. Brecher E. Sussman N: History of human sex research and study, in Saddock BJ, Kaplan HI, Freedman AM (eds.): The Sexual Experience. Baltimore, William & Wilkins, 1976, p. 73
5. Hollender M: The medical profession and sex in 1900. Am J Obstet Gynecol 108: 139, 1970
6. Gagnon JH: Sexuality and sexual learning in the child. Psychiatry: 28:212–228, 1965
7. Van de Velde T: Ideal Marriage: Its Physiology and Technique. New York, Random House, 1930
8. Dickinson RL: Human Sex Anatomy. Huntington, NY, Krieger Pub. Co., 1969
9. Benjamin H: The Transsexual Phenomenon. New York, Julian Press, 1966
10. Kinsey AC, Pomeroy WB, Martin CE: Sexual Behavior in the Human Male. Philadelphia, WB Saunders, 1948
11. Kinsey AC, Pomeroy WB, Martin CE, Gebhard D: Sexual Behavior in the Human Female. Philadelphia, WB Saunders, 1953
12. Masters WH, Johnson V: Human Sexual Response. Boston, Little, Brown, 1965
13. Masters WH, Johnson V: Human Sexual Inadequacy. Boston, Little, Brown, 1970
14. Stoller RJ: Sex and Gender: On the Development of Masculinity and Femininity. New York, Science House, 1968
15. Money J, Ehrhardt AA: Man & Woman, Boy & Girl: Differentiation and Dimorphism of Gender Identity from Conception to Maturity. Baltimore, The Johns Hopkins University Press, 1973
16. Green R: Sexual Identity Conflict in Children and Adults. New York, Basic Books, 1974
17. Money J: The development of sexology as a discipline. J Sex Res 12:83–87, 1976
18. Lehfeldt H: Introduction. J Sex Res 1:1–2, 1965
19. Baker LG: The rising furor over sex education. Family Coordinator 18:210–216, 1969
20. Thomas JL: Sexuality and the total personality. SIECUS Newsletter 1:3, 1965
21. Hottois JW, Miller N: The Sex Education Controversy. Lexington, MA, DC Heath, 1975
22. General Committee on Family Life, The United Methodist Church: What Church Leaders Can Do to Improve Family Life and Sex Education in School, Church and Home. Nashville, The United Methodist Church, 1970
23. Drake G: Is the Schoolhouse the Proper Place to Teach Raw Sex? Also, SIECUS: Corrupter of Youth. Tulsa, Christian Crusade Publications, 1968
24. Lentz G: Raping our Children. New Rochelle, Arlington House, 1972
25. World Health Organization: Education and Treatment in Human Sexuality: The Training of Health Professionals. Technical Report No. 572. Geneva, Switzerland, WHO, 1975
26. Byler R, Lewis G, Totman R: Teach Us What We Want to Know. New York, Mental Health Materials Center, 1969
27. Kohlberg L: Moral stages and sex education, in Calderone MS (ed): Sexuality and Human Values. Chicago, Association Press/Follett Pub. Co., 1975, p 111
28. Gilligan, C: Sexual dilemmas at the high school level, in Calderone MS (ed): Sexuality and Human Values. Chicago, Association Press/Follett Pub. Co., 1975, p 98

Harold I. Lief

2
Sex Education in Medicine: Retrospect and Prospect

RETROSPECT

Remarkable changes have taken place in the sex education of medical students and physicians in the last 18 years. This chapter describes the changes that have occurred since 1960, the present status of sex education for health professionals, and future prospects.

By 1960 only three medical schools had formal programs of training in human sexuality. The first of these was the University of Pennsylvania. In 1952 Emily Mudd, then Director of the Marriage Council of Philadelphia and the Division of Family Study, instituted an elective course in sexuality for medical students. Over 90 percent of the senior medical students elected the course.[1] Subsequently, William Masters at Washington University in St. Louis presented a series of lectures for medical students, and Frank Lock and Clark Vincent at Bowman-Gray organized seminars for residents in obstetrics and gynecology that were also open to students.[2]

In the early 1960s, through addresses to professional organizations and papers in professional and popular journals, this author called attention to the "woefully inadequate" training of medical students in human sexuality.[3,4] With the help of a group of noted medical educators and support from the Commonwealth Fund, the Center for the Study of Sex Education in Medicine (CSSEM) was organized in 1968.[5] At that time, according to a survey by Coombs, 29 medical schools had developed formal courses in sexual function and dysfunction.[6] The picture began to change rapidly. By 1974, 106 medical schools included programs of instruction in this area.[7] Thus, in approximately 14 years, human sexuality had become an accepted part of the medical curriculum.

Nevertheless problems still remained. If the program was not an integral part of the curriculum, independent of the special concerns or charisma of one or more teachers, the course in sexuality might be abandoned when those teachers left the institution. A high priority had to be assigned to "institutionalization" and to training a core group of teachers who could then teach others, thereby creating a sufficient pool of trained personnel within the institution. CSSEM held seven regional workshops for faculty from 94 medical schools to discuss curriculum design, teaching methods and techniques, and dissemination of new information. An important by-product of these workshops was the establishment of both formal and informal communication networks among interested medical teachers.

Another important problem was the attitude and feelings of medical students.[8] Sexuality and sex carry such an emotional "charge" that this part of the curriculum differs from many other medical subjects which are less influenced by the physician's feelings. The ease and comfort with which a medical student or physician deals with the sexual problems and concerns of patients is an extremely significant aspect of patient management. If a physician is uncomfortable, he may do more harm than good. Moreover, attitudes affect acquisition of information and development of skills. If the medical student is uncomfortable, he or she is less open to new information and finds it very difficult to develop interviewing skills.

The scarcity of clinical facilities has been a serious problem in training medical students in human sexuality. As more and more patients began to demand treatment for sexual dysfunctions and the outlook for successful treatment improved, primarily due to the pioneering work of Masters and Johnson[9] and the psychotherapeutic methods of Kaplan,[10] medical schools began to develop sex therapy clinics. In 1960 only one medical school, the University of Pennsylvania, had suitable facilities for the treatment of sexual dysfunctions. The Marriage Council of Philadelphia, as its name implies, was not set up solely for treatment of sexual dysfunction, but since 75 percent of patients who come for marital therapy have a sexual dysfunction, a large clinical population was available for those medical students who wanted to undertake specialized training. However, it was an entire decade before other medical schools began to develop sex therapy clinics.[11] In 1970 four more such facilities were established; six were developed in 1971; eight in 1972; twelve in 1973; sixteen in 1974; and eight in 1975. Of the 55 schools that had sex therapy facilities in 1975, 19 had separate and distinct therapy clinics.

The mid-1960s saw other professional developments. Major medical societies and organizations began to schedule workshops, seminars, and special sessions devoted to human sexuality. The AMA passed a resolution expressing a need to incorporate "appropriate learning experiences for physicians in the area of counseling related to sexual attitudes and behavior." The AMA Board of Trustees appointed a committee to prepare the book *Human Sexuality,*[12] and in 1977, the Board named a task force to write a new text for medical students and physicians dealing with human sexuality and sex counseling. The American College of Obstetricians and Gynecologists issued a pamphlet entitled *Sex Education as a Professional Responsibility.*[13] *Pediatric Clinics of North America* devoted an entire issue to the sex education of the physician.[14] Special workshops were developed by the American College of Physicians and the American Urologic Association, and an increasing number of papers on human sexuality have been presented at annual meetings of the American Psychiatric Association. Several new professional journals appeared.

Physicians were not the only professionals who became interested in sex therapy. Psychologists, social workers, nurses, clergymen, educators, and some social scientists joined the ranks of those jumping on the sex therapy bandwagon. This led to a proliferation of sex therapy "clinics" said to number in the thousands. Outright quacks are probably less of a problem than professionally trained people who have not had adequate training in sex counseling and therapy. Thus, the development of standards for training and accreditation has become a critical issue. An initial conference on the ethics of sex education, therapy, and research was held in St. Louis in January 1976,[15] followed by a second conference in January 1978.

SPECIAL ISSUES

Attitudinal Teaching and Learning

Slovenko once said that in one way or another, almost every person is more interested in sex than in any other subject.[16] This great interest is accompanied by strong, often intense feelings, creating a special climate for teaching and learning. It is the rare human being who can be relatively objective and nonjudgmental about sexual matters, and medical students are no exception. Attitudes are composed of values, feelings, and beliefs that may interfere with the physician's management of a patient.[17] For example, the student or physician who believes that homosexuality is a perversion may have great difficulty in being compassionately concerned with a homosexual patient. One who believes that abortion is murder under all or almost all circumstances may have difficulty even inquiring about the feelings of a woman who is uncertain whether she wishes to carry her fetus to term. If the physician believes that most young people are promiscuous, he or she may have trouble giving contraceptive counseling to an unmarried teenager. A physician who is shocked by extramarital sex may reveal this reaction to a patient who wishes to talk about his or her marital infidelity.

Specific inappropriate or troublesome attitudes, added to the anxiety medical students usually have about interviewing and the very general feeling that sex is the most private and intimate of behaviors, contribute to making sexual interviewing and history-taking difficult for the medical student.[18] He or she may feel embarrassed or anxious and, on occasion, to make matters more disquieting, may experience troublesome sexual feelings. The student often feels that he or she is unique in having these emotional reactions or sexual feelings, and this increases his or her sense of shame. These emotions often lead to maladaptive defense mechanisms, such as avoidance, being "preachy" or directive, anger at seductive behavior (or its converse, susceptibility), or an attempt to generalize from the student's own sexual experiences. It is this type of medical student or physician who, if these defenses break down, is most susceptible to "acting out" sexually with patients.

Avoidance may be very direct, such as changing the subject abruptly. Other forms are more indirect; for example, the physician may give the patient pat, superficial, cliche-ridden reassurances such as "this is a phase and it will pass," or "I'm sure it will work out in time" or, to a postcoronary patient, "take it easy," or "why are you so concerned about sex?"

Delivering a sermon about appropriate values is another frequent stance, especially of older physicians. Imposing one's values on the patient is a temptation to be strongly avoided, yet many doctors succumb to this temptation as an easy way out that maintains their self-image as moral human beings. This is almost always perceived by the patient as patronizing, increasing the patient's feelings of inferiority, and frequently leads to a reactive resentment. In the absence of discussion with colleagues or of wide reading in the field, the physician may assume that his or her own experiences are normative when, in fact, they may not be. A common example is the physician who regards oral sex as perverse.

Vincent described the process of attitudinal training for medical students and physicians in this area of medical practice as desensitization, sensitization, and integration, by which he meant that the student has to become more *comfortable* with his or her own feelings (desensitization) and thus become more sensitive to the feelings of patients (sensitization), after which the student can begin to connect his or her feelings and the empathy with the patient's feelings with the body of knowledge which he or she is attempting to absorb (integration).[19] I believe the sequence is more accurately described as follows: (1) initial sensitization, (2) desensitization, (3) resensitization, and (4) integration. Students have to become *more aware* of their own feelings (sensitization) before they can begin to become desensitized (comfortable); then they must become resensitized to their own feelings in a more appropriate fashion before beginning the process of integration. Typically, medical schools have used erotic films with or without small group interactions to develop this process. Approximately 90 percent of the medical schools use erotic films in their teaching.[7]

There is still a debate as to whether these films should be combined with small group interaction, or whether they can accomplish the process alone. This author firmly believes that small group interaction is a key element in the process, and he has described these techniques as confrontation, consensual validation, and implosion.[20] Confrontation is the process by which the medical student is sensitized to his or her own feelings through erotic films, patient demonstrations, or interviewing "teaching subjects" (e.g., homosexuals, transsexuals, or transvestites who are brought in from the community to talk about their particular forms of gender orientation). In confrontation the student becomes aware of his or her own feelings, sometimes in a rather dramatic fashion. Role-playing is another technique that is used effectively to meet this objective. Students may play the role of patient, doctor, or observer of the doctor-patient interaction and, in this fashion, examine the kinds of feelings that occur in each participant of the threesome.

Consensual validation occurs when students begin to compare their attitudes with those of their peers. They may find that they are not as unique as they thought, or some students may find that in one or more dimensions they are somewhat set apart from most of their colleagues. At any rate, this technique seems to reduce the student's reliance on his or her own sexual experiences and attitudes in counseling patients.

Implosion is a specialized form of confrontation in which the students' senses are bombarded by visual, auditory, and, in a few instances, tactile sensations to sensitize them to their own feelings. A popular method, pioneered by Ted McIlvenna of the National Sex Forum, Herbert Vandervoort, and Richard Chilgren is Sexual Attitude Restructuring (SAR).[20a]

Whatever methods are used, a cardinal objective of teaching human sexuality is to increase the student's comfort so that he or she will be able to make a patient comfortable, and the patient can then discuss his or her problems with some degree of freedom.

Skill Development

The basic problem in most programs for medical students is either the unavailability of patients or the difficulties of finding curriculum time and faculty time for medical students to conduct interviews with patients under close supervision. Consequently, most medical schools rely on patient demonstrations or on role-playing. A teacher interviews a patient in front of a group or presents a videotape of a patient interview. Only a few programs have incorporated actual interviewing and patient management as part of their training program. Unlike other aspects of medical teaching and learning, the student rarely has the opportunity to interview a patient with a sexual problem, and even more rarely is he or she able to receive adequate supervision. Thus, learning is more by reading and watching others than by doing. This is the chief reason why most medical school programs are still too superficial. I hope that the advent of sex therapy clinics in medical schools will bring about fundamental changes whereby students will have more opportunities to learn by doing than by watching.

Education, Counseling and Therapy

One of the major difficulties in setting forth measurable objectives is the inability to define precisely the parameters of what most practicing physicians should be able to do in sex counseling. An early attempt to achieve greater precision was made by Vines and Lief, who presented a conceptual scheme organized around hierarchical levels of competence (Table 2-1).[21] The well-informed physician should be able to counsel patients about sexual anatomy, physiology, and the range of sexual behaviors. It is not too difficult to describe in greater detail what the physician as an *educator* ought to be able to do in his or her office practice; it is more difficult to draw the line between counseling and therapy, although the sex therapist can be described readily. The sex therapist should have a range of education and counseling skills, including the capacity to perform individual and marital psychotherapy. In this view, the sex therapist is a highly trained specialist.

One of the major tasks of the sex counselor is to increase communication about sexual matters between the partners. For this reason, conjoint couple counseling is usually preferable to individual therapy. Couple counseling is unfamiliar to almost all medical students and, indeed, to most physicians. Since few will have had the opportunity to interview couples in medical school or in residency training, this will have to be learned during practice by trial-and-error. (Our Center is attempting to work out a method of supervision of sex counselors and therapists who practice at a distance, via videotaped interviews, so that sex counseling skills, including couple interviewing, can be enhanced.)

A second task of the sex counselor is to know how and when to recommend to the couple the "pleasuring" or sensate-focus exercises described by Masters and Johnson.[9] The "prescription" is relatively easy to learn but often difficult to apply in practice. Resistances to pleasuring exercises are frequent, and sabotage of the prescription varied, frustrating, and perplexing. The beginning counselor is apt to mishandle the resistances. In any case, with most couples a mechanical approach to sex counseling does not work. To carry out effective sex counseling, some understanding of the nature of the couple's interaction is necessary. Thus, in addition to sex counseling, the counselor must learn at least the rudiments of marriage counseling. Clearly, these are difficult, probably impossible, tasks for most students to accomplish during medical school training. Teachers can hope that a climate can be established which will encourage students to try to learn this form of treatment, either by trial-and-error or by additional supervision in the early years of practice. We are a long way from accomplishing these objectives.

A third aspect of counseling is to learn how to make an appropriate referral once the physician recognizes that his or her own limitations prevent successful management of the patient's problems. In medical school, attention should be given to methods of appropriate referral, while teaching students how to recognize when they are beyond their depth. Clearly, the severity of individual or marital psychopathology is the key determinant of whether the physician should refer the patient to a specialist. In that case, he or she not only has to know how to make the referral, but how to select the appropriate therapist. Whether to send a patient or a couple to a psychiatrist, or to a marital or sex therapist, demands some capacity to make an appraisal, including a diagnosis, of the patient or couple (Table 2-1)*

Institutionalization of the Teaching Program

As indicated previously, when key teachers leave, some programs either deteriorate or are prematurely terminated because of failure to have effective teachers. Each institution must train a corps of teachers so that if one or two key faculty members leave, the program can be continued. The workshops for medical faculty conducted by CSSEM did a great deal to develop cadres of teachers in many medical schools, but this work has to be continued. To this end, seminars for teachers of human sexuality in medical schools should be held periodically. In every medical school the program director should make sure that junior faculty members are recruited into the faculty as teachers, and that their development can continue.

---

*The conceptual scheme set forth here by Vines and Lief[21] is not unlike that of the PLISSIT model developed by Annon.[22]

Table 2-1
The Physician's Roles and Tasks in Sex Counseling and Therapy

Level of Diagnosis of Sexual Problem	Patient Need	Professional Task	Professional Role
Sexual ignorance	To know	To provide accurate information	Inquirer-Educator
Situational discomfort-anxiety	To relax	To reduce or to eliminate immediate causes of sexual dysfunction	Counselor
Interpersonal distance-conflict	To reorient the relationship	To reshape dyadic system	Marital Therapist
Historical intrapsychic conflict	To explore tension between intrapsychic and interpersonal systems	To explore the interface between historical conflict and sexual discomfort-dysfunction	Psychotherapist
All of the above	Flexible use of new repertoire of sexual behaviors	Formulating hierarchy of patient needs and incorporating those into a sequence of treatment	Sex Therapist

Teaching Residents

We still do not know the effects of the training of medical students upon their practices, even the extent to which they undertake to treat patients with sexual dysfunctions. Nor do we know whether they deal with these problems effectively. Studies of the integration of student training into medical practice should be carried out. Another high-priority objective is the sex education of residents in the primary-care specialties. Sex education of family-medicine residents has been conducted in only a few places. Four medical schools provide training in sex counseling to family-medicine residents as a definite part of their curriculum, and five other schools encourage participation in interdisciplinary programs.

Departments of obstetrics-gynecology and psychiatry are more committed to such teaching. However, in specialties other than psychiatry, sex counseling is still a very minor aspect of the residency curriculum. It seems to be almost nonexistent in training pediatricians and urologists. Efforts to train family care specialists have to be greatly increased during the next decade.

Continuing Education for Physicians

Scores of workshops and seminars on sexual topics have been held for physicians in practice, but these hardly suffice for the development of skills. A three-day workshop or even a two-week course does not prepare the practicing physician to become an effective sex counselor. For this reason, new techniques need to be developed so that those in the field can actually obtain supervision for their work with their own patients. We are attempting to use long range videotaped supervision for physicians and other professionals who wish to enhance their skills as sex counselors and therapists. If this turns out to be a feasible technique, regional centers for such supervision can be established with the physician paying a fee for supervision. These regional centers could then become self-supporting.

Interprofessional and Interdisciplinary
Teaching and Training

There are issues with regard to appropriate roles and tasks. As many non-physicians move into the field of sex counseling and therapy, there is competition for this particular turf. Rivalry among the various professionals could be minimized if one were to emphasize tasks, rather than roles. Defining the variety of tasks in the field of sex counseling and therapy, as we are beginning to do, may reduce professional competition. Some link with medicine must be maintained in any sex clinic, for not only do many sexual dysfunctions (e.g., impotence and dyspareunia) have some organic basis, but many patients with psychogenic sexual dysfunctions report a significant medical history affecting their sexual attitudes and behavior. Medical knowledge is essential in assessing the significance of the medical history, as well as in weighing the etiological significance of biological factors. Sex education, counseling, and therapy roles may be assigned irrespective of the educational or professional background of the therapist, provided there is adequate medical supervision.

At this time, there is no Department of Sexology in the medical schools of the United States. Sexology includes information from all medical disciplines, and from the biologic and social sciences as well. Hence, there is every reason to believe that a separate department, interdisciplinary in outlook and staff, would be a welcome development. Medical school training programs certainly should be interdisciplinary so that students recognize that the field is not bounded by any one department's fences.

Aspects of Curriculum Design

In *Sex Education in Medicine,* three sample curricula are offered as examples of different conceptions of curriculum design.[7],* One curriculum places heavy emphasis on the social and behavioral sciences; another emphasizes medical practice; and the third stresses experiential or attitudinal learning. In short courses of approximately 40 hours, the selection of topics and methods of presenting them have been of primary concern to teachers. Other issues have also come to the fore. Should the training program be concentrated in a short period of time or should it be spaced out over many weeks? To what extent can teaching be done in large groups, a method which is more economical of faculty time? Should the program stress affective or attitudinal learning or the dissemination of information? How much attention can be given to the actual development of skills in a limited period of time? Can this subject be taught effectively when the course is elective rather than required?

Some investigators have compared "time-condensed" programs with weekly lecture or seminar ("spaced") programs. Vines reported that the intensive or massed sex-education program increased the comfort of students conducting interviews with simulated patients more than spaced sex education.[23] However, Marcotte et al reported that a spaced course in sex education was effective in increasing students' cognitive sexual knowledge and their tolerance for various sexual behaviors.[24] Marcotte judged his findings on the basis of the Sex Knowledge and Attitude Test (SKAT),

*See Part V for other program descriptions.

whereas Vines, using independent appraisal of videotapes, based his evaluations on comfort during interviews, close to the physician's actual task.

Evaluation Techniques

Since methods and results of evaluation are dealt with in detail in Chapter 11 (Williams and Miller), only a few comments are in order. Clearly, the major task in evaluation still remaining is to discover the extent to which information and skills conveyed in courses on human sexuality are actually applied in practice. Only Vines' study has made an attempt to evaluate this facet of skill development, and that study had the disadvantage of using a simulated instead of a real patient.

The SKAT has been a remarkably useful instrument. A survey conducted by the CSSEM found that approximately 50 percent of the medical schools use SKAT.[7] The test can serve three valuable purposes: (1) to test the effectiveness of the courses being taught; (2) as a teaching instrument, since the items themselves can serve as topics for class discussion; and (3) to gather data about the sexual information, attitudes, and behavior of medical students and other groups. The SKAT has been administered to more than 35,000 students, and the accumulated data have been useful in establishing norms for such groups as college students, medical students, nurses, and graduate students. The data have been analyzed for sexual differences, and correlations have been made with background data and information about sexual behavior.[25] Despite the usefulness of this instrument, it is necessary to develop other techniques that study the degree to which the objectives of courses in human sexuality have been integrated into actual practice. A step in this direction is the patient-management-problem method, using stepwise choices akin to programmed teaching. This work has been pioneered by Marcotte in both pencil-and-paper and video format, but has not yet been widely distributed.[26] Another method, admittedly difficult, is direct observation, as in the studies by Peterson et al and Clute.[27,28]

One technique that has been under-utilized is the use of unobtrusive measures. For example, Mudd and Fleiss found that in routine physical examinations, genital and rectal examinations were frequently omitted; when "deferred," they were postponed indefinitely.[29] Similar studies recording a sexual history would no doubt demonstrate that these are omitted at least as often. Perhaps following a course of training in human sexuality given to primary care physicians, unobtrusive surveys of primary care residents' histories could be made to determine the degree of carry-over from the course to their work. Techniques of evaluation of physician performance have been reviewed by Payne, Lyons, and

Barro.[30-32] Additional evaluation techniques might be developed through the use of videotapes sent to competent supervisors, as has been mentioned earlier in this chapter.

FUTURE PROSPECTS

Unquestionably, the teaching of human sexuality has now found a definite place in the medical curriculum. However, it is still not deemed to be of sufficient importance by the most influential medical teachers, perhaps because the enrichment and quality of life is still secondary to concerns with its prolongation. Therefore, it has yet to achieve its appropriate integration into didactic and clinical teaching. This outcome will perhaps have to await three developments: (1) a shift from the treatment of illness and the prevention of death to the prevention of illness and the enrichment of life, (2) more general availability of specific sex therapy, and (3) development and acceptance of standards for training and accreditation in the field of medical sexology. In the meantime, stabilization of the gains already made is a necessary prelude to further advancement in the field. Stabilization will occur when there is an adequate corps of teachers in each medical school and when there is sufficient administrative support for the teaching of human sexuality.

A distinct possibility is the organization in some medical schools of a Department of Medical Sexology, which would bring the fruits of biology, medicine, psychology, and sociology to bear on the enormous range of topics subsumed under the heading of sexology or human sexuality. The formation in a few universities of doctorates in human sexuality indicates the gradual academic acceptance of the field; as more research becomes "respectable" and more funding becomes available, the field will begin to develop more innovative approaches to the teaching of human sexuality.

I look forward to a time when research and clinical endeavors in the treatment of people with sexual problems will serve as one of the most important bridges among the clinical specialties and as a very significant link between the basic and the clinical sciences. Just as sex therapy is having an integrative effect on the practice of psychotherapy in general, so may sexology prove to have an integrative effect in medical education and practice.

REFERENCES

1. Appel KE, Mudd EH, Roche PQ: Medical school electives on family attitudes, sexual behavior, and marriage counseling. Am J Psychiatry 112:36–40, 1955
2. Lock FR: The challenge of change: Inaugural Address. Obstet Gynecol 24:481–487, 1964

3. Lief HI: What medical schools teach about sex. Bull Tulane Med Faculty 22:161–168, 1963
4. Lief HI: Sex education of medical students and doctors. Pacific Med Surg 73:52–58, 1965
5. Lief HI: New developments in the sex education of the physician. AMA 212:1864–1867, 1970
6. Coombs RH: Sex education for physicians: Is it adequate? Family Coordinator 17:271–277, 1968
7. Lief HI, Karlen A: A Survey of sex education in U.S. medical schools, in Lief HI, Karlen A (eds): Sex Education in Medicine. New York, Halsted Press, 1976, p. 25–34
8. Woods SM: Sex education in medical schools, in Money J, Musaph H (eds): Handbook of Sexology. Amsterdam, Excerpta Medica, 1977, p 1107–1120
9. Masters W, Johnson V: Human Sexual Inadequacy. Boston, Little Brown, 1970
10. Kaplan HS: The New Sex Therapy. New York, Brunner/Mazel, 1974
11. Lief HI, Miller WR: Sex therapy clinics in medical schools. Paper delivered at International Acad Sex Research meeting, Bloomington, Ind., Aug 3, 1977
12. American Medical Association Committee on Human Sexuality: Human Sexuality. Chicago, AMA, 1972
13. American College of Obstetricians and Gynecologists, Committee on Maternal Health: Sex Education as a Professional Responsibility. Norwich, N.Y., Eaton Laboratories, 1965
14. Homel SR (ed): The physician and sex education. Pediatr Clin North Am 16:327–528, 1969
15. Masters W, Johnson V, Kolodny R: Ethical Issues in Sex Therapy and Research. Boston, Little, Brown, 1977
16. Slovenko R: Sexual Behavior and the Law. Springfield, Il, C Thomas, 1965
17. Athanasiou R: A review of public attitudes on sexual issues, in Zubin J, Money J (eds): Contemporary Sexual Behavior: Critical Issues in the 1970s. Baltimore, Johns Hopkins University Press, 1973, p 361–390
18. Mudd JW, Siegel RJ: Sexuality–the experience and anxieties of medical students. New Engl J Med 281:1397–1403, 1969
19. Vincent CE (ed): Human Sexuality in Medical Education and Practice. Springfield, Il, C Thomas, 1968
20. Lief HI: Obstacles to the ideal and complete sex education of the medical student and physician, in Zubin J, Money J (eds): Contemporary Sexual Behavior: Critical Issues in the 1970s. Baltimore, Johns Hopkins University Press, 1973, p 441–453
20a. Garrard J, Vaitkus A, Chilgren R: Evaluation of a course in human sexuality. J Med Educ 47:773, 1972
21. Lief HI, Vines NR: The physician's roles and tasks in sex counseling and therapy. Presented at a workshop of the American College of Physicians, Phila., April 1976
22. Annon JS: Behavioral Treatment of Sexual Problems: Brief Therapy. Hagerstown, Md., Harper & Row, 1976
23. Vines NR: Student Comfort While Assessing Sexual Concerns. Ph.D. Dissertation, School of Education, University of Pennsylvania, 1976
24. Marcotte DB, Geyer PR, Kilpatrick DG, et al: The effect of a spaced sex education course on medical students' sexual knowledge and attitudes. Br J Med Educ 10:117–121, 1976
25. Lief HI, Miller WR: Masturbatory attitudes, knowledge and experience: Data from the Sex Knowledge and Attitude Test (SKAT). Arch Sex Behav 5:447–467, 1976
26. Marcotte DB, Held JP: A conceptual model for attitude assessment in all areas of medical education (submitted for publication)
27. Peterson OL, Andrews LT, Spain RS, et al: An analytical study of North Carolina general practice: 1953–54. J Med Educ 31 (12), Part 2, 1956

28. Clute KF: The General Practitioner: A Study of Medical Education and Practice in Ontario and Nova Scotia. Toronto, University of Toronto Press, 1963
29. Mudd JW, Fleiss JL: Physical examinations of hospitalized adults. J Med Educ 48:1140–1147, 1973
30. Payne BC, Lyons TF: Office Care Study. Ann Arbor, University of Michigan School of Medicine, 1972
31. Payne BC, et al: The Quality of Medical Care: Evaluation and Improvement. Chicago, Health Services Monograph Series, Hospital Research and Educational Trust, 1976
32. Barro AR: Survey and evaluation of approaches to physician performance measurement. J Med Educ 48:1047–1093, 1973

John Vasconcellos
Douglas Wallace

3
Legislating Sex Education
for Professionals

INTRODUCTION

The phrase "legislating sex education for professionals" might strike readers of this volume as being incongruous; somehow the "need" to mandate education of any kind for professionals does not fit with the generally accepted definition of what a professional is or does. Yet the legislature of the State of California saw a need to pass such legislation in 1976, the first such legislation of its kind to be signed into law in the history of the United States. This chapter will trace the history of two bills from their roots in the social environment through the legislative process to the executive or enactment phase. Consideration will be given to the rights and obligations of the State and how these interact with public need.

SOCIAL ROOTS

The decades of the 1960s and 1970s have been characterized by the confluence of many social and technological developments. This merging of several often conflicting philosophies, attitudes, and life styles may be seen most readily in the area of human sexuality. Phenomena such as the youth culture, the rise of the human potential movement, the women's liberation movement, the antiwar protest, the increasing influence of electronic mass media, and the development of increasingly effective contraceptives have all contributed to an increasing societal concern with sexuality. The mass media's focus on sexuality has helped to foster greater candor and self-disclosure and has made sexuality an acceptable topic for "polite" discussion. The affluent society, with its emphasis on enhancing the quality of life, has resulted in a reevaluation of sexuality and its contribution as an enriching component of relationships. The "body is beautiful and natural" became an acceptable mode of thought, if not lifestyle, as people became more concerned with "natural foods" and "natural functioning footwear."

These basically positive social influences, however, were currents in a society which has traditionally viewed human sexual function with a mixture of revulsion and obsessive preoccupation. The new sexual adjectives of "natural," "honest," "affectionate," conflicted with older pejorative labels of "dirty," "immoral," "disgusting," "obscene," as well as "sacred," "private," and "mysterious." Individuals and couples found themselves caught between inhibiting value-systems by which they were reared and the new social mandate to be sexually liberated; unfortunately the new mandate was often as repressive as the old.

Despite the chaos and confusion, or perhaps as a result of it, a move to redefine sexuality was started. Sexuality was being redefined away from genitalia to eroticism, away from the old dichotomy that held "sex" to be a function of the genitals, while sexuality was a cerebral event at best. The traditional negativity toward the body and the sexual function was not only being undermined at the conceptual level, it was being challenged at the behavioral level as well. Surveys of public opinion and behavior demonstrated repeatedly that sexuality was, in its largest sense, ubiquitous; it permeated every aspect of the human condition. Unfortunately, this information only added to the stress experienced by many individuals as they began to consider the implications of making the transition from where they were with their sexuality to a point which reflected an affirmation of it. As this subjectively experienced sexual distress became more acute for greater numbers of people, health care professionals began to receive more requests for solid sexual information and counsel. The health care consumer began to regard sexuality as a component of life deserving of professional attention. This attention was usually sought during a visit to a physician, as they were perceived to be the only provider of sexual health care.

Physicians were seldom prepared to provide this new type of care. The AMA recognized this lack of preparedness when it adopted a resolution at its annual meeting in 1973 encouraging the formal instruction of physicians in human sexuality at undergraduate, graduate, and continuing medical education levels. The resolution also called upon medical education institutions and organizations to respond promptly and effectively to this area of need. The institutional response to this call was limited primarily to introductory level courses for medical students. Public demand, on the other hand, was increasing dramatically. This situation of imbalance between consumer demands and the ability of health care providers to deliver quality care provided the impetus for the legislation to be discussed below.

LEGISLATIVE ACTION

Legislative bodies have two general tasks which must be accomplished if effective legislation is to be developed and enacted. One is an informational task; the other is one of limitation.

The informational task. Legislative bodies must inform themselves as to what the public needs are, and what resources are available to meet those needs. This task is accomplished through numerous public and private hearings, meetings, briefings, individual research, and the efforts of lobbyists. Staff aides and assistants also play an important role in developing the informational base to support the positions which an individual legislator may wish to take on a particular issue. Which issues become the subject of formal legislative proposals is a function of the individual legislator and his or her values, attitudes, and perception of need, both personal and public.

Two sociopolitical considerations dictate whether a bill is introduced. One is a consideration of readiness; the perception that both the public and the legislature are ready to address themselves to the issue or question being raised. The second consideration is timeliness; is there an immediacy to the issue, does the issue require immediate attention? It should be noted that a consideration of these factors may often overcome perceptions of considerable need, with the resulting inaction oftentimes leading to unfortunate consequences.

The limitation task. Completion of this task is more often than not accomplished as a result of political negotiation, as it involves a determination of the appropriate legislative response and, in turn, the specific language of the legislation. The capacity of the state government also becomes an important consideration; that is, can the state respond in a valuable and meaningful manner? Many bills, when signed into law, direct that other components of state government carry out specific tasks. These components may be large departments such as a health department, or smaller bureaus or regulatory agencies. An implicit assumption is made that the bureaus or agencies will have the necessary expertise and resources to accomplish the mandated task. This assumption may be made even though it is known to be untrue, because the legislature may be acutely aware of its own lack of expertise or resources to perform the task itself.

State Regulation of Interpersonal Transactions

The role of the state in regulating or effecting change in the social environment is a critical issue, for it is central to the determination of whether or not the state should act in a particular instance, and if so, how it should respond. The state has a right to assist its citizens to lead more fulfilling lives, to ensure the safety of its citizens, and to help construct adequate environments in which to raise children. These rights are derived from the state's constitutional responsibility to provide for the education of children, to provide for the health and safety of all its inhabitants, and to provide conditions which facilitate the pursuit of happiness. With regard to human sexuality, the state may then provide for sex education, regulate those interpersonal exchanges wherein one person is in an inferior position (e.g., rape, incest and child molestation), and promote sexual health by ensuring that individuals who deliver health care services are qualified to do so. The latter provision usually takes the form of regulation through licensure and certification procedures. The idea of legislating sex education for professionals came out of a series of hearings conducted by the Assembly Permanent Subcommittee on Health Personnel in 1975. The purpose of these hearings was to explore the desirability of establishing government regulatory mechanisms on the newly emerging fields of sex counseling and sex therapy.

TWO SEX EDUCATION BILLS

Assemblyman John Vasconcellos was invited to attend the hearings as an observer because of his demonstrated interest in matters pertaining to medical education and human sexuality. Evidence presented at the hearings suggested that those professions which were currently licensed to provide sex counseling services (e.g., physicians, psychologists, and social workers) were providing lower quality sex counseling to their patients and clients than those calling themselves "sex counselors," who were currently unlicensed. Simple observation indicated that most of the sex counselors had gone to the trouble and expense to acquire some expertise in the field by attending some type of training program; most of the physicians and others had not. It was astonishing to learn that the licensed professionals had not recognized their own need to secure additional training in support of the activities in which they were currently engaged. This indicated a lack of awareness of their own sexuality and an apparent lack of sensitivity to the needs of their patients. It also reflected the mystification and ambivalence toward sexuality existent in society. A similar lack of awareness was being displayed by many medical schools in the state. Training of medical students in human sexuality was either nonexistent or it was given cursory treatment. Thus the legislation grew out of a perceived need to ensure that those who were currently licensed to provide sex counseling services were sufficiently aware and capable of doing so.

Two bills were introduced into the Assembly. One would require

... any person seeking or renewing a license, registration, or first renewal of such license as a licensed clinical social worker, or any person seeking a license as a marriage, family and child counselor or psychologist to show evidence of completed training in human sexuality, as defined, as a condition of licensure or registration (Assembly Bill No. 4178, p 2).

The second bill was very similar, in that it would require

... an applicant for a physician's and surgeon's certificate or an applicant applying for renewal of such certificate ... to show by evidence that he has completed training in human sexuality ... (Assembly Bill No. 4179, p 1).

The intent of these bills was not to get the identified professionals to become learned in the area of human sexuality, but rather to get them to increase their level of self-awareness regarding their own sexuality so that their personal sexual values and attitudes would not interfere with their providing counsel to their sexually distressed patients or clients. Another rationale for the bills was educational. For although the State has a direct constitutional responsibility to provide for the education of school-age children, it must remain aware of those generations who are not in school, who may not be sexually aware, who will experience sexual difficulties, and who will likely seek assistance from licensed practitioners. The State should ensure that those licensed to provide sex counseling are qualified to educate those generations out of school, who by virtue of their lack of sex education may be disturbed about their sexuality.

It should be noted that the two bills did not specify the content of the training in human sexuality. Rather, human sexuality was defined simply as "the study of a human being as a sexual being and how he or she functions with respect thereto." While this definition represents a holistic conceptualization of human sexuality, it is also "limited" in the legislative sense previously discussed. Each regulatory agency is free to choose the definition most fitting the professions it serves, and further, they can specify the minimum requirements regarding the type and quantity of training deemed necessary to ensure the delivery of adequate sexual health-care services. The role of these regulatory agencies will be considered again after we have seen the bills through the legislative process.

The bills were introduced into the Assembly with the full expectation that two to three years would be required to educate the legislators to their importance. The bills were sent to the Health Committee where they were heard and considered with little opposition. They were then sent to the Ways and Means Committee because of the administrative costs involved should the bills become law. Again there was little opposition. The bills next went to the floor of the Assembly, where with little debate, they were passed overwhelmingly as some of the more conservative members lined up to support them. The rapidity with which the bills moved through the Assembly was totally unexpected, as there is generally such a fear of sexuality among many legislators that they will reflexively vote against any legislation which might be considered pro-sexual.

The Senate, a traditionally more conservative body, was expected to be more difficult. Only two favorable votes of the six needed to get the bills out of the Senate Health and Welfare Committee could be anticipated. While the bills were being held in committee, the California Medical Association intensified its lobbying effort against the bills, concerned that making training in human sexuality a legislated requirement for recertification might be too stringent. The Association suggested an amendment which would have the word "recommended" substituted for the word "required," with the Board of Medical Quality Assurance, the regulatory agency for medical specialties, to consider making the training a requirement as part of their continuing medical education program. They pledged to drop their opposition to the bill if their amendment were accepted. During a subsequent hearing, one of the most conservative members of the Senate inquired of Assemblyman Vasconcellos whether the amendment was acceptable to him. It was. The Senator replied by saying that he would then move the bills out of committee; but he also added that he would like to know where he might take one of the courses described during the hearings. That this legislator, who one would have not expected to have been curious about the subject, indicated such self-awareness regarding his own need for information was an indication of the attractiveness and timeliness of the bills. The response of the Senate Finance Committee was also indicative of the bills' attractiveness, as it took up consideration of the bills with no opposition and no debate. When the bills were sent to the floor of the Senate for consideration they were placed on the Consent Calendar, which meant that there was no opposition and no debate required. Returning to the Assembly for concurrence, the bills were passed overwhelmingly. The Governor received the bills, and after intensive lobbying efforts by his advisors overcame his skepticism, the bills were signed into law. Training in human sexuality was now required as a precondition for licensure for some health professionals and strongly recommended for others.

To obtain passage of the bills there had to be a readiness both in the public and in the legislature, and this readiness had to occur approximately at the same time in both spheres; for though the legislature may be somewhat ahead of the general public in its consideration of various issues, individual legislators are not willing to get so far out that they are no longer able to communicate with the public. To do so would be against common sense and self-preservation as an elected representative. The public was ready for the bills, as there was no adverse reaction or backlash from any constituents; they evidently believed that this was a legitimate area for legislative activity.

Another factor was timing. Ten years ago the dialogue about sexuality on the Assembly floor was of "locker room" mentality, conducted behind closed doors with hand across the mouth and accompanied by a lot of tittering. When it came out on the floor it was embarrassing to those possessed of some sensitivity and self-awareness regarding sexuality. In addition, the fear of sexuality which was common in society at the time, and the fear of the politician worried about reelection, combined to produce paralysis when sexual topics were considered. In 1973 a bill concerning consensual sexual relations between adults precipitated extensive debate in the Assembly. This debate, however, represented a turning point in the consideration of legislation concerning sexual issues for it was of exceptional quality, with the various arguments and viewpoints being put forth directly and cogently. The Assembly had demonstrated that it could consider sexuality as an integral component of the social order. It reaffirmed this development by the manner in which it considered the sex-education-for-professionals bills.

A third factor which facilitated passage of the legislation was the untenable position in which the professionals were placed. Assuming that the professionals were informed of the bills and were organized as a political force, it would have been embarrassing for them to come forward and testify that they should not have this education or training. To do so would have required them to deny that they were being asked by their patients or clients for sexual information or counsel, an unlikely situation as it was common knowledge that they have always been asked about sexual issues.

A fourth and final factor which was of importance in securing passage of the bills was the increasing popularity of the holistic conceptualization of human beings and their relationship to their environment, and the concomitant development of a concept of social competency which held that individuals should be educated, by whatever means, to a certain level of social functioning (i.e., the individual by the time he or she reaches the age of majority should be able to function in the society in such a manner as to make a contribution to society as well as to their own growth and development). It is unfortunate that many people had not accepted this new conception of human ecology, particularly as it concerned sexual behavior. It should be noted that it is not the obligation or the right of the state to enter into such value conflicts and mandate a solution; rather it is the responsibility of the state to raise the question—is not there a better alternative?—and then to permit the people to make their own choices based upon an informed self-awareness and freedom from fear or repression.

ACTIONS OF STATE BOARDS AND AGENCIES

The legislative function, aside from oversight responsibilities, ends when the bills are signed into law. It is then the responsibility of the state agencies and boards to determine what the legislature meant and to make the legislation operational. As of this writing, the Board of Medical Quality Assurance has submitted its determinations and recommendations concerning medical-student instruction in human sexuality to the legislature and governor for approval. The Board determined that: the instruction must be a minimum of 30 clock-hours, involve a multidisciplinary faculty; cover the topics of sociocultural determinants of sexual attitudes and values, variations in sexual behavior including homosexuality, the nosology and etiology of common sexual dysfunctions, techniques for sexual history-taking, and office management and appropriate referral of sexual problems and sexual trauma. The instruction should include the use of explicit sexual materials such as films, slides, and interviews; and at the end of the course of instruction, the student be able to take a sexual history and develop an appropriate patient management plan which may include appropriate referral. A task force was established to facilitate the necessary curriculum development and to consider the inclusion of human sexuality in the continuing medical education of physicians.

The agencies which regulate the practice of psychologists, licensed clinical social workers, and marriage, family, and child counselors have yet to make their final determinations. There is some indication that they will recommend the following: a minimum of ten clock-hours of didactic instruction in human sexuality to be conducted by an approved or accredited educational institution, with the focus of instruction directed toward increasing the awareness of the course participants as to the importance of sexuality in a holistic model of human behavior. As these agencies are only concerned with licensure and certification, they are likely to leave the content of the course of instruction to the discretion of the educational institution or course faculty, perhaps with some input from the professional associations of the respective professions.

Administrative difficulties may delay the final implementation of the new requirements. However, the issue has been raised and each of those affected must at least begin to consider the implications which their current level of sexual self-awareness and comfort may have for their ability to provide their patients or clients with quality sexual health care.

SUMMARY

Considered from the perspective of a legislator, the major lesson learned from the experience was that people are often more ready to embrace new ideas and modes of behavior than we legislators think they are, and that quite often we do not raise the questions or issues at the legislative level because of this misperception, when in reality, we are the ones who are not ready to take the necessary actions to confront the problem. It is important for people elsewhere, who may be involved in or concerned with the legislative process, to believe in the possibility that appropriate and effective legislation can be passed, if such is required; and perhaps more importantly, to know that important questions and issues concerning human sexuality can be raised, and that an arena can be created wherein they can be heard. This is not to deny the real costs involved, one of which is the time and effort that is required to become comfortable with one's own sexuality, but rather to hold out the hope that with the development of increased self-awareness we may be better able to effect a more humane environment in which to raise sexually healthy children and to affirm our own sexuality.

PART II

Designing a Curriculum in Human Sexuality

Norman Rosenzweig
F. Paul Pearsall

Introduction

Although human sexuality per se was not generally taught, traditional medical education has long included instruction in sexual anatomy and physiology, at least as these subjects have been traditionally understood. The direct observations of Masters and Johnson, however, have clearly demonstrated that traditional teaching has been sorely inadequate, and many so-called "facts" that had been transmitted in this fashion were erroneous. It is obvious that accurate information about sexual anatomy and physiology are essential not only for the practice of medicine, but for all those who seek to help others with their sexual life. Oliver Bjorksten provides a comprehensive review of the issues involved in teaching these traditional subjects in nontraditional ways to heterogeneous student groups of varied educational and philosophical backgrounds.

Anatomy and physiology, however, are not enough for a comprehensive curriculum in human sexuality, and the chapter by Stayton provides an extensive overview of the multiple considerations that must be taken into account by anyone attempting to prepare a course on human sexuality. Stayton considers the curriculum within the context of the anxieties and emotional biases of the student to be taught, and emphasizes the need to begin where the student is rather than where we expect students to be. The point is made here, as it is repeatedly throughout this volume, that there cannot be adequate assimilation of information without some attitude restructuring, which many of the authors refer to as "sensitization-desensitization" in the manner of McIlvenna and the Sexual Attitude Reassessment approach. This is only to repeat that curriculum design in human sexuality is not a task that can be approached in a

49

purely academic fashion; the teaching methodology must be considered simultaneously with the course content.

Three chapters in this section call special attention to particular content areas that deserve some consideration in the design of any core curriculum, but require added emphasis and elaboration where special audiences are being addressed. So long as venereal disease remains a major public health problem, it would be a gross omission if the subject were not included in any course on human sexuality, to laymen or professional alike. But as Aronoff emphasizes, it is essential that the physician and those who counsel others on sexual matters have a realistic understanding of the nature and scope of the problems of sexually transmissible diseases. In addition, Aronoff shares with us his personal experiences and views on how this difficult subject can best be incorporated into a human sexuality curriculum.

Cole also addresses a subject that both teacher and student would often prefer to ignore or gloss over—sexuality and the physically handicapped. Confronting this aversive attitude toward the disabled which is shared even by the health care professional, Cole addresses the need to help faculty members become comfortable with impairment and the impaired person before they can teach others techniques and skills for facilitating sexual adjustment of such persons.

Just as it used to be considered acceptable to investigate sexuality through studies of animal behavior, there was one college department that had sanction to study human sexuality—provided it was confined to studies of primitive peoples. This was probably because people in polite Western society could wall off the anthropologists' observations as pertaining to heathen practices of savages. Gebhard points out how far we have come from this notion. Cross-cultural studies of sexual practices are no longer used to justify the notion that non-Western societies are subhuman, but rather to place into transcultural perspective many of the cherished notions of Western civilization regarding what is right and proper sexual behavior. Gebhard thereby emphasizes the ethnocentric biases of most professionals, and the relevance of such biases to the attitudes of students and teachers of human sexuality.

William R. Stayton

4
The Core Curriculum: What Can Be Taught and What Must Be Taught

INTRODUCTION

As training in human sexuality for the health professional becomes more widespread, it is important to consider what can and must be taught in the core curriculum. Concerns of this chapter include the reasons why the health professional needs a human-sexuality educational experience, the objectives of such training with suggestions for implementation, and a comparison of a comprehensive curriculum with one which includes only the basic essentials. Materials for this overview are drawn from the outstanding curricula already tested in medical or graduate schools, from the guidelines set forth by the American Association of Sex Educators, Counselors and Therapists (AASECT),[1] and from this writer's own experience with the suggested curriculum.

RATIONALE FOR A SEXUALITY CURRICULUM

In order to function competently, the health professional needs to be keenly aware of his or her own attitudes, feelings, and judgments surrounding all areas of sex, and must have a basic body of knowledge as well as skills for treating sexual concerns of the patient or client. This education and experience is essential to counteract the growth-limiting attitudes and societal realities present in the United States. Anxiety and emotionality surround the field of human sexuality today. As Judd Marmor has so well stated: "Sexual behavior is so intimately entwined with moral issues, religious and cultural value systems, and even aesthetic reactions, that those who attempt to deal with it too open-mindedly are likely to be charged by their contemporaries with being immoral or amoral, if not illegal."[2]

Several factors have contributed to the high level of discomfort and anxiety which so many people, including health professionals, feel about the whole subject of sex. Four major anxiety-producing factors can be identified:

1. *Sexual Trauma.* In our American culture, expression of sexuality has been repressed, and the majority of people are traumatized in regard to their natural sexual curiosity, fantasies, and need. A person is born sexual with the potential capacity of responding erotically to any number of sexual stimuli. As the acculturation process occurs in the developing individual, limitations are placed on the individual's sexual behavior. Appropriate sexual expression has traditionally been limited to married, monogamous, heterosexual relationships, and within these relationships variations of sexual behavior have also been limited. All this has had the effect of programming a person away from his or her own natural sexual responsivity. Autosexuality, homosexuality, and apart from marriage, even heterosexuality are negatively programmed in most persons. Thus any discussion of these matters creates trauma, anxiety, and confusion. Confusion arises because there is an internal struggle between natural sexual interests and appropriate culturally sanctioned interests.

2. *Sexual Ignorance.* Many segments in our society value sexual ignorance. There is a proscription against knowledge because it is believed that knowledge increases irresponsible behavior. This claim is unsubstantiated by research; nevertheless, my observations and experiences lead me to believe it is a widely-held view. In my clinical experience, many people seem to self-select ignorance, as knowledge of sexual matters might require them to be more responsible for their interests and actions; it is so much easier to blame parents, upbringing, religion, God, and ignorance for their sexual inhibitions. In fact, sexual inhibition is the most prevalent sexual dysfunction today.[3] Sexual ignorance contributes to inhibition of natural sexual desire.

3. *Sexual Secretiveness.* Another problem in a sexually repressive culture is the value placed on being secretive. It is not appropriate to discuss sexual behaviors. This secretiveness has not only afflicted lay persons but health professionals as well. Too often professional training exacerbates secretiveness because sexuality is approached from a pathological perspective, thus increasing the professional's trauma and ignorance.

4. *New Phenomena in the Sexual Life Cycle.* Today we are faced with some new phenomena in the field of human sexuality which challenge our traditional religious and moral value systems. At least five will be mentioned briefly.[4]

First, there is a Biblical injunction to "be fruitful and multiply." This has been the formula for human survival until recently when it has suddenly become the formula for human disaster. It took until 1850 for humankind to populate the earth to 1 billion persons. Today in the late 1970s we have 4 billion. Yet our concepts regarding proper sexual behavior still center around the procreative function.

Second, with the advent of contraception, it is now possible to separate procreational from recreational sex. Yet we have not developed moral or ethical value systems based on a need for recreational sex with its behavioral implications.

Third, adolescence has been expanded so that it is no longer a transition stage of 2–4 years between childhood and adulthood, but rather a major stage in life lasting possibly 10–15 years. We have not creatively taken into account the sexual needs and demands of that important stage in the life cycle.

Fourth, there are sex roles and there are sex-coded roles. Sex roles are well defined and unquestioned: males can impregnate; females can lactate, gestate, and menstruate. Most other behavior is sex coded by a particular time and culture. Today virtually every sex-coded role is being challenged. The effect of this challenge on family life and sexuality is profound; it is both healthy and frightening, but neither males nor females seem to be emotionally equipped as yet to handle the implications of changing sex-coded roles.

Fifth, one of the most neglected areas of research and clinical practice has been sexuality and the aging process. People now live longer. Today 10 percent of our population (over 20 million persons) are over the age of 65. An important concern of older persons is their sexuality and "proper" sexual expression. Much has been learned about the sexual capacity of aging persons, but there is much more to know. One thing we do know is that given a good self-image, healthy attitudes toward sex, meaningful sexual experience throughout early and middle adulthood, an attractive (to the person) partner, and reasonably good health, there is no reason why one's capacity and interest in sex cannot grow and deepen with age, especially after retirement, when there is time to cultivate one's sexual responsivity.

Whether we like it or not, these and other subtle forces have created a revolution which is changing our lives. The health professional is placed in a position of being the "expert," and yet he or she may know less and be more traumatized, ignorant, and secretive than the patient or client. Even the professional who has adequate sexual knowledge may be unable to be of any help to a patient or client because of his or her own anxieties and attitudes about sexuality. It is clear that education and training in human sexuality is essential for the professional.

OBJECTIVES OF A SEXUALITY CURRICULUM

Every sexuality curriculum for the health professional must include experiences and course work in three areas of training.

Desensitization—Resensitization

Some of the outstanding programs in the country, such as that at the University of Minnesota Medical School, have revised their curriculum in human sexuality to meet the needs of a traumatized, ignorant, and secretive student population, through the "demythologizing of sexual behavior, desensitization to hasty or emotional overreaction to sexual stimuli, and resensitization toward gentle, humanistic, and professional understanding of the sexuality of both self and others."[5] This writer agrees that this objective is essential in the education of any professional involved in human-sexuality issues. The program mentioned, known as Sexual Attitude Restructuring (SAR), was developed in cooperation with the National Sex Forum of San Francisco, the originators of an implosion model of desensitization through the use of explicit films of persons, couples, and groups involved in sexual activity. Research conducted at the University of Pennsylvania School of Medicine, through the Center for the Study of Sex Education in Medicine, revealed that students who participated in the implosion model were significantly more comfortable in confronting sexual issues in patients than those who viewed the same films over a period of weeks and those who saw no films.[6] The format of using explicit films followed by small group discussions is now a part of human-sexuality programs in many medical and graduate schools throughout the country. AASECT also considers the SAR an important first step in training professionals in human sexuality.

An alternative method of desensitization, which may be used with or without the films, was developed by the author and Nathan W. Turner, both of whom served as the Family Life and Sex Education team at Marriage Council of Philadelphia when this alternative was developed. This approach uses fantasy and recall of significant events in the psychosexual life-cycle of the individual as outlined by Erik Erikson.[7]

The format includes questions centered around each stage in the life cycle: prenatal, infancy, early childhood, play age (5–8), school age (9–12), adolescence (13–19), and adulthood. The questions are designed to help students probe their psychosexual development to gain insight into those events and experiences that shaped their attitudes toward various areas of sexual behavior and sexual relating. Personal reflection on each question also helps to identify the feelings surrounding each experience, attitude, or judgment.

Group discussions allow experience in talking about a subject that has been secretive and broadens one's view of "normal" human sexual behavior and response. Health professionals who are aware of their own feelings and attitudes toward sexual behavior and responses feel more comfortable and are less likely to impose their opinions, judgments, and anxieties on the client or patient.

Knowledge Building

Once the professionals' anxieties have been reduced, the second phase of knowledge building is instituted. The professional must know the physical, psychological, emotional, and behavioral aspects of human sexuality. The breadth of knowledge required depends, in part, on the degree to which the professional is involved in the treatment of sexual problems, from diagnosis and referral to therapy. The content of this phase will be discussed thoroughly in the next two sections of this chapter.

Skill Development

The third phase of the core-curriculum program includes skill development in treating the sexual concerns of the patient or client. Once the professional has become comfortable regarding sexual development, behavior, and expression, he or she must then learn how to apply this new attitude and knowledge to help another person. For some professionals, such as the general medical student, this phase would include taking a sex history, sorting out the sexual concerns of the patient, and making the proper referral to a sex therapist. This professional needs to be informed of the various treatment models available and the appropriateness and effectiveness of each.

However, for the professional who wants to perform sex therapy, further training is necessary, including supervision by a qualified sex therapist. Training opportunities are discussed at the end of this chapter.

The following course objectives from the University of Indiana Medical School and the University of Minnesota Medical School summarize well the objectives in training programs for health professionals in the area of human sexuality:[8]

1. To increase the student's awareness that:
   a. a wide variety of sexual problems exist,
   b. many of these problems are presented to the health professional,
   c. the professional needs more than his or her personal experience and private opinions to help these clients and patients,
   d. the professional's judgment is frequently handicapped by his or her own personal taboos, biases, and overreactions to sexual information and stimuli.
2. To make the student more tolerant of the wide spectrum of "normal" human sexual responses.
3. To force the student to think about the various points of view in controversial sexual issues.
4. To "desensitize" the student against hasty or over- reaction to sexual stimuli.
5. To "resensitize" the student to become gently, humanistically, and professionally involved in understanding clients' and patients' sexuality.
6. To help the student decide whether he or she will include or exclude the management of sexual problems in his or her professional practice.
7. To convince the student that a professional treating sexual problems has the right of access to very personal data from those he or she serves.
8. To introduce the professional to:
   a. some diagnostic tools,
   b. some therapeutic techniques,
   c. some preventive procedures and materials.

CONTENT: WHAT CAN BE TAUGHT

Before describing the kinds of courses which can be taught in this field, I will briefly discuss the importance of the methods that are used. In order that a professional be both knowledgeable and sensitive to sexual issues and how they affect persons, I believe it is necessary to use both affective and cognitive methodologies in presenting course material. Of course, the SAR is an experiential model. But within the body of academic work, it is highly recommended to help students confront the material as it relates to attitudes and personal responses. For example, instead of telling about sex and the aging process, it would be advantageous to have older persons who are open about their experiences share with the class, have general discussion, and relate this to the material read and studied in class. Throughout this section there will be suggestions for using an affective model of education.

The practicing professional can find opportunities to take part in an effective experiential course in human sexuality through participation in short-term workshops such as the AASECT Advanced Studies Institute which allows participants to relive their own psychosocial-sexual development via film, fantasy, and discussion. These experiences are coupled with cognitive data from research. In a course format, experiential learning is included in the SAR portion of the course as well as in a continued relating of knowledge to one's own experience and understanding.

The knowledge building content of the course can be organized to follow in sequence the stages of development as outlined by Erik Erikson. The content as outlined below follows the suggested curriculum of AASECT.[9] It is recognized that in some programs, such as in a medical school, some of the content would be covered in other courses.

1. **The Process of Reproduction.**
   Biology . . . Heredity . . . Sex Determination . . . Menstruation. Conception . . . Pregnancy . . . Embryology . . . Childbirth . . . Multiple Births . . . Infertility and Sterility . . . Contraception . . . Abortion . . . Population Control.
2. **Sexual Development.**
   Sexual Components of Physical, Mental, and Emotional Growth during Infancy . . . Prepuberty Period . . . Puberty . . . Early Adolescence . . . Late Adolescence to Adulthood . . . Fixation and Arrested Development . . . Sexual Responsiveness in Early Adulthood . . . Middle Age and Old Age . . . Menopause and Climacteric.
3. **Sexual Functioning.**
   Male and Female Anatomy and Physiology . . . Masturbation in Infancy . . . Childhood, Adolescence, and Maturity . . . Nocturnal Emissions . . . Sex Dreams and Fantasies . . . Male and Female Homosexuality . . . Sexual Variations and Other Erotic Minorities . . . Male and Female Coital Response . . . The Sexual Dysfunctions of the Male and Female . . . Myths and Fallacies Relating to Sexual Functioning.
4. **Sexual Behavior.**
   Cultural Values Relating to Sex . . . Religious Views of Sexuality and Sexual Behaviors . . . Laws Relating to Sexual Varietism.

5. **Sex and Gender.**
   Male and Female Sexual Characteristics (primary and secondary) . . . Hermaphroditism and Transsexualism . . . Masculinity and Femininity . . . Gender Roles and Stereotypes . . . The Liberation Movements.
6. **Marriage, Family and Interpersonal Relationships.**
   Courtship and Mate Selection . . . Sexual Adjustment in Marriage . . . Sexual Communication in the Family . . . Sex Education in the Home . . . Parents as Gender Models . . . Psychology of Family Relations . . . Sex in Changing Marriage Patterns . . . Mate Swapping . . . Group Sex.
7. **Sex and Health.**
   Sex-related Biological Anamolies and Anatomical Malformations . . . Sex and Hormones . . . Venereal Disease . . . Sex and Mental Health . . . Sexual Anxiety and Conflict . . . Sex and Neurosis.
8. **The Study of Sex.**
   History of Sex Beliefs and Attitudes in Western Culture . . . Sex in Other Cultures . . . Sex Among Primitive Peoples . . . Sex in Subhuman Species . . . The Scientific Study of Sex . . . Findings of Major Sex Studies . . . Current and Future Directions in Sex Research.

An effective way to implement part of the course content is to bring in guests who represent the various erotic minorities, such as members of the "gay" community, transsexuals, transvestites, and one of the paraphilias (if possible) to share their experiences and perceptions. This can be a vital addition to the desensitization and resensitization process.

Other essential parts of course content include: (1) taking a sex history, (2) introduction to various counseling modalities in treating sexual problems, and (3) opportunity to develop skills for consultation, collaboration and referral.[10]

An effective technique for teaching sex-history-taking is to have the students pair off and take the sex history from each other and then discuss the experience as to degree of comfort, usefulness of data gathered, and insights and learnings about that data-gathering process.

When presenting the various treatment models, it is suggested that practicing therapists who represent the various modalities, such as rational-emotive therapy, behavioral therapy, insight therapy, or psychoanalysis, present the basic concept of their treatment and illustrative case histories.

Role-playing is very useful in teaching the skills of consultation, collaboration, and referral. An interdisciplinary approach can help the student learn about various medical, religious, legal, psychological, and sociological resources and what each can offer. The more the health professional is comfortable with and knowledgeable about the available resources, the easier it will be for him or her to make a successful referral.

CONTENT: WHAT MUST BE TAUGHT

When time is limited, certain basic content areas must be covered in the health professionals' training.

Desensitization and Resensitization. Basic to any training in sexuality is some type of desensitization program. The most rapid and effective means involves the use of films and a person trained in the SAR technique. When these resources are unavailable, the fantasy and recall technique may be substituted. These techniques are described in detail earlier in this chapter.

Issues and Research in Human Sexuality. Following some type of desensitization process, it is helpful to highlight critical issues and current research in sexuality throughout the life cycle. A discussion of the development of gender, gender identity, sex roles, sex-coded roles, and sexual orientation is very important. If at all possible, invite a transsexual to meet with the students so they can experience and learn from someone who was discordant in their physiological and gender-identity development and can understand the process the person went through to become integrated as a whole person in mind and body.

Techniques of Taking a Sex History. Learning the technique of taking a sex history from a patient or client is basic in the training of the health professional. A method of accomplishing this was described in the previous section of this chapter and has proven to be effective.

The Sexual Response-Cycle. Understanding the phase of the sexual response cycle, both physiologically and psychologically, and the effect that illness or anxiety can have in disrupting the sexual response cycle, is essential to any health professional who may deal with sexual concerns.

Erotic Variations. This part of the curriculum would include the erotic variations in human experience including autosexuality, homosexuality, bisexuality, heterosexuality, and the paraphilias. The author has found that it is extremely beneficial to have a representative(s) of the various erotic minorities meet with the students.

Alternative life styles that persons are choosing with integrity today can also be explored. These alternatives include: monogamous nuclear relationships, single parenthood, childless relationships, singlehood, second-chance monogamy or serial marriage, communal living, cohabitation, swinging and group sex, group marriage, open-ended relationships, and family network systems including the voluntary extended family.[11] It should be noted that these lifestyles can be chosen by persons regardless of sexual orientation.

Sexual Issues Encountered in Health Practice. The material in this section can be made specific to the student's professional objective, e.g., sexuality in OB/GYN practice, family medicine, pediatrics, social work, and nursing. Included in this section would be study of sex and handicapped or spinal cord injured patients, and sexuality and the aging process.

Treating Sexual Dysfunction. A basic curriculum would include material on the definition, etiology, and treatment modalities of sexual dysfunction, including developing the skills for consultation, collaboration and referral as discussed in the previous section of this chapter.

FURTHER TRAINING OPPORTUNITIES

There are an increasing number of opportunities for health professionals who seek further training in human sexuality. A list of accredited training programs can be obtained from the American Association of Sex Educators, Counselors and Therapists, the American Association of Marriage and Family Counselors, the Sex Information and Education Council of the United States, and the Eastern Association of Sex Therapy.

A student who has had adequate course material and wishes to continue training through supervision from a qualified sex therapist may refer to the *National Register of Certified Sex Therapists,* obtainable through AASECT. A number of medical and graduate schools also offer supervised clinical internships. It is generally agreed that proficiency as a sex therapist is best facilitated through supervision, using audio recording, videotaping, and observation through the one-way-vision mirror, as well as individual and group case conferences.

SUMMARY

This chapter has presented a rationale and objectives for the sex education of the professional, suggested methods for implementation of a program, discussed what can and must be taught in the core curriculum, and identified sources of information on further training opportunities for the professional who would like to include sex therapy in his or her professional service.

REFERENCES

1. American Association of Sex Educators, Counselors and Therapists: The Professional Training and Preparation of Sex Counselors and the Professional Training and Preparation of Sex Educators. Washington, D.C., AASECT, 1973
2. Marmor J: "Normal" and "deviant" sexual behavior. JAMA 217:165–170, 1971
3. Kaplan HS: Interview: "Quack" sex therapy. Med Aspects Hum Sexuality 11:32–47, 1977
4. Money J, Tucker P: Sexual Signatures: On Being a Man or a Woman. Boston, Little, Brown, 1976, p 7
5. Chilgren RA, Rosenberg P, Cole T, et al: A process of attitude change in human sexuality, in Maddock JW, Dickman DL (eds): Human Sexuality: A Resource Book, vol 1. Minneapolis, The Medical School, University of Minnesota, 1972
6. Vines NR: Responses to Sexual Problems in Medical Counseling as a Function of Counselor Exposure to Sex Education Procedures Incorporating Erotic Film. Ph.D. Dissertation, University of Pennsylvania, 1974
7. Maier HW: Three Theories of Child Development, 2nd ed. New York, Harper & Row, 1969
8. Maddock JW, Dickman DL (eds): Course objectives: Human Sexuality: A Resource Book, vol 1. Minneapolis, The Medical School, University of Minnesota, 1972
9. American Association of Sex Educators, Counselors and Therapists: The Professional Training and Preparation of Sex Counselors. Washington, AASECT, 1973, p 7–8
10. American Association of Sex Educators, Counselors and Therapists: The Professional Training and Preparation of Sex Counselors. Washington, AASECT, 1973, p 9–10
11. Mazur RM: The New Intimacy: Open-Ended Marriage and Alternative Life-Style. Boston, Beacon Press, 1974

Oliver Bjorksten

5
Teaching Sexual Anatomy and Physiology

INTRODUCTION

Traditional medical education has long included instruction in human sexual anatomy and physiology.[1] However, recent in vivo observations by Masters and Johnson have demonstrated that much traditional teaching was inadequate and many of the "facts" so transmitted were erroneous.[2] It is obvious that accurate information about sexual anatomy and physiology are essential for the practice of medicine, psychology, family planning counseling, marital therapy, and of course, sexual therapy. In an effort to help the sex educator incorporate the modern discoveries into his or her curriculum effectively and efficiently, this chapter will consider problems facing the educator and the student, teaching methods and strategies, the issue of *who* needs to know *what*, and curriculum planning.

PROBLEMS IN TEACHING SEXUAL ANATOMY AND PHYSIOLOGY

Some of the major problems encountered in teaching sexual anatomy and physiology are mentioned below and are further considered elsewhere in this volume. In planning an educational endeavor, it is vital that the teacher carefully consider each of these problem areas and choose methods and strategies which will best overcome them.

Heterogeneous Composition of Student Groups. This is unquestionably the greatest single problem facing the sex educator. Groups are often composed of students who vary widely in experience, knowledge, capability, and motivation. Such a group tends to exhibit more intense rivalry, competition, contempt for one another, and professional jealousy than would a more homogeneous group. Several facets of this basic problem must be considered in planning a particular class or course:

1. **Motivation.** Students who plan a career in surgery, community mental health, or pastoral counseling may have little interest in learning about complex physiological mechanisms, while those who plan to practice sex therapy may be disappointed if the teacher is not thorough enough. The instructor faces the challenge of demonstrating the relevance of these subjects to a variety of clinical situations.
2. **Educational Background.** Not all students, even those in medical school, have a basic knowledge of gross anatomy or human physiology. The instructor must consider how to relate course material to what the students know so they can integrate the new information effectively.
3. **Ability to Think in Biological Terms.** Many students interested in sex therapy have had no prior training in biological sciences and may have trouble understanding even the most basic concepts and assumptions. This can be the case with social work students, psychologists, and pastoral counselors. Other students are highly sophisticated biologists and may become bored if presentations are too elementary.
4. **Purpose for Which Knowledge is Sought.** The involvement of a student who approaches this subject as an interested layman will be quite different from that of a student who plans to enter clinical practice involving sexual problems. The teacher must decide how "practical" the teaching should be, and the number and complexity of examples to be used.

Course Parameters. A teacher rarely has unlimited time and facilities for teaching a subject, and he or she must usually reach a compromise between optimum and practical goals and methods. This problem is especially evident in teaching sexual anatomy and physiology, which many students consider of less intrinsic interest than such topics as sexual dysfunctions, paraphilias, and sexual attitudes.

Resistance to Acquiring Knowledge. In addition to the usual problems of students, such as overwork, competition by other courses, test anxiety, and intellectual limitations, sexual subjects often stimulate specific resistances. These may include moral conflicts, professional pride, embarrassment at public discussion of sexual topics, and unwillingness to betray any degree of ignorance. Physicians, for example, are often reluctant to question teachers freely about sexual subjects when non-medical students are present. Furthermore, the student may experience cognitive dissonance as he or she must reevaluate many previously learned ideas, attitudes, and "facts" (or possibly myths) in the light of new information.

Overestimation of Knowledge. Postgraduate students often overestimate how much they already know about the biological aspects of sexuality. The clearest example is the well-trained physician who has forgotten some basic science material or who has not reviewed recent advances in sexual anatomy and physiology.

METHODS OF TEACHING SEXUAL ANATOMY AND PHYSIOLOGY

A number of teaching methods will be reviewed in this section. It is important that the teacher choose those methods which are most likely to confront the students' problems and at which he or she is most proficient. For example, a competent but humorless teacher probably should not attempt to entertain students with a series of poorly presented jokes.

Didactic Presentations. Lectures are a very efficient means of conveying information to large numbers of students in a relatively short time, particularly when outline notes are provided for each presentation. However, they do have the well-known propensity to become boring unless the material is of great interest or the lecturer has some ability to entertain the audience. This method permits comparatively little student-teacher interaction, but this problem can be overcome by dividing the lecture audience into small discussion groups following the didactic session. A purely verbal presentation may not be effective for teaching sexual anatomy, which requires students to comprehend spatial concepts.

Group Discussion. This method, which promotes student-teacher interaction, may not be the most efficient means of introducing new information, but it can have great value in desensitizing anxiety about discussing sexual topics in public and encouraging students to admit specific areas of ignorance. It works best where the groups are homogeneous in composition. Chapter 9 discusses this approach more fully.

Demonstration Techniques. Several demonstration methods are available:

1. Audio-visual materials are valuable for communicating information, and they also help to desensitize students to dealing with sexually

explicit materials. Films have the advantage of actually showing many sexual physiological phenomena, and slides are particularly useful for visualizing anatomical relationships which are very difficult to explain in words.

2. Anatomical dissection is one of the best methods for teaching detailed sexual anatomy, but it is usually limited to the medical profession.

3. Laboratory demonstrations, while usually requiring animal material, can provide model systems for the student to study and manipulate in order to better understand relevant physiological variables.

4. Models of sexual anatomy are especially useful in learning in vivo anatomical relationships which will later be used in clinical practice. A relatively new teaching method involves performance of sexological examinations of "surrogate patients" who are themselves experts in sexual anatomy and can teach students while the genital examination is being performed. Students not only learn sexual anatomy, but they become more comfortable talking with patients during the examination. This method also provides direct feedback to students about their examination methods and skill.

Reading. The time-honored method of teaching most students is to provide them with reading materials on sexual anatomy and physiology. While probably the most efficient method, the teacher has little control over whether students have actually read and understood the material. Materials are available from the comic book to the textbook level, which lessens the problem of matching reading material to the students' level of knowledge. Illustrations can be helpful to biologically experienced students; but they may be virtually incomprehensible to other students, who are apt to have the greatest difficulty conceptualizing a three-dimensional picture of sexual anatomy.

Programmed Learning. An exciting newer approach to teaching sexual material is the programmed textbook. It has the advantage of allowing students to progress at their own pace, and can be combined with videotape demonstrations which the student plays at appropriate points in the text. The best example is *The Programmed Learning System for Psychiatry* (which has a chapter on human sexuality) produced by the Department of Psychiatry of the Medical University of South Carolina.[2a]

Lectures on basic aspects of sexual anatomy and physiology can be videotaped. This method frees the teacher from the onerous task of repeating the same material with each course, permits the use of more sophisticated demonstration techniques, and enables the teacher to devote more time to answering questions.

TEACHING STRATEGIES

There are many ways in which the sequence of components of a sex-education program can be arranged to suit the particular needs of various student groups. The choice of a "game plan" depends greatly on the motivation and experience of the group. A major consideration is the level of comfort the group has in discussing sexual topics in public. For many groups, it is necessary to begin with an intensive desensitization program, such as a Sexual Attitude Reassessment (SAR) program, to increase this level of comfort and promote questions and discussion of particular areas of ignorance.[3] (It has been shown that an intensive program is more effective than the same materials presented in a "spaced" fashion over several weeks.) Unfortunately, many medical school curricula are too highly structured to provide adequate time for an intensive SAR program. Chapter 19 discusses this approach in more detail.

The teacher may consider placing a student in a clinical situation which confronts him or her with specific areas of ignorance and thus promotes active questioning by the student. While this method is often powerful, it is inefficient and frequently not comprehensive.

The educational "context" one chooses often affects the teaching strategy. A course in human sexuality is only one context in which sexual anatomy and physiology can be taught. Another is as part of an intensive workshop experience which may last several days. While these experiences are valuable at the time, there is serious question as to the degree of retention by participants after they return to their usual work environments. An advantage of the workshop model is that a great deal of material can be presented in a relatively short time, and there is often sufficient anonymity so that participants are more willing to ask questions which reflect their ignorance. The therapist-patient relationship, in which the patient asks questions which require the therapist to fill gaps in his or her knowledge, is a potentially educational context. Another extremely useful strategy is to involve both members of a professional couple in the educational experience. This method can promote a healthy competition which motivates both professionals.

WHO NEEDS TO KNOW WHAT

Students can come from almost any training background, but the most common fields are medicine (medical students, family practice, psychiatry, gynecology, urology), psychology (clinical and educational), social work, counseling, clergy (pastoral counseling), family planning, and nursing. Each of these training backgrounds differs in the amount of mandatory exposure the students have to anatomy and physiology; and even within the same field, exposure varies. For example, some psychologists have taken many courses in physiological psychology and are as well informed about sexual anatomy as gynecologists, while other psychologists have never been exposed to this material.

The kind of practice in which the student eventually engages dictates the required level of training. A partial list of these areas includes the following:

1. Research in human sexuality
   a. Physiological
   b. Attitudinal
2. Practice of sex therapy
3. Practice of medicine
   a. Primary care (family practice, internal medicine)
   b. Specialty practice (psychiatry, gynecology, urology)
   c. Nursing
4. Practice of psychology
   a. Clinical
   b. Experimental
5. Social Work
   a. Clinical counseling
   b. Team functioning in a medical or institutional setting
6. Pastoral Counseling
   a. Formal counseling
   b. Informal counseling as part of ministerial duties
7. Family planning
   a. As part of general duties
   b. Specific practice of sex counseling in family planning clinic
8. Teaching
   a. Medical students
   b. Psychology students
   c. Social work students
   d. Seminary students

At the risk of grossly oversimplifying a complex problem, and not giving sufficient credit to the motivation and ability of some students, Table 5-1 is offered as a guideline in planning the level of material to be taught to various student groups.

Table 5-1
Who Needs to Know What

Education Level*	Student-Training Background	Utilization of Training
I. Detailed course in anatomy and physiology, including current research findings, relationship to disease states, pharmacology, and issues of medical management with respect to sexual functioning	1. Medicine 2. Psychology (if prior exposure to anatomy and physiology) 3. Students (medical, some psychology)	1. Sex therapy 2. Research 3. Practice of medicine (especially psychiatry, gynecology, and urology)
II. Detailed course in anatomy and physiology with *superficial* consideration of relationship to disease states and pharmacology	1. Medicine 2. Psychology (if no prior exposure to anatomy and physiology) 3. Students (medical, some psychology, social work and family planning)	1. Practice of medicine, psychology, and social work (counseling) 2. Sex therapy (minimal level) 3. Sex education 4. Physical therapy
III. Basic anatomy and physiology with minimal reference to disease states and pharmacology	1. Medicine 2. Psychology 3. Social work 4. Family planning 5. Students (some psychology, social work, family planning, pastoral counseling)	1. Practice of medicine, psychology, social work, and family planning 2. Sex counseling 3. Occupational therapy

Table 5-1 continued

IV. Basic anatomy and physiology	1. Medicine (?) 2. Psychology (?) 3. Social work 4. Family planning 5. Pastoral counseling 6. Sex education (?) 7. Students (pastoral counseling, some social work, medical(?))	1. Clinical practices (general) 2. Some sex counseling (but not sex therapy)
V. Superficial sexual anatomy and physiology	No advanced training	Personal growth

*See Appendix (pp. 75–76) for a more detailed definition of each level of anatomy and physiology education.

CURRICULUM PLANNING

Current Knowledge

The gross anatomy of the sexual system has been known for a long time, and the reader would do well to review some of the many excellent sources which cover this material.[2,4,5] Sexual physiology is another matter. Since 1966 there have been more publications on human sexual physiology than in all the previous years combined.[6] Although there are many good reviews of sexual physiology,[4,7,8] the sex educator must regularly review this literature. Basic sexual physiology is beyond the scope of this chapter, but some of the current fruitful areas of investigation, with which the instructor should be familiar, are given below:

1. *Measurement of the sexual response in males and females.*[9-11] Some limitations have been found in the objective measurement of parameters in this field, but it is still a valuable area of investigation.

2. *Neurological correlates of the sexual response* at various levels of the nervous system, including the autonomic nervous system [GSR, pupillary response,[12] effects of autonomically active drugs[13-15]], central nervous system activity during sexual responses as measured by EEG and indepth electrodes,[16,17] and the role of neuro-transmitters in the sexual response.[18-20] Obviously there are numerous interactions between various levels of neurological activity during the sexual response, such as autonomic and cognitive variables, but these are as yet poorly understood. Other promising areas of investigation include measurement of nocturnal tumescence to differentiate psychogenic from organic sex problems[21,22] and examination of sexually relevant reflexes.[23]

3. *Hormonal factors in the sexual response* per se, as well as their relationship to the inclination to initiate sexual activity.[24-26] Apparently, hormonal factors relate to both facilitation and inhibition of sexual activity.

4. *The relationship of pheremones to human sexual activity.*[27] Since some pheromones (copulins) may be active in humans, speculation as to their role in sexual functioning has allowed researchers boundless fantasies.

5. *Visceral changes during the sexual response.*[28-30] Arterial blood flow, cardiac activity, uterine response, arterial pH, blood pressure, and even fetal heart rate during maternal orgasm have been investigated.

6. *Vascular activity during the sexual response.*[31] Methods include measurement of heart rate, pulse volume, EKG, penile volume, and vaginal blood flow.
7. *Subjects' responses to sexually explicit materials.*[32-34] Physiological as well as psychological variables have been examined.
8. *Physiological responses occurring as a consequence of traumatic sexual experiences* such as rape or pelvic surgery. Investigators postulate that various forms of conditioning occur as a consequence of sexual trauma and that these responses can be physiologically measured. This area may serve as a model system for sexual pathology in general, and thus represents one of the most clinically relevant new directions in sex research.
9. *Quantitative examination of muscular correlates of the sexual response* by such means as the EMG. This is a very new area of research which appears to be one of the most potentially fruitful from a clinical perspective. In addition to measuring absolute levels of muscular tension, patterns of muscle activity may be identified which will permit differentiation of "normal" and pathological patterns. Such results, if obtained, could conceivably aid in diagnosis of organic versus psychogenic sexual disabilities.

There are many other new areas of research into sexual physiology, and it is incumbent on the sex educator to be aware of these developments in order to prepare students for changes which are bound to occur in the field, as well as to encourage students to pursue sex research.[35,36] Probably the most important deficiency in the field of sexual physiology is the lack of a comprehensive, unifying theory. At the present time, we are in a data gathering phase of development, and any theory could be premature. We hope that integrating concepts will be forthcoming in the near future.

Curriculum Design

Since teaching sexual anatomy and physiology involves so many problems, it may be useful to consider some aspects of the curriculum design process, especially if any of the obvious signs of educational failure are present. These signs include students not attending class, not knowing the material, sleeping in class, asking many questions about material which has already been covered, not asking any questions at all, and not taking notes.

The following steps in course development may be considered minimal:

A. Preassessment
  1. Students
     a. Prior training, knowledge, and experience
     b. Motivation (required versus elective course)
     c. Resistance to learning
        1. Time available to study (amount of competition from other courses)
        2. Attitudes and stereotypes which block new learning
        3. Ability of students
        4. Heterogeneity of class
  2. Utilization of Training
     a. Research
     b. Practice of sex therapy
     c. Practice of medicine, psychology, social work, etc.
     d. Counseling of patients
     e. Personal edification
B. Planning the Course
  1. Sequence of course elements (e.g., often it is valuable for sex education courses to begin with a desensitization program so students come to feel freer about asking questions, and then present didactic material)
  2. Teaching Strategy and Methods
     a. Large classes
     b. Small groups
     c. Practical experience.
     d. Demonstrations (e.g., use of models of dissection)
     e. Programmed learning
     f. Readings
  3. Materials
     a. Readings (choosing the appropriate level of complexity)
     b. Models (both inanimate and human)
     c. Audio-visual materials
        1. Sexual explicit materials
        2. Didactic inputs (e.g., Programmed Learning System chapter on human sexuality)
     d. Patient demonstrations
        1. Gynecological and urological surgery
        2. Psychiatric consultations
  4. Time Available
     a. Total time available
     b. Timing in relation to other course elements and overall training (e.g., it is often most valuable for medical stu-

dents to have sex education courses as they begin clinical rotations, and not in the beginning of the first year,
even though it may be easier to schedule then)
5. Relevance of teaching methods and strategies to utilization
of knowledge (e.g., although a pastoral counselor or social
work student could learn much from dissecting the human
pelvis, it would be much less relevant to that person than to
a medical student)

C. Implementation

Once planning is completed, one must be able to carry out the
plan effectively and anticipate problems. Programs often fail for
the most minor reasons: students don't like the teacher's tone of
voice, the chairs are uncomfortable, the room is too cold,
audio-visual materials are of poor quality. Preparing for such
contingencies can often be done by joining forces with other
faculty and by having someone available to do necessary minor
chores.

D. Postassessment (Feedback)

1. Process Feedback

a. While course is in progress (gaining information from
students about how they like the *manner* in which the
course is being taught)

b. After the course is over (gaining information from students about how they liked the manner in which the
course as a whole was taught)

c. Observing students to see if they are incorporating
information and attitudes which are conveyed and
modeled by faculty. (Observations may either be made
informally or by use of rigorous observational instruments.)

2. Content Feedback

a. Knowledge gained by students as compared with the
amount possessed prior to the course. This can be measured by a variety of methods, including pre- and post-
testing with standardized instruments and assessment of
clinical competence. (This topic is more fully covered in
Chapter 11.)

b. Long-term follow-up of students. This is probably the
best method of assessing effectiveness of the teaching
method, but few such studies have been made.

E. Replanning

Responding to feedback about an educational effort is very complex. Most educators are aware that classes have different

characters, and it is often difficult to assess whether students' opinions are idiosyncratic or truly representative, even when the majority responds in the same way. Although teaching methods can be adjusted (based on process feedback) while the course is in progress, only the final assessment of gained knowledge should be grounds for redesigning the entire teaching effort. The educator must be willing to examine the source of dissatisfaction and blocks to student learning so that these can be eliminated and other alternatives substituted. He or she should be prepared for the painful possibility that the most important element in student dissatisfaction is the educator.

CONCLUSION

The teaching of sexual anatomy and physiology differs from other areas of human sexuality because this material can be taught at greatly varying degrees of complexity. Thus, the sex educator faces numerous problems in planning and implementing a teaching program on these topics. Problems relate mainly to varying degrees of knowledge of students, purposes to which the teaching will be put, materials available for teaching, and the teacher's level of knowledge and ability. The task is not insuperable, but it does require considerable planning and effort by the teacher and diligence by the student.

APPENDIX

Level of Sexual Anatomy and Physiology

Level I represents thorough consideration of the gross and microscopic anatomy, including embryology of primary and secondary sex organs, preferably including experience in the dissection of them. The anatomy of other parts of the body which relate to sexual functioning is also included in this level (such as central and peripheral nervous systems, endocrine glands, and circulatory system). Physiological aspects at this level include: peripheral or "end" organ responses during sexual activity, neuroendocrine factors in reproduction and sexual response, visceral responses during sexual activity (e.g., heart, uterus), and neurological aspects of sexual response (e.g., EEG, autonomic factors, neurotransmitters). In addition, the relationship of pharmacological agents and disease processes to sexual functioning would be considered in detail. Newer areas of investigation would be mentioned, (such as studies of pheromone activity, methodology of measuring genital response, neuroendocrine patterns in sexual activity, and nocturnal penile tumescence in normal and sexually dysfunctional people).

Level II represents a thorough consideration of the gross anatomy of the primary and secondary sex organs, possibly including experience in dissection. Anatomy of other related body parts may be covered superficially. Physiological considerations would include peripheral organ responses, basic concepts of endocrinology, and neurological and visceral activity during sexual activity. The relationship of sexual functioning to pharmacological and disease processes would be superficially covered.

Level III represents a consideration of the gross anatomy of the primary and secondary sex organs and exposure to the physiology of the end-organ responses during sexual activity. Reference would be made to the effects of pharmacological agents and disease states upon the sexual response.

Level IV represents only basic sexual anatomy and physiology for the professional. This level would be primarily aimed at increasing professionals' awareness that further study would be necessary to become knowledgeable about these subjects. (The majority of workshops present sexual anatomy and physiology at this level.)

Level V represents a superficial exposure to sexual anatomy and physiology in lay terms.

REFERENCES

1. Shaw JR: Scientific empiricism in the middle ages: Albertus Magnus on sexual anatomy and physiology. Clio Med 10(1):53–64, 1975
2. Masters WH, Johnson VE: Human Sexual Response. Boston, Little, Brown, 1966
2a. Randalls PM, McCurdy L, Powell WS et al (eds): The Psychiatry Learning System: A Multimedia Self-Instructional Course in Basic Psychiatry, 2nd ed. Charleston, S.C. Medical University of South Carolina Press, 1974
3. Bjorksten O: Sexually graphic material in the treatment of sexual disorders, in Meyer J (ed): Clinical Management of Sexual Disorders. Baltimore, Williams & Wilkins, 1976
4. Kaplan HS: The New Sex Therapy. New York, Brunner/Mazel, 1974
5. Gray H: Gray's Anatomy, 28th ed. Philadelphia, Lea and Febiger, 1966
6. Schiavi RC: Sex therapy and psychophysiological research. Am J Psychiatry 133(5):562–566, 1976
7. Guyton AS: Textbook of Medical Physiology, 4th ed. Philadelphia, WS Saunders, 1971, p 951–971
8. Sarrel FM: Sexual physiology and sexual functioning. Postgrad Med 58(1):67–72, 1975
9. Jovanovic UJ: The recording of physiological evidence of genital arousal in human males and females. Arch Sex Behav 1(4):309–320, 1971
10. Laws DR: A comparison of the measurement characteristics of two circumferential penile transducers. Arch Sex Behav 6(1): 45–52, 1977

11. Hoon PW, Wincze JP, Hoon EF: Physiological assessment of sexual arousal in women. Psychophysiology 13(3), 196–204, 1976
12. Peavler WS: Pupillary dilation as a measure of sexual arousal. A reply to Hamel. J Psychol 90:113–114, 1975
13. Tennet G, Bancroft J, Cass J: The control of deviant sexual behavior by drugs: A double blind controlled study of benperidol, chlorpromazine, and placebo. Arch Sex Behav 3(3):261–272, 1974
14. Everett GM: Pharmacological and biochemical aspects of sexual aggressive behavior in animals and man. Psychopharmacol Bull 11(3):44–45, 1975
15. Hollister LE: Drugs and sexual behavior in man. Psychopharmacol Bull 11(3):44, 1975
16. Heath RG: Pleasure and brain activity in man. J Nerv Ment Dis 154:3–18, 1972
17. Cohen HD, Rosen RC, Goldstein L: Electroencephalographic laterality changes during human sexual orgasm. Arch Sex Behav 5(3): 189–199, 1976
18. Securteri F: Serotonin and sex in man. Pharmacol Res Comm 6(4):403–411, 1974
19. Securteri F, Del Bene E, Fonda C: Sex, migraine and serotonin interrelationships. Monogr Neural Sci 3:94–101, 1976
20. Karczmar AG: Neurological, neurotransmitter, and pharmacological aspects of sexual behavior. Psychopharmacol Bull 11(3):39–40, 1975
21. Karacan I, Williams RL, Guerrero W, et al: Nocturnal penile tumescence and sleep of convicted rapists and other prisoners. Arch Sex Behav 3(1):19–26, 1974
22. Karacan I, Hursch CJ, Williams RL, et al: Some characteristics of nocturnal penile tumescence during puberty. Pediatr Res Comm 6(6):529–537, 1972
23. Dick HC, Bradley WE, Scott FB, et al: Pudendal sexual reflexes. Electrophysiologic investigations. Urology 3(3):376–379, 1974
24. Kraemer HC, Becker HB, Brodie H, et al: Orgasmic frequency and plasma testosterone levels in normal human males. Arch Sex Behav 5(2):125–132, 1976
25. Reinisch J: Fetal hormones, the brain, and human sex differences: A heuristic, integrative review of the recent literature. Arch Sex Behav 3(1):51–90, 1974
26. Goy RW, Goldfoot DA: Neuroendocrinology: Animal models and problems of human sexuality. Arch Sex Behav 4(4):405–420, 1975
27. Sokolov JJ, Harris RT, Hecker MR: Isolation of substance from human vaginal secretions previously shown to be sex attractant pheromones in higher primates. Arch Sex Behav 5(4):269–274, 1976
28. Fox CA, Fox BA: Blood pressure and respiratory patterns during human coitus. J Reprod Fertil 19:405–415, 1969
29. Fox CA, Wolff HS, Baker JA: Measurement of intra-vaginal and intra-uterine pressures during human coitus by radio telemetry. J Reprod Fertil 22:243–251, 1970
30. Nemec ED, Manfield L, Kennedy JW: Heart rate and blood pressure responses during sexual activity in normal males. Am Heart J 92(3):274–277, 1976
31. Littler WA, Honour AJ, Sleight P: Direct arterial pressure, heart rate and electrocardiogram during human coitus. J Reprod Fertil 40(2):321–331, 1974
32. Steele DG, Walker CE: Male and female differences in reaction to erotic stimuli as related to sexual adjustment. Arch Sex Behav 3(5):459–470, 1974
33. Colson CE: The evaluation of pornography: Effects of attitude and perceived physiological reaction. Arch Sex Behav 3(4):307–324, 1974
34. Schmidt G: Male-female differences in sexual arousal and behavior during and after exposure to sexually explicit stimuli. Arch Sex Behav 4(4):353–365, 1975
35. Weiss HD: The physiology of human penile erection. Ann Intern Med 76:793–799, 1972
36. Little BC, Zahn TP: Changes in mood and autonomic functioning during the menstrual cycle. Psychophysiology 11(5):579–580, 1974

Michael S. Aronoff

6
Teaching About the Sexually Transmissible Diseases

Most lectures on venereal disease lack interest and relevance, and it is small wonder that many participants in sexuality courses skip this presentation. This chapter focuses on critical aspects of an effective presentation which other educators may use in their own curriculum development. Changing concepts and the need for better education about these diseases are discussed by Grant.[1]

Few health care providers are adequately prepared by professional schools to manage sexually transmissible diseases. Students enter medical school with a vague understanding of two problems, syphilis and gonorrhea. They soon learn that there are actually five different major venereal diseases: syphilis, gonorrhea, chancroid, lymphogranuloma venereum, and granuloma inguinale. My total medical school education concerning these five disorders was probably less than one hour and involved didactic material only. Two years out of medical school I entered a practice where the patients were largely sexually active persons 18–25 years old. I soon recognized that a dozen or more health problems could be sexually transmitted and that some of these problems were more important to my patients than the original list of five diseases.

My experience with patients, medical students, and professional health care providers revealed two things: a concern about disease as it related to sex and a lack of knowledge about such diseases. I attempted to deal with these problems as I began designing and presenting lectures for both professional health-care providers and nonprofessional groups.

I began my presentation with the title "Sexually Transmissible Diseases." This expressed a concept that there were more than the two classical diseases of which the public is usually aware. However, two mistakes were obvious in those early presentations. First, I began the lecture with a complete and sometimes esoteric presentation of syphilis and gonorrhea. This was a mistake, because the time devoted to those two diseases left little time to discuss the remainder of the lengthy list. The audience was generally already most familiar with syphilis and gonorrhea, and no matter what I tried, I could not maintain their interest. My second major mistake was that I did not make certain that the accompanying audio-visual materials portrayed these diseases in situations relevant to the audience.

These and other mistakes surfaced when I presented an entire seminar course to medical students concerning the "Pharmacology of Sexually Transmissible Diseases." On a week by week basis, I discussed minute details of 14 diseases. Then, on the last day of the class, I presented a film showing a couple having intercourse. One of the partners in the film had a genital lesion that appeared to be syphilis. I was confident that everyone would be able to recognize a genital chancre. The class did see the lesion, and they began asking questions about the sexually transmissible diseases as though I had never lectured. At that time I decided that consideration of sexual behavior and the relevance of sexuality to the transmission of disease and to the audience was of such vital importance that sexually explicit material should be incorporated throughout rather than only at the end of a lecture or lecture series.

It wasn't long before my embryonic educational scheme met another challenge. My audiences had been largely homogeneous; then I made a presentation to a seminar course on human sexuality. The audience was a mixed group of health care providers and consumers from various disciplines. I had no specific plan for that presentation; however, a strategy evolved from participant criticism as well as my intuition. That strategy is based on four major points: (1) begin the discussion with those diseases most frequently encountered in the lecturer's experiences and end with those least encountered; (2) incorporate sexuality as it relates to disease transmission at the outset and interweave it in the entire presentation; (3) include aspects of the doctor-patient relationship and stresses on that relationship created by the patient's sexuality and the doctor's attitudes toward various sexual behaviors; (4) provide for audience interaction in various forms, such as question-answer and role rehearsal.

It is convenient to begin each presentation with a brief description of those persons who are at risk of contracting a sexually transmissible disease. Most popular discussions center on the three P's (permissiveness, promiscuity, and the pill), but there is no clear relationship between these factors and degree of risk.[2] Permissiveness is a vague concept that relates more to attitudes and feelings than to actual behavior. Promiscuity, as the term is commonly applied, has little to do with risk unless the behavior of one's partners is also considered.

To illustrate this point, compare one man who has three partners, all of whom have sexual intercourse only with him, to another man who has only one partner, but whose partner has a number of other consorts. In this situation, the more promiscuous man will never acquire gonorrhea as long as his three partners are uninfected at the outset and remain loyal to him, but the second man is at some risk because of the behavior patterns of his partner.[2]

Because of the pejorative connotations, the term promiscuity should not be used. The relationship of the pill to the prevalence of sexually transmissible diseases is complex and depends on the patient and the specific disease.

A sexual act as it applies to disease transmission is any act where the genitals of one person come in contact with any body part of another person. This definition therefore excludes masturbation and oral-oral contact. Disease transmission occurs when an infectious agent is transferred from one person to another. Audiences grasp this concept best if statistics, graphs, and charts are avoided.

Next, it is appropriate to introduce the list of diseases that are currently believed to be transmitted in some measure by sexual contact. I present the disorders as they are seen by me, somewhat in the order of decreasing frequency. It is important that the audience understand the structure of this list. Most appreciate the relevance of this presentation when they see nongonococcal urethritis and condyloma acuminata close to the top. This introduction should include the common vernacular term for some of the diseases, (i.e., warts, yeast, cold sores, crabs).

I use the following list:

1. Nongonococcal urethritis
2. Condyloma acuminata
3. Molluscum contagiosum
4. Candidiasis
5. Trichomoniasis
6. Gonorrhea
7. Herpes genitalis
8. Pediculosis pubis
9. Scabies
10. Syphilis
11. Hepatitis
12. Chancroid
13. Lymphogranuloma venereum
14. Granuloma inguinale

Several important aspects of this list should be discussed. The list does not adhere precisely to my own definition of sexually transmissible. There is some doubt about the exchange of microorganisms in granuloma inguinale. Furthermore, the list is not all-inclusive. Some would include Group B streptococcal infection, Haemophilus vaginalis vaginitis, inclusion conjunctivitis, cytomegalovirus disease, and the Marburg virus disease. It is also true that molluscum contagiosum is not the third most frequently encountered disease in my practice. I place it next to condyloma acuminata because the lesions are similar in appearance. If students react to my list by pointing out the deficiencies and inconsistencies, I have the satisfaction of knowing that they are paying attention.

Taking each disease separately, I discuss etiology, mode of transmission, incubation period, clinical course, diagnosis, and treatment. Concise descriptions of these aspects of each disease are available.[2,3] It is important that the lecturer be very familiar with the most recent factual information concerning the sexually transmissible diseases. Periodic examination of the *Cumulated Index Medicus* will provide current references. More or less detail can be included depending on the audience and the available time.

Some areas of special concern might include the benign nature of some of the diseases and the asymptomatic carrier state. Treatment failure, drug allergy, other complicating health problems unrelated to sex, and recidivism are other topics for expansion. These special concerns may be presented to the audience just as they are discussed with the patient. A patient who has nongonococcal urethritis should be informed about the benign, recurrent nature of the disease. Patients who are not properly counseled may develop other sexual distresses, such as impotence and fear of intimate relationships. Reassurance must be presented in the proper context of concern to prevent the patient from becoming complacent about recurrent urethritis. Gonococcal urethritis is not always easily differentiated from nongonococcal urethritis. The asymptomatic carrier state of gonorrhea must also remain a concern. So, while reassuring a patient of the benign nature of his recurrent nongonococcal urethritis, it is also necessary to emphasize the importance of reculturing with each new episode.

In dealing with herpes genitalis infections, the clinician must be alert to the development of fears by the patient that he or she is carrying an incurable disease. Transmissibility of this disease in the absence of apparent lesions has not been documented. Since patients and audiences ask about the relationship between herpes genitalis and cancer, the teacher or clinician must be prepared to put the statistics in perspective and emphasize the positive approach to cancer surveillance using Pap testing. Some problems, such as the period of transmissibility of hepatitis-B, have not yet been resolved. The speaker must deal with popular misapprehensions about these diseases, as revealed by audience interaction.

At the conclusion of the "facts" presentation, audience questions generally relate to disease prophylaxis. It is wise either to incorporate a separate section on this topic or to discuss prophylaxis specifically as each disease is presented.

Audio-visual materials should be selected to highlight and clarify the specifics of each disease. It is easy to acquire an adequate collection of 35mm slides. Inexpensive medical illustration cameras are available. These convert typewritten material to projection status and allow one to photograph diseases as they appear in the office or clinic. Those who do not have direct access to patients may ask their local VD clinic to photograph some cases. It is also possible to purchase medical illustration slides from some pharmaceutical companies.[4]

At some convenient point early in the presentation it is important to discuss sexual activity as it relates to a specific disease. The lecturer must be careful not to imply that any particular disease is the likely result of a given sexual act. It is clear that an understanding of sexual behavior is necessary, and that one can understand a sexual act without personalizing it. Analogies are useful in clarifying this. For example, a non-smoker can provide good health care to a patient with chronic lung disease. Yet, the non-smoker must ask the patient questions about smoking, such as frequency, inhaling, and what is inhaled. Similarly, a non-drinker can provide good health care to a patient with liver disease only if he or she can be comfortable taking a history from that patient which includes questions about alcohol use.

An important part of the presentation, usually placed near the end, is a discussion of the doctor-patient relationship as it exists in the management of the sexually transmissible diseases. I have experienced and I have noticed in my peers many pressures, discomforts, and pleasures that result from this relationship. One who lectures about these diseases must be prepared to share both negative and positive clinical experiences. Some of the topics pertinent to those experiences include: working with the patient's sexual preferences and behaviors, treatment failure, recidivism, case reporting, and confidentiality. Helping the patient deal with his or her partners is another challenge to the doctor-patient relationship.

In discussing the stresses upon the doctor-patient relationship, I present my approach to the patient's sexual preferences and behavior. I make a conscious effort not to assign gender to a patient's partner. I have found that when I use terms such as "partner" or "contact" rather than "boyfriend," "girlfriend," "husband," or "wife," my patients seem willing to assign a gender when it is appropriate. In addition, I neither express assumptions about the patient's behavior nor judgments about specific sexual behaviors. For example, before obtaining a culture test for gonorrhea, I explain the importance of obtaining that specimen from all orifices where there has been sexual contact. I list the orifices: throat, anus, urethra, cervix. I ask the patient, "Should I culture all of the above or some of the above?" By that point the patient hopefully has gained enough confidence to respond honestly.

The final ingredient of the presentation is the interaction between audience and instructor. Some teachers prefer having questions asked as the topic is being presented, while others want a defined forum at the conclusion. Time and audience size may suggest the appropriate approach; limited time or large audiences may preclude an ongoing exchange. However, dealing with audience questions can be one of the most rewarding aspects for the educator. It is vital to acknowledge a questioner verbally, listen carefully to the question, and then restate the question from the podium. The lecturer should use the questioner's own words as he or she has heard them and ask, after repeating the question, if it has been heard correctly. Then, a brief, clear response should be made. Any uncertainty about the response should be honestly stated. No question is considered a "dumb question." Assume that if the questioner had the answer, the question would not have been asked. If questions are being asked while the presentation is in progress, it is well to allow the sophistication of the questions to guide the tone, pace, and complexity of the presentation.

Another form of audience interaction involves role-playing or situation rehearsal. When time permits, this can be one of the most meaningful aspects of the presentation. I ask for a volunteer from the audience to play the role of physician while I play the role of the patient. One premise for this encounter is that the "physician" will have 12 minutes, the actual length of my standard office appointment. In that time the "physician" must take a history, outline strategies for diagnosis, treatment, contact tracing, reporting, and follow-up. As the patient, I usually begin with a simple complaint. I will then introduce some situations that stress the encounter (e.g., gay patients, multiple partners, marital relationships, inadequate or inappropriate prior care). I may also select some of the more difficult diagnostic problems. These stresses, plus the 12-minute time limit, generally evoke some empathy for the clinician. After each 12-minute "appointment," I discuss the problem areas that have been obvious.

Role rehearsal provides limitless variations. A useful technique in teaching professional health care providers is to have members of the class play both roles. Observation of the student playing the "patient" role may reveal some important stereotyping of how he or she thinks patients with a sexually transmissible disease behave.

Time is a critical factor. The amount of time available varies according to the curriculum. I have been able to make a single 3-hour presentation using the structure outlined above, omitting role rehearsal but incorporating a 30-minute break. The purpose of the session generally dictates the amount of time necessary. Purposes can vary from preparing a health care provider to diagnose and treat these problems to informing consumers who have a personal interest. In the middle, of course, are the people who deal with another aspect of the patient's sexual health but who must be able to recognize these diseases.

It is clear that every sexuality curriculum must include a specific presentation on these diseases. When the purpose has been defined and the time appropriated, it is necessary to use that time economically. Therefore, careful selection of content and approach is essential.

The teacher must set priorities for his or her objectives. These objectives may be the teaching of general subject matter, specific technical skills, or understanding of interpersonal relationships. Some students may require all of the above; others may have variable needs. The lecturer must attempt to assess the needs of the audience. This assessment will not always be correct, but audience interaction usually reveals invalid assumptions.

No two instructors will prepare the same way. Essential elements of my preparation include a working outline, selection of audio-visual aids, and attention to the physical facilities. Without a working outline, I have a tendency to digress, and since I generally lose track of time, digression is disastrous. Reworking my outline prevents boredom on my part. Next to hyperventilation, boredom is the worst thing that can happen to me during a lecture. Working without a prepared outline one afternoon, I looked at one of my slides and could find nothing interesting about it. My thoughts drifted to some other topic; I panicked; I hurried; I lost contact with my audience.

I select audio-visual material with some attention to a style that will maintain my interest. I am also careful to provide and set up my own hardware; it is important to me to know that the projectors will function and that spare bulbs and extension cords are available.

A few strategic sips of a soft drink will generally abort hyperventilation. While I do not usually wear a wrist watch, referring to the clock helps me pace my lecture. If all else fails, bladder pressure from the soft drink signals time for a break.

Everyone must develop his or her own strategy for teaching about the sexually transmissible diseases. The single most important influence upon the evolution of my presentation has been the critical comments made by various audiences. I have tried to encourage criticism and alter my presentation when necessary.

In my opinion, the best teacher is one who motivates students to remember the greatest part of the presentation, and who instills a desire to learn more about the subject independently.

REFERENCES

1. Grant J: Microbiology in venereal disease: The quest for concept. J Intl Res Commun Med Sci, 2:11. 1974
2. Wiesner PJ, Tyler CW Jr. (eds): Venereal disease in obstetrics and gynecology. Clin Obstet Gynecol 18(1):31–32, 1975
3. Cherniak D, Feingold A: VD Handbook. Montreal, the Handbook Collective, 1972
4. Netter FH: The Ciba Collection of Medical Illustrations vol 2, Reproductive System. Slides. Summit, NJ, Ciba Pharmaceutical Co, 1965

Theodore M. Cole

7
Teaching for Professionals in the Sexuality of the Physically Disabled

THE HISTORY OF EDUCATION AND RESEARCH

While studying human sexuality curricula in American medical schools, Ebert and Lief pointed out that sexuality training programs for medical students were almost nonexistent before 1954.[1] There were 3 programs in 1960; and by 1968, 30 medical schools offered sexuality curricula. In 1975, nearly all medical schools reported substantial sex education programs for their students.

The history of interest in sexuality and physical disabilities has followed a similar course. A review of eight professional journals from the field of rehabilitation medicine and allied disciplines shows that articles written about sexuality prior to 1971 dealt almost exclusively with medical and reproductive aspects of sexuality. From 1967 to 1970, only three articles in those eight journals dealt with psychosocial and behavioral aspects of sexuality. During the same four years, only one paper on psychosocial or behavioral aspects of sexuality in the physically disabled was presented at annual meetings of the American Congress of Rehabilitation Medicine (ACRM) and the American Academy of Physical Medicine and Rehabilitation (AAPM&R). This is especially noteworthy because these journals and national conventions are designed to offer significant and up-to-date information for professionals who work with the physically disabled.

Things began to change in 1971. During the next four years a total of 16 papers dealing with the psychosocial and behavioral aspects of sexuality appeared in these same eight journals, and 11 presentations were made at the annual meetings. In 1975 and 1976 alone, 20 papers appeared in these journals, and 10 presentations were made at ACRM and AAPM&R annual meetings.

In a recent analysis of trends in research relating to the care of the physically disabled, Ozel and Kottke identified ten clinical areas, including human sexuality, which have not attracted a strong research interest.[2] Only 1.85 percent of the papers delivered at annual scientific meetings of the major rehabilitation professions between 1972 and 1976 reported research on human sexuality. Thus, while sexuality of the physically disabled has been more widely discussed in the last five years, it still attracts little research attention.

MYTHS

Myths and misunderstandings often arise around groups of people who display three characteristics: they are a minority; members are clearly identifiable; and society harbors fears or aversions toward them. Many physically disabled people meet all three criteria and thus become objects of social bias. Discrimination, in turn, fosters the growth of contrived tales and stories designed to set this group of people even further apart from "normal society." Only recently has it been recognized that many myths about sexuality and the physically disabled are widely believed by members of the medical profession and allied health professionals who provide services to the physically disabled in the United States.

Figure 7-1 symbolizes such a myth. The satyr, a sylvan deity demigod often depicted with the tail and hindquarters of a horse, the trunk of a man, and the head of a goat, was thought to be given to riotous merriment and lasciviousness. From this mythical figure comes the word satyriasis, meaning an insatiable sexual appetite in the male. It is interesting to wonder if the ancients invented the satyr after seeing a person such as appears in the right-hand portion of Figure 7-1. This picture was drawn from a photograph of a boy with a development disability of the spinal cord, leading to hip, knee, and ankle contractures and compensatory hyperextension of the back. In addition, the drawing depicts an exuberent growth of hair resembling a horse's tail over the area of the spinal defect. The total image is of particular interest since spinal injury creates the potential for intermittent penile erections not influenced by psychogenic stimulation but reflexly caused by internal or external physical stimulation of the pelvic viscera or genitals. Is it possible that the ancient Greeks, viewing an adult with this developmental disability and with reflex penile erections, assumed that his sexual appetite was insatiable?

More recently, Robert Penn Warren in his novel, *All the King's Men*, describes the life of a quadriplegic as one of paralysis, hopelessness, and

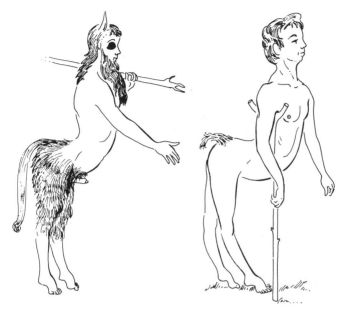

Fig. 7-1.   The satyr.

impending death.[3] The classic book, *Lady Chatterley's Lover* is about a lady who is sexually frustrated in consequence of her husband's paralysis and turns to another man.[4] The implicit message is that the paralyzed, crippled, or disabled man cannot satisfy a woman's sexual appetite.

On the other hand, there is a common belief that disabled people do not wish to express their sexuality or that sex is not important to them. People with conspicuous disabilities may be thought to have unpleasant body odors or even to be mentally retarded. Some believe that a handicapped individual should be segregated or disposed of in order not to allow him to propagate "his own kind." Or, in another manifestation of social bias, some believe paternalistically that the disabled should accept or appreciate anything that is given to them and that they have no right to compete with their able-bodied peers or to be selective or seductive in their sexual preference.

Medical and educational literature has reinforced these myths. Money states that the paraplegic's "index on the popularity parade . . . is at the bottom of the list. . . . Paraplegia is sexually totally disabling."[5] Fox, in writing about the need to separate sex education for able-bodied children from sex education for children with cerebral palsy, downplays the importance of sexual fantasy.[6] He states that sex is a bodily pleasure and a physical joy expressed through our bodies, not our minds, and that sex in the head "titillates without fulfilling." He doubts that the body of a handicapped person could give pleasure to its owner and recommends that sex education emphasize sublimation as a substitute for sex for handicapped children.

Cole et al report that many disabled people do not accept these myths.[7] In a comparison of able-bodied single and married medical students with single and married spinal-cord-injured adults, he found that disabled people entered more quickly into a sensitive discussion of sexual topics than did the able-bodied medical students; and they displayed less defensiveness and more openness. In contrast to Fox's admonition, the role of fantasy was found to be very strong in the disabled group. Some reported that their partners' sensory experiences were additive to their own. Others complained about the paternalistic attitude of their physicians. We concluded that if any myth about sexuality is to be dispelled, it is the myth that sex cannot or should not be discussed frankly with a physically disabled person, and we suggested that in many respects disabled people demonstrated that they were *more* capable of dealing with anxiety-producing material in a direct and tolerant manner than were many of the able-bodied people with whom they were compared.

CURRICULUM COMPONENTS

Sexual Self-Awareness.   As in any sexuality course, the first unit should be sexual awareness training of the professionals themselves. This topic is discussed in detail in Part V.

Disability Self-Awareness.   The second area of self-awareness is the attitude of the professional toward physically disabled people and his or her reasons for wanting to become trained in the area of sexuality. Ideally, motivation should reflect a desire to offer comprehensive services to disabled people. Some professionals will recognize that by developing comfort and skill in the area of talking about sexuality, they will see a spreading effect to other sensitive issues which are vital to a successful treatment program. In addition, the professional may recognize that it is difficult to harbor a paternalistic attitude toward a patient or client and simultaneously engage in a sincere and honest exchange of feelings about sexuality and disability.

Attitudes and Expectations.   A third major area of awareness training for the professional concerns understanding the attitudes and expectations which disabled people may hold for their own sexuality. A disability in no way frees an individual from restrictive or disabling attitudes toward sexuality. The disabled person may not only have recently acquired physical disabilities but preexisting sexual difficulties as well. Early in the course of their disability some people may have an incomplete notion of the impact of the disability on their sex lives. Such people may seem naive and be challenging to treat. Others may be overwhelmed with fear and anxiety about their disability, and conclude that sexual activity is neither expected nor appropriate. Some disabled people may develop negative attitudes toward the professionals with whom they are working. Being physically impaired and unable to exert independence may cause resentment toward able-bodied people who walk in and out of counseling offices or hospital rooms. Although resentful, they are also dependent upon the professionals who are to help them regain their physical and mental health. The professional must recognize that these attitudes may exist, and should help the patient or client to discuss them as part of the counseling process.

Categories of Disabilities

Different disabilities have differing effects on the handicapped person. In an earlier paper, I divided disabled persons into four groups, depending on the age of onset and the progressive or stable nature of the condition (Figures 7-2–7-5).[8] Type I disabilities are stable and have their onset in early life or before sexual maturation. Examples include congenital brain injury such as cerebral palsy or limb amputation in early life. People with these disabilities never experience a period of "normalcy," and they may be denied experiences which lead to psychosexual maturation. As a result, they may enter the adult world, where they are expected to be sexually sophisticated, lacking the requisite social skills and knowledge.

Type II disabilities also have their onset in early life or before sexual maturation, but they are progressive in nature. Two examples are juvenile rheumatoid arthritis and juvenile diabetes mellitus. The child or adolescent with such a disorder can never be confident that his or her body will be the same next year as it is this year. Not only may these persons go through life being different, but they may lack a stable base from which to plan their lives. Because of the progressive nature of their disability, they may be regularly involved with medical therapies and have to divert energy into maintaining health.

Type III disabilities have their onset in adult life or after sexual maturation and are nonprogressive. Examples include traumatic spinal cord injury and traumatic amputation of the penis. People with these disabilities are able to recall a period in life when they were able-bodied or "normal." This point of reference may serve them well in regaining a

Type of disability: **Stable**
Time of onset: **Prepuberty**

	Masturbation	Coitus	Fertility	Conspicuous to Society
Brain Injury				♂ ♀
Spinal Cord: Motor and Sensory loss	♂ ♀	♂	♂	♂ ♀
Skeletal: Amputation, Deformity	♂ ♀	♂ ♀		♂ ♀
Altered Body Growth				♂ ♀
Heart Disease				
Blindness				♂ ♀
Deafness				♂ ♀

Fig. 7-2.   Relationship of physical disability to sexuality.

Type of disability: **Progressive**
Time of onset: **Prepuberty**

	Masturbation	Coitus	Fertility	Conspicuous to Society
Diseases of the Brain			♂ ♀	♂ ♀
Diseases of the Spinal Cord	♂ ♀	♂	♂	♂ ♀
Musculo-Skeletal Diseases	♂ ♀	♂ ♀	♂	♂ ♀
Metabolic or Deficiency Diseases				♂ ♀
Heart Disease				♂ ♀
Blindness				♂ ♀
Deafness				♂ ♀

Fig. 7-3.   Relationship of physical disability to sexuality.

Type of disability: **Stable**
Time of onset: **Postpuberty**

	Masturbation	Coitus	Fertility	Conspicuous to Society
Spinal Cord: Motor and Sensory loss	♂ ♀	♂	♂	♂ ♀
Spinal Cord: Motor paralysis only	♂ ♀			♂ ♀
Skeletal: Amputation, Deformity	♂ ♀	♂ ♀		♂ ♀
Genital amputation, Deformity	♂ ♀	♂ ♀	♂	
Disfiguring injuries				♂ ♀
Enterostmy	♂ ♀	♂	♂	
Blindness				♂ ♀
Deafness				♂ ♀

Fig. 7-4. Relationship of physical disability to sexuality.

Type of disability: **Progressive**
Time of onset: **Postpuberty**

	Masturbation	Coitus	Fertility	Conspicuous to Society
Heart Disease		♂ ♀		
Stroke				♂ ♀
Diabetes Mellitus	♂ ♀	♂	♂	
Muscular Dystrophy				♂ ♀
Multiple Sclerosis	♂ ♀	♂	♂	♂ ♀
Skeletal: Amputation, Deformity	♂ ♀	♂ ♀		♂ ♀
Renal Disease, end stage	♂ ♀	♂	♂	

Fig. 7-5. Relationship of physical disability to sexuality.

previously established psychosexual identity. Furthermore, they may have learned some of the interactional skills necessary to develop sexual relationships with other adults. They may be able to modify these skills to serve them as disabled people. However, the bitterness or anger which may attend the abrupt onset of a stable postadolescent disability may leave scars on the personality which encumber the rehabilitation process.

Type IV disabilities have their onset in adult life and are progressive. They include such common disorders as progressive heart disease, cerebral vascular disease, and end-stage kidney failure. Since the onset is gradual and the course is progressive, there is an opportunity for slow adjustment to the disabling process. However, like people in Type II, they may lack a stable base from which to plan their lives. They, too, may be asked to divert time and concern into maintaining their own health. They cannot look upon themselves as "well even though disabled."

As shown in Figures 7-2–7-5, the male and female symbol in each square indicates that a sexual concern or dysfunction may exist in the area of masturbation, coitus, or fertility, or it may influence one's body image. This does not mean that the individual must necessarily have a sexual concern or dysfunction, but rather that the skilled clinician will explore this area before ruling out the need for intervention.

In our work with spinal cord injured people, we have found that the duration of disability may play an important role in the person's awareness of a sexual concern or dysfunction. In a sample of patients recently discharged from our spinal cord injury center, almost half of them felt that their sexual adjustment was good at the time they left the hospital. Only 9 percent stated that it was poor. However, a year or two later, as many as 38 percent of this same group stated that their sexual adjustment was poor. This finding suggests an early lack of awareness of the magnitude of the changes in their sexuality.

CURRICULUM CONTENT

Content falls into three categories: (1) medico-mechanical aspects of sexual function, (2) psychosocial aspects, (3) those interpersonal aspects of sexuality which affect the partner.

Medical Aspects of Disability

It is beyond the scope of this chapter to enumerate the medical and physiological aspects of the myriad of disabilities which may affect man and woman. However, the professional should be aware of some of the physiologic alterations which the disability imposes on sexual function.

For the purpose of a medical analysis, we will limit this consideration of sexuality to genital and reproductive aspects only.

At one end of the spectrum is the loss of the genitals themselves. Diseases which result in penectomy or orchiectomy pose clear possibilities for male sexual dysfunction. Vulvectomy, vaginal closure, hysterectomy, and oophorectomy pose the possibility of similar sexual dysfunctions for the female. Mastectomy may also produce a sexual dysfunction due to loss of a body part intimately associated with sexuality, sensuality, and procreation. In patients with such medical conditions, the professional should discuss with patients the meaning of their sex organs to them, and explore the potential for an expanded view of sexual performance and gratification. The author is aware of a young man who, for treatment of cancer, required a half-body amputation just above the pelvic brim. When he and his wife were asked about their sex life together, they both described it as active and satisfactory. Clearly, this disability suggests that if other aspects of the postdisability adjustments are adequate, sexual performance and gratification can be achieved even without the presence of the genitals.

Less vivid but still devastating dysfunction can be seen in people who lose sensation in their genitals due to metabolic or nervous system diseases. Not only will the individual receive less sensation, but physical orgasm may not occur and potency and fertility may be lost in the male. Some may conclude that loss of fertility and sensation means loss of sexual feelings in general. They may invest great energy in protecting themselves behind a barrier of seeming indifference to sexual stimulation, forgetting that the largest sex organ in the body remains intact within the skull.

Medical conditions that lead to loss of genital function, such as developmental or degenerative abnormalities of the organs themselves or of the circulation supplying them, may be equally disabling. The male who is unable to achieve erection due to vascular insufficiency may see himself as less of a man that he was before. The woman whose vagina is atrophic or obstructed by scar tissue may see herself as unable to perform as a female, even though her disability is limited to her genitals.

For some people, the limitations imposed upon them by orthopedic or neurologically handicapping conditions may limit their usual repertoire of sexual activities. Severe arthritis of the hips may make traditional positioning for sexual intercourse impossible and lead the woman to conclude that she can no longer engage in coitus with her partner. In other cases, mechanical adaptive equipment necessary to drain urine from paralyzed or incontinent bladders may be so unacceptable that even the partner becomes convinced that the organs no longer can be used for sexual pleasure.

Psychosocial Aspects of Disability

The professional should recognize that sexual dysfunction following medical disability may not be physiologically related to the disability. Some people may attribute sexual dysfunction to the physical disability in order to avoid accepting the psychological components. However, in most situations, the psychological aspects of sexual dysfunction may be as disabling as the medical ones. For example, female anorgasmia, whether primary or secondary, may occur in a woman whose medical condition cannot completely explain the loss of orgasmic capacity. Similarly, dyspareunia and sexual aversion may also accompany a medical disease or disability and be only tangentially related to the physiological changes caused by the disability. Vaginismus is another example. The woman with multiple sclerosis and skeletal muscle spasticity may experience vaginismus on the basis of the involuntary muscular contractions of the outer third of her vagina secondary to spasticity caused by her disease. However, it is well known that anxiety in some patients with central nervous system disease can heighten spasticity. Separation of the medical from the psychological causes will be necessary before useful therapy can commence.

For the male, the sexual dysfunctions of premature ejaculation, erectile dysfunction (impotence), and retarded ejaculation may be manifestations of medical illness or psychological reaction to illness. We have known a number of men who have clear-cut central or peripheral nervous system disease which, by itself, could explain the loss of genital function. However, we have noted that with counseling and the removal of anxieties, genital function returns. These cases point out that medical problems which seem to explain sexual dysfunction may only serve as a shroud behind which the person may hide. Who among us is willing to accept his or her own inadequacy as an explanation of a sexual dysfunction when we have the option of blaming a medical problem over which we have no control?

Interpersonal Aspects of Disability

The third area of content to which the professional should attend is the sexuality of the spouse or partner. The issues here involve an interpersonal dysfunction. Imagine the able-bodied spouse whose sexual frame of reference to the partner is dramatically altered by a disfiguring burn on the partner's face, or whose partner has survived a life-threatening myocardial infarction and who is consciously or unconsciously withholding sexual advances because of fears that sexual activity may risk the partner's life. In these cases, couple counseling is essential to reduce sexual dysfunction.

TEACHING STRATEGIES

Recently a number of medical facilities have found that the professional who has a physical disability may have an added asset as a counselor, and some institutions have trained disabled people to enter counseling professions. Research by Mitchell suggests that a counselor in a wheelchair is received more favorably than an able-bodied counselor, especially by females.[9] Other institutions are asking disabled people to take instructional roles because learners may listen more willingly to them than to able-bodied instructors.

A second important strategy in teaching is self-disclosure, which does not imply explicit disclosure of one's personal sexual activities, but rather a willingness to express one's own feelings about sexuality. Through self-disclosure the professional gains first-hand experience with the discomfort which clients-to-be may experience when they are asked to talk about their sexuality. This strategy has been amply demonstrated to be effective in the Sexual Attitude Reassessment (SAR) models which have found wide acceptance in medical schools. Although it may be anxiety-provoking for the professional to self-disclose in front of peers or disabled persons, the experience can be healthy and productive.

Another strategy that has been extensively used in training programs for rehabilitation professions is to have the professional spend a day attempting the usual tasks of relating to family and colleagues while sitting in a wheelchair. When done prior to formal or structured learning, this experience creates a more receptive frame of mind toward the facts of disability and societal attitudes toward disabled persons.

Part VI of this book lists some reference articles, movie titles, and videotapes which are helpful in learning about sexuality in the physically disabled. Sexually explicit movies and videotapes, followed by small group discussions of the feeling which they evoke, are useful for engendering empathy. Small discussion groups have been used extensively in medical school curricula, often being facilitated by disabled former patients. The disabled facilitator makes it possible for the professional to experience learning from people who, under other circumstances, would be regarded as patients or clients. Another useful technique is to listen to testimony by panels of former patients. The poignant stories which they tell about their experiences while in treatment, or while out in society, often are very effective in learning how a professional's attitude can impair attempts to provide services.

Learners can also profit from handling and examining equipment and devices used by disabled people. This includes equipment related to sexual function such as vibrators and dildos, as well as equipment used by the physically disabled to accomplish activities of daily living, such as catheters, fecal drainage bags, braces, and wheelchairs.

Sexual function can be enjoyable even in the presence of denerva-
tion, amputation, or deformity. However, accepting that idea challenges
some of the sexual attitudes and myths which many of us hold. Certainly,
such acceptance may cast a new light on experiences with sexual concerns and dysfunctions we may have had in our own personal lives.

STRATEGIES FOR SKILL TRAINING

Once the learner has added content to an already established awareness of self and the disabled person, he or she must integrate them into
counseling and practice them repeatedly. For some professionals who
have never done sexual counseling, "getting the first attempt over with"
is an essential first step in the practice phase of the curriculum. The
professional who is reluctant to practice talking about sex with real or
simulated patients or clients should be urged to give it a try. The curriculum should include supervised opportunities for the learner to try
counseling with the new awareness and information.

Practice is best done when the learner is in a safe environment.
There, the professional can match new attitudes and information with
previous counseling skills to see how effective they are. Disabled people
can play a unique role in a sexuality curriculum by serving as simulated
patients or clients. When trained, they can provide very real opportunities
for the professional to practice counseling techniques. Practice can be
conducted in the same small discussion groups with which the professional has been associated during the content phase of the curriculum.
Constructive criticism by the group can be beneficial. This method has
been used extensively in the University of Minnesota's Program in
Human Sexuality. For five years we have conducted training programs
for rehabilitation professionals in the area of sexual interviewing and
counseling. With training, disabled people or their spouses can reach into
their own experiences or those of other disabled people with whom they
have associated to find situations to enrich the practice sessions. We have
shown the value of practice by studying a group of physicians who had
participated in a curriculum dealing with sexuality and physical disability.
Prior to training, we found that patients with certain types of physical
disabilities tended to receive more or less permission to have and discuss
sexual problems and to receive information. Elderly patients and patients
with diseases other than spinal cord injury received considerably less
permission to discuss their sexuality. Following training, all groups of
patients reported more permission and information received from their
physicians.

Depending upon skill, interest and work assignment, each professional may find his or her own level of appropriate involvement. Annon has suggested a four-tiered scheme of involvement.[10] At Level I, the professional gives permission to the disabled person to have a sexual concern or dysfunction, to bring it up and discuss it. This can be done by asking leading questions, initiating talk about sensitive subjects, or by simply listening to the spoken or body language of the disabled person. All helping professionals should be able to function at Level I. Failure to do so may deny permission to patients to discuss the problems and concerns which they may be facing. At Level II, the professional provides limited information, typically educational and nonpersonal, for general problem-solving. At Level III, the professional provides specific suggestions about sexual concerns or dysfunctions. This implies that the counselor has taken a sexual history and is knowledgeable about sexuality and the particular sexual disability. Level IV involves intensive therapy which should be attempted only by professionals thoroughly trained in counseling.

The goal for a curriculum in education and sex counseling for the physically disabled is the integration of awareness, content, and practice into the everyday work-setting. It is more appropriate for sexuality to be dealt with in this fashion than to be sensationalized and given separate handling. The negative message of separate handling is that sexuality is too touchy to be dealt with as one of the everyday activities of living. Integration into the daily work-setting of the professional, on the other hand, sets the expectation that sexuality, like other aspects of disability adjustment, will be dealt with at appropriate, recurrent intervals and at a level which fits the situation. Thus, a social worker, nurse, or physician may provide useful "permission" to the patient who at the same time is receiving help with social, nursing, or medical problems caused by a physical disability. Or, the professional may provide "limited information" or even "specific suggestions" for sexual difficulties just as he or she deals with other aspects of medical care or patient education. The professional who is trained in disability adjustment and relationship counseling may provide "intensive therapy" for those whose concern or dysfunction cannot be adequately met by the other three tiers of patient-professional interaction.

CURRENT TRENDS

Although sexuality of physically disabled people has become more widely discussed since 1971, it is by no means generally agreed that sexuality is as important an issue as other problems facing the hospitalized patient. Some centers are reassessing the recent acceptance of the importance of sexuality in institutional settings. In a recent study, Hanson and Franklin questioned spinal cord injured men about the relative importance of their sex organ function in comparison to the use of their legs, arms and hands, and bowel and bladder.[11] In a hospitalized sample, they found that the majority of patients ranked sex as being the least important of the other major functional losses. In contrast, staff members viewed the loss of sexual function as substantially more important. Spergel et al examined the relative importance of sexuality compared with other rehabilitation issues.[12] In questioning his hospitalized sample, he found that during the early stages of the rehabilitation program, sex was reported as less important than the other variables of ambulation, activities of daily living, muscle strengthening, pain relief, mobility, and transportation.

However, if one restrictively defines sexuality as sex-organ function, or if one surveys institutionalized patients still in the early stages of disability adjustment, the broader and deeper meanings of sexuality may be overlooked. Sexuality is more than genitality and certainly more than sex acts. To limit the concept of sexuality to genitality is to exclude those whose physical disabilities have caused their genitals to be lost, denervated, or damaged. To confine sexuality to intercourse is to reduce the richness of sexual expression. The latter becomes especially clear when one considers solitary masturbation.

We prefer to define sexuality more broadly as intimacy. Intimacy is of vast importance to human beings, whether able-bodied or disabled. Everyone is capable of it, young or old, married or single, male or female. Intimacy can be practiced at all levels, between all people. It includes adults interacting with adults, adults interacting with children, and children with each other. Comfort with intimacy may influence how one person interacts with another, how patients work with staff, as well as how a person communicates with his or her sexual partner.

Professional literature and periodicals circulated to the disabled community convey the message that sexual rehabilitation should be expected from health professionals and institutions. One day sexual activity may be thought of as one of the activities of daily living which many adults repeat at regular intervals and with which the rest of their lives and activities are intertwined. Institutional prohibitions which have, until recently, discouraged intimacy between the hospitalized person and his or her spouse are giving way. In some centers, privacy rooms are now available to patients who can use them with their partners for intimate exchange which may or may not include genital activity. Perhaps in the not too distant future, the neglect of sexual rehabilitation of the physically disabled will no longer be considered benign; it will be called negligent.

REFERENCES

1. Ebert RK, Lief HI: Why sex education for medical students? in Green R (ed): Human Sexuality: A Health Practitioner's Text. Baltimore, Williams & Wilkins, 1974, p 1–9
2. Ozel AT, Kottke KJ: Trends in research in physical medicine and rehabilitation. Arch Phys Med Rehabil (in press)
3. Warren RP: All the King's Men. New York, Harcourt Brace Jovanovich, 1974
4. Lawrence DH: Lady Chatterly's Lover. New York, New American Library, 1972
5. Money J: Sexual Problems of the Chronically Ill, in Wahl CW (ed): Sexual Problems: Diagnosis and Treatment in Medical Practice. New York, Free Press, 1967, p 266–287
6. Fox J: Sex education—but for what? Spec Educ 60:15–17, 1971
7. Cole TM, Chilgren RA, Rosenberg P: A new program of sex education and counseling for spinal injured adults and health care professionals. Paraplegia 11:111–124, 1973
8. Cole TM: Sexuality and physical disabilities. Arch Sex Behav 4(4):389–403, 1975
9. Mitchell JC: Disabled counselors: perception of their effectiveness in a therapeutic relationship. Arch Phys Med Rehabil 57:348–352, 1976
10. Annon J: The use of vicarious learning in the treatment of sexual concerns. Paper presented at Annual Meeting of American Psychological Association, Chicago, 1975
11. Hanson RW, Franklin MR: Sexual loss in relation to other functional losses for spinal cord injured males. Arch Phys Med Rehabil 57:291–293, 1976
12. Spergel R, Rosenthal D, Albert B: Sex—a rehabilitation issue: What priority and when? Abstract from Official Program of American Congress of Rehabilitation Medicine, San Diego, 1976

Paul H. Gebhard

8
Anthropological Considerations in Sexuality Curriculum

Anthropology can make an essential contribution to any educational effort to improve the efficacy of a health-service professional. Most such professionals derive from the middle or upper socioeconomic levels of our society and because of this—plus the demands made upon them to earn the advanced degree necessary to the position to which they aspire—have neither experienced nor witnessed the diversity of human sexual behavior which they will encounter later in their clients or patients. These professionals will have been insulated from many sexual realities, especially those of the lower socioeconomic level and ethnic minorities. Health-service individuals will find it difficult to comprehend how behaviors and attitudes contrary to their own backgrounds are sometimes functional and rational accommodations to socioeconomic environments. It will be far easier for them to regard such differences as dysfunctional or pathological. Moreover, the professional is naturally prone to view sexuality through a European-American conceptual lens. His or her perception of ranges, norms, and needs is based upon this cultural background and upon a necessarily limited personal experience.

In brief, the professional is culture-bound, and anthropology's value lies in its power to break these intellectual shackles and permit the therapist or counselor to see and better evaluate the physiological, cultural, and psychological realities which must be dealt with in order to assure effective and humane behavioral or attitudinal modification.

Achieving true clinical objectivity through emancipation from one's own culture and experience is not easy. At the intellectual level one must give up many psychiatric and psychoanalytic axioms such as the trauma of witnessing parental coitus, the oedipal complex, the inherent value of the incest taboo, and the assumption that years of behavioral conditioning can be nullified quickly. At the emotional level one must relinquish sacrosanct value judgments such as the belief that ideally an affectional relationship must precede sociosexual activity, and that certain behaviors are intrinsically harmful to the individual or society. I shall attempt to illustrate how cross-cultural data can assist the professional in achieving this desirable objectivity, but before doing so I must emphasize the obvious: one's clients or patients must live in a society which has its own values, regardless of whether these are rational or irrational. In modifying a person's behavior or attitudes the professional must make some compromise between social demands and idiosyncratic needs. One must not try to produce a complete conformist to social mores nor some free spirit perpetually in conflict with society.

The first truth anthropology offers is that man is neurophysiologically an animal and hence some of his capacities and behaviors are genetically determined and species specific, as is the case in all other life forms. Being a mammal, man can be expected to share many sexual traits with other mammals, particularly those which are phylogenetically closest to humans. While these inborn capacities and behavior patterns are obscured by learning and conditioning, they continue to exist as factors which must be considered. As far as we know, all humans share the same sexual response sequence, the same neurophysiological traits, and (in varying degree) the same need for sexual expression, although the modes and frequencies of such expression are largely culturally determined. As the new science of sociobiology matures, we can hope to learn more about what part of sexuality is genetically determined and hence less amenable to modification. We must bear in mind that as one progresses upward (a value-laden wording) from the lower mammals (e.g., rodents) to primates and man, individual variation and the power of conditioning become increasingly manifest. The stereotype of the lower mammals is replaced by the enormous variation in the sexual behavior of the higher mammals. This greater variability is undoubtedly the result of the human's more developed cerebral capacities which allow learning and conditioning to dominate inherent behavior patterns. It is possible that over the millenia conditioning so frequently conflicted with the estrus cycle that ultimately the cycle was overwhelmed or bred out, so that humans, alone of all mammals, escaped this cyclical hormonal control of sexuality.

The extreme variability in humans includes not only preferences and techniques but also sex drive—a combination of physiological capacity and psychological needs. This fact has important social and clinical implications. Some humans need, or feel they need, one or more orgasms per day; others of the same age and in good health report they are satisfied with a few orgasms per year, or even none. The magnitude of such a difference exceeds that of any other physiological phenomenon. The clinician, therefore, must not fall into the trap of trying to define normality on some purely quantitative basis. Hypo- or hypersexuality are value judgments, and often the reference point is the clinician's own frequency. The reference should be the client or patient: is he or she functioning at a sexual frequency (with or without orgasm) markedly less or more than what seems to have been a satisfactory baseline.

Both the health-service professional and the sex researcher operate with the handicap of ignorance as to what degree human behavior represents innate capacity. While positive, the correlation is only of a moderate order at best. Many of us have known individuals who, with new partners or in altered environments, have radically increased frequencies of sexual behavior, not merely for a brief period but for years. It is clear that most humans function at some fraction of their sexual potential. Even taking into account the probability that different genetic groups have different capacities, anthropological findings seem to corroborate the preceding statement. Donald Marshall discussed with male Polynesian informants what they considered to be the normal frequencies of marital coitus at different ages.[1] Marshall learned that at age 18 there were generally three copulations per day—an average of about 20 per week if one includes four days per month lost because of menstruation. The frequency was reduced by age, becoming two or three per week by age 48.

Alan Merriam found African Bala tribesmen withstood a decrease in sexual activity due to age even better.[2] He questioned ten men aged 23 to 66 daily for ten days as to whether they had engaged in coitus in the preceding 24 hours. He repeated this interrogation a month later. All averaged 1.0 to 1.9 copulations per day; those who missed a day had compensated for the omission on some subsequent day. These frequencies are far in excess of that in the United States.

Conversely, Karl Heider reported that at least one society, the Dani of New Guinea, has minimal sexual needs.[3] The Dani delay the sexual consummation of marriage two years, have a five-year postpartum taboo on marital coitus, and apparently have no compensatory activities. They express no feeling of deprivation and seem relatively unconcerned about sex. Heider states that they are as physically healthy as neighboring tribes who are much more sexually active.

In addition to demonstrating that there are great differences in capacity, anthropology vividly illustrates another axiom: human sexual attitudes and behavior are extremely malleable. Humans are highly conditionable, and even a basic, inherent sex drive can be modified enormously by social pressure and learning. A society not only determines the social and psychological importance of sex but also whether it is perceived as a highly-valued pleasure or as a revolting chore. For example, Margaret Mead studied the Manus women of the Admiralty Islands who unanimously agreed that coitus was unpleasant for them.[4] On the other hand there are many groups, particularly the Polynesians, whose females greatly enjoy coitus and usually experience multiple orgasms.[1,5] This human quality of plasticity has been witnessed in the United States during the past century when a previously considered onerous marital duty has metamorphosed into an enjoyable right for many females. While the power of the therapist—or any professional attempting to modify others—is far less than that of society, recognition of the degree of human capacity for modification is both encouraging and frightening.

Mention of modifying or controlling attitudes and behaviors leads to another anthropological truth: all known societies have governed to a substantial degree the sexuality of their constituent members. All cultures share three universal traits: some form of marriage, condemnation of rape within the group, and restrictions as to who is eligible as a sexual partner or spouse.

Marriage appears to be a device to reduce time-and-energy-consuming competition. Assuring two or more individuals of an available sexual partner or partners permits devoting more energy to vital matters such as food production. The concept of marriage as an essential for the protection of females and infants is weakened by observation of nonhuman animals and by recognition that this protective function could be served by arrangements other than marriage, such as communal child care.

Prohibition of intragroup rape is necessary to avoid resentments and hostilities which would be socially disruptive.

Restrictions applicable to eligibility as sexual partners and spouses are less easily explained. All societies employ some combination of endogamy, keeping the choices within the social group or some subdivision thereof, and exogamy, keeping the choices outside of the nuclear family or some social unit close to the individual. Endogamy strengthens group solidarity yet tends to isolate the group. While it may dilute loyalty, exogamy offers political and economic advantages through the establishment of reciprocal obligations with more people. A Western society tends to be endogamous by discouraging marriage with foreigners or persons of different religions, races, and backgrounds. The same society embraces exogamy by prohibiting marriage with relatives extending out as far as first cousins.

Other disciplines might suggest a fourth universal: the desire for privacy during coitus. This is a tenable suggestion, which I prefer to reject because in many societies the desired privacy is not actual but psychological. In a one-room hut, parents will copulate while their children and resident relatives feign sleep. The unmarried couples copulating side by side in the mixed-gender dormitories of Borneo and of the Muria tribe in India politely ignore those next to them.[6]

Aside from the three anthropological universals, societies have imposed extremely different sexual regulations. Even behaviors which the average clinician or social scientist would consider to be inescapably dysfunctional or pathological have been incorporated into the normative behavior of various societies without evident damage. For example, female adultery is permitted or condoned in some cultures; male bisexuality is the norm in a number of societies; and perhaps the most dramatic illustration—the Lepcha of India encourage sexual activity between preadolescents and adults.[7]

Most societies have evolved a system of exceptions to prevailing regulations while still exerting control over sexual behavior. These exceptions probably evolved as repeated occasional adaptations to problems rather than as social planning. It is almost as though people recognized that they cannot be perpetually conforming, that it is socially and psychologically advantageous to have certain vacations from, or loopholes in, the restrictions. There are two categories of such exceptions. Those based upon kinship permit extramarital heterosexual activity ranging from obscene joking to coitus between certain kinspersons which are otherwise prohibited. The kinspersons most commonly thus privileged are generally the siblings of one's spouse. One might say that a halo effect surrounds marriage; the sexual rights accorded to a spouse extend in dilute form to his or her siblings. For example, while adultery may be generally prohibited to a male, the prohibition does not apply to his brother's wife or his wife's sister. This desire to confine sexual interaction to in-law peers is emphasized when a spouse dies: the widower is expected to marry any unmarried sister of his deceased wife (the sororate system), and the widow is expected to marry a brother of her late husband (the levirate). Thus the ties of marriage, with their valuable reciprocal obligations and loyalties, are preserved.

Often in Western societies, vestiges of this phenomenon may be seen. The sororate and levirate systems, exhorted by the Bible, were rather common until the 20th century in North American society.

The sexual permissiveness between peer in-laws is by no means absolute. It must be exercised only occasionally to avoid serious physical or affectional competition with marriage. Interestingly enough, in those societies wherein homosexuality is normative, there is no equivalent system based upon kinship. A male has no particular access to his male lover's brothers.

The sexual joking relationships of preliterate societies, frequently confined to brothers-in-law, sisters-in-law, and cousins, may be viewed as a means of expressing and thereby reducing sexual tensions between persons who might have married one another. First cousins are included along with peer in-laws because many societies encourage or demand cousin marriage; this trend is still extant in Europe and Appalachia. Not simply an exposition of anthropological exotica, this discussion has implications for our own society in which sexual joking and physical contact between brothers- and sisters-in-law are considered more permissible than with anyone else. Also, in situations where males and females of roughly the same age work together in close proximity, sexual joking frequently develops to defuse sexuality. Societies apparently recognize that males and females of approximately the same age who are forced into continual proximity because of kinship or working situations are going to be sexually attracted to one another, and control this attraction by allowing it partial expression.

The second category of exceptions to regulations is based not upon kinship but upon special occasions ranging from magico-religious rites to secular festivals. Such "ceremonial license" temporarily permits not only premarital and extramarital activity but on occasion, high-taboo behavior such as rape, incest, prostitution, and the deflowering of a bride by someone other than the bridegroom. In enfeebled form, ceremonial license exists in Western society. During festivals such as Fastnacht (Germany) and Mardi Gras (United States and France) hugging, kissing, and petting with complete strangers is acceptable, and to some even coitus is excusable. In still more attenuated form, ceremonial freedom permits the custom of kissing under the mistletoe or at the stroke of midnight on New Year's Eve; flirtation and petting at cocktail parties or church "socials" no longer evoke recrimination and censure.

With increasing sexual permissiveness, it is likely that temporary exceptions to the prevailing sexual restrictions will not suffice for many people. We will probably develop some system based not on kinship or ceremonial license but upon affectional relationships and the concept of individual freedom. It is difficult to foretell if this will be an acceptance of clandestine affairs or "open marriage" or a continued revival of communal living. Whatever evolves, the professional should anticipate and be prepared to cope with the problems such a change, even though gradual, will bring.

All scientists and clinicians dealing with human behavior acknowledge the power of learning and conditioning; in the realm of sexuality an anthropological phenomenon appears to conflict with this scientific axiom. In a small number of societies, pubescent and adolescent males are physically segregated from the community, and whatever sociosexual activity they have is of necessity with other males. Upon attaining an age regarded as adulthood they reenter the community, evidently abandon homosexuality and establish heterosexual relationships which shortly lead to marriage. There is a scarcity of data regarding young females, but it appears they experience a parallel deprivation of heterosexual contact. The sex researcher, accustomed to explaining some homosexuality as primarily the result of conditioning, is baffled by this sudden and complete conversion to heterosexuality. Actually, conditioning has not been mysteriously overridden but is operant in disguise. The young people have been given the belief and expectation that their homosexual, or at least homosocial, phase will inevitably be replaced by heterosexuality. (It would be most interesting to know if their masturbatory and homosexual activity is accompanied by heterosexual fantasy.) A less dramatic but comparable change in overt sociosexual behavior may be seen in the abandonment of the homosexuality common in gender-segregated schools. In brief, it is not what one does that is of paramount importance; rather it is how one views the behavior and what one expects will occur.

This brings us to a cardinal point: no sexual act has an inherent social or psychological value. It is the cultural and situational elements which determine the value and meaning of sexual activity. Even those who would maintain that all coitus has value because it may result in reproduction must admit that procreation may result in social or individual damage. Accepting the relativistic statement made above logically leads to an absolutely vital question for all of us: with what meanings shall society invest various sexual behaviors? Or, stated in another way, what controls can some proportion of the members of society legitimately exert on themselves and other members? In attempting to answer, the professional is at once forced into making value judgments.

If the problem is approached from a purely secular, rational viewpoint, society and the professional should seek to prevent or change only behavior which demonstrably and usually causes physical or emotional damage or which causes more unhappiness and social friction than happiness and tranquility. Unfortunately, from an anthropological viewpoint, a completely rational approach is impossible at the present state of social and intellectual evolution. Were we to adopt this rationale, we should not only prohibit rape but also severely limit tobacco, alcohol and sugar consumption, regulate procreation, and institutionalize the grossly obese until they learn to curb their self-destructive appetites. Realizing that rationality cannot always prevail, we must allow people freedom to do things which adversely affect them providing that their behavior does not adversely affect others to a substantial degree. The essence of freedom is not only the unfettering of one's self but the obligation to allow others to do things of which one disapproves. So the problem distills to the question of the limits of individual freedom.

In general, subscription to the idea that what consenting adults do sexually in private should not be subject to social control is laudable; when one focuses on specific cases, this idea has flaws. Should society tolerate serious injury or death in a consensual sadomasochistic relationship? Aside from this sadomasochistic qualification, there is validity in the consenting adult philosophy even though there may be unfortunate sequelae such as emotional disturbance and divorce. Freedom has a price.

The consenting-adult philosophy leaves untouched the extremely important question as to control and guidance of the non-adult. This question contains within it another: how does one define adulthood? One immediately thinks of criteria: adequate knowledge of social functioning, economic independence, and other social awareness. These attributes are not accurately determined by chronological age, and we cannot afford to have courts or special evaluators deciding when each individual becomes an adult. A physical definition is reasonable: the average age at which the developmental processes of adolescence ends. This generally occurs in the late teens and is marked by cessation of rapid growth in height. By the time final stature is attained, one has adult physical capabilities and, assuming our educational system is reasonably efficient, a passable knowledge of how to conduct one's self. Having defined the threshold of adulthood as 17 or 18, what about the non-adult?

Many scientists and clinicians are ambivalent as to childhood sexual activity. Some feel that prepubertal heterosexual play need not be discouraged since it can be a useful learning prelude, as it is in various preliterate societies, to adult sexual life. Others would argue that such permissiveness would establish in the children sexual patterns and needs which would bring them into conflict with social and religious mores when they became adolescent.

Prepubertal homosexual play poses a similar but more acute problem. Because of the attitudes characteristic of our society most professionals would discourage homosexual play if it reached an intensity or exclusivity leading the parent and consulted professionals to believe it would result in a predominately homosexual orientation in adult life. They would not knowingly allow children to develop what would likely be a handicap in later life. Virtually all persons who were exclusively or nearly exclusively homosexual when I interviewed them felt that children should not be encouraged toward homosexuality, or at least not so conditioned that by the time they reach adulthood the decision as to their sexual orientation already had been determined.

From a rational viewpoint, a parent or clinician should discourage any pattern of sexual behavior which could be expected to make later life unusually difficult. A touch of masochism, fetishism, transvestism, voyeurism, and certain other paraphilias may add a little welcome variety to sexuality, but a person deeply committed to such behaviors is almost certain to have great difficulties in finding and keeping sexual partners and runs an increased risk of social censure, guilt, and possibly lowered self-esteem. Ordinary heterosexual life is difficult enough; one should discourage the development of additional imperative compulsions with their concomitant problems of gratification within our culture.

At this juncture someone will inquire about child-adult heterosexual contacts. Would not such initiation be a beneficial introduction to adult heterosexuality? While in some particular cases this might well be true, in general one cannot but fear the likelihood of duress and exploitation, and mistrust the tutelage of the adult whose motivation is more probably gratification than altruism.

Any professional dealing with human sexual needs and behaviors cannot escape the problem of what is best for society as a whole as opposed to what is best for a particular individual. Not only must the professional struggle privately with the issues I have mentioned (plus others I have not), but he or she may be called upon to give opinions before courts or legislative bodies. The responsibility the professional owes to clients, patients, and society is heavy. Anthropology can lighten this burden by offering for inspection what amounts to numerous experiments by diverse societies in dealing with the problems of human sexuality, and in so doing, inculcate the professional with cultural relativity and objectivity. Both are necessary for effective and humane therapy and social planning.

REFERENCES

1. Marshall D: Sexual behavior on Mangaia, in Marshall DS, Suggs RC (eds): Human Sexual Behavior: Variations Across the Ethnographic Spectrum. New York, Basic Books, 1971, p 123
2. Merriam A: Aspects of sexual behavior among the Bala, in Marshall DS, Suggs RC (eds): Human Sexual Behavior: Variation Across the Ethnographic Spectrum. New York, Basic Books, 1971, p 89–90
3. Heider K: Dani sexuality: a low energy system. Man (New Series) 11:188–201, 1976
4. Mead M: Growing up in New Guinea, in Mead M (ed): From the South Seas. New York, William Morrow, 1939, p 165
5. Suggs R: Marquesan Sexual Behavior. New York, Harcourt, Brace & World, 1966
6. Elwin V: The Muria and Their Ghotul. Bombay, Geoffrey Cumberlege, Oxford University Press, 1947
7. Gorer G: Himalayan Village: An Account of the Lepchas of Sikkim. London, Michael Joseph, 1938

PART III

Teaching Methodology for Curricula on Human Sexuality

Norman Rosenzweig
F. Paul Pearsall

Introduction

Most educators now agree that presentation of factual material in a direct or didactic fashion is not a suitable approach to teaching human sexuality. There is a general recognition that the emotional biases and resistances of both student and teacher must be confronted and dealt with before cognitive learning can occur. This section addresses some methodologies for bringing about such attitude reassessment and change, and also considers the problems of assessment.

Flatter discusses the use of group discussion to emphasize the human, universal, and personal aspects of sexuality and the ubiquity of sexual anxiety among those raised in Western cultures. Group discussion can facilitate desensitization and resensitization, although, as Flatter reminds us, there are difficulties associated with the use of groups that the educator should be aware of and attend to.

Briggs presents a personal review of the use of audio-visual materials in courses in human sexuality. Her approach is so straightforward that it is difficult to realize that general acceptance of the utilization of these materials is a fairly recent phenomenon. How much the social climate has changed can be illustrated by the contrast between the receptions given to the work of Ellis and Kinsey, respectively. Havelock Ellis' *Studies in the Psychology of Sex: Sexual Inversion* was declared a "lewd wicked bawdy scandalous and obscene libel" in 1898 by an English court. The work was seized as obscene and Ellis was attacked by professionals and lay groups as a corrupter of morals. A half-century later Kinsey's *Sexual Behavior in the Human Male* appeared, under the imprimatur of a commercial rather than a scientific publisher, and the book became a best seller. Indeed, according to noted attorney Morris Ernst, Kinsey's works themselves made a large contribution toward modification of public attitudes "by providing a different, and documented point of view about social behavior."

What had happened in the interim between Ellis and Kinsey was a significant change in the position of Western courts (British and U.S. in these cases) toward enforcement of censorship. Morris Ernst had himself participated in one of the landmark decisions as attorney for the defendant in United States versus Ulysses in 1933. By 1957 the U.S. Supreme Court attempted to distinguish sex from obscenity. In the words of Justice Brennan, "The portrayal of sex, e.g., in art, literature and scientific works, is not in itself sufficient reason to deny material the constitutional protection of freedom of speech and press."

Some of the first audio-visual materials used by pioneer educators in human sexuality were in fact items that had been confiscated by the authorities enforcing the censorship statutes. But as the censorship of sexual materials abated there appeared an explosion of explicit erotic materials; and sex educators, sometimes with serious misgivings, utilized this readily available commercial material in their courses. Many of these works were crude, however, and soon certain groups such as the National Sex Forum, EdCoa, and others began producing films expressly for education in human sexuality. The reader is referred to McIlvenna's paper in Part V, as well as the Appendix by Bantis, in addition to Briggs' chapter, for further information on this subject. Although sexually explicit, these films did not portray sexual athleticism and minimized some of the obvious earlier agism and sexism, depicting rather genuine relationships between people. The sensitivity and lack of commercialism which these films seemed to show encouraged many who had been timid to employ such audio-visual materials in sex education courses. These explicit materials had the effect not only of arousing the sexual feelings of students, but also, when accompanied by the opportunity for self-examination and discussion in small groups, tended to lessen rather than increase the student's sexual anxiety. Such "desensitization" thus lowered the psychological barriers to absorbing and really learning the cognitive content dealing with sexuality. Briggs' chapter deals not only with the philosophical considerations, but also discusses the practical issues involved in the use of such media. It must be borne in mind, of course, that use of such media is still not universally accepted or approved of, and the educator must be sensitive to possibilities of backlash.

A thorny problem in any pedagogical endeavor is the development of adequate assessment instruments. This problem is even more important in sex education when new approaches and direct work with student attitudes are employed. The subject is dealt with in a thorough and professional fashion by Miller and Williams. As they emphasize in the last chapter of this section, where we will go with sexuality curricula depends to a large extent on learning much more specifically and operationally where we were and where we are in terms of the purpose, outcome, and impact of the sexuality program.

John Flatter

9
The Use of Small Groups in Sexuality Programs

INTRODUCTION

Men and women are, by their very nature, social beings. Their sexual attitudes are formed and maintained largely through social interaction. Therefore, any meaningful sexual attitude reexamination should occur within a context that provides for social group interaction. The small group experience provides such a context. Moreover, unlike the rather unplanned and random attitude formation that occurs with one's initial sex education, the sexual attitude reassessment group has the potential advantage of providing for a systematic reexamination of one's attitudes and values, and of comparing them with those of others who come from varying cultural and family environments.

While it is generally agreed that group experience is desirable, and that interaction with one's peers is a necessity for meaningful attitude exploration and reassessment, little has been written about specific goals, structures, and processes of sexual attitude reassessment groups. The attitude reexamination group, as with other types of groups, can be ineffective as a learning experience, or may even be destructive to the emotional integrity of some members. Process and outcome in sexual attitude reassessment groups is dependent upon many mutually interactive factors, most of which have not been analyzed or clarified in the literature. Little has been written about group goals, what should happen in the group experience (including participant behavior and appropriate interactions), and what facilitator skills and behaviors are necessary for promoting attitude reexamination. The purpose of this chapter is to discuss the various issues involved in planning, execution, and evaluation of the small group experience, including facilitator functions and skills, as well as the use of group games and activities. More specifically, a behavioral model for group process and facilitator intervention will be described.

GOALS

Perhaps one of the major characteristics of one's own initial attitude formation and value-system development is the general ambiguity of what has been acquired. Unfortunately, many professionals are among those with ambiguous sexual attitudes and unclear value systems. Unquestionably, what is needed now are learning experiences which help bring awareness and clarity to one's attitudes, feelings and values. Sexuality workshops can provide such experiences. However, attention must be paid to the planning and implementation of the workshops if they are to be successful. In his book, *The Age of Discontinuity,* Drucker suggested that one reason why organizations are not successful is because they lack clear-cut criteria for measuring success.[1] Without goals, interaction lacks direction. Without direction, effectiveness is impossible. This is most applicable with respect to sexuality workshops, and most certainly to small group discussion.

Addressing himself to behavior contract groups, Egan observes that "there is a great deal of evidence indicating that groups achieve a high degree of effectiveness of operationality only through clear-cut goals and defined means of achieving these goals."[2] This observation holds true for sexual attitude reexamination groups as well.

If the discussion group is to minimize the ambiguity of earlier attitude formation and is to become an effective learning experience, the first and primary issue is definition of group goals: what does the group experience hope to accomplish? What occurs within the group experience is inexorably tied to its goals; and these goals are, in turn, dependent upon, and must be articulated with, the overall purpose of the sexuality workshop.

Although content and procedures may differ, there is general agreement that one important purpose of sexuality workshops is to provide a series of learning experiences involving both cognitive and affective dimensions, through which there is movement toward an increased degree of participant tolerance of one's own sexual attitudes, feelings, value systems, and sexuality, and those of others. Thus, the overriding goal of the group experience is to promote an increased level of tolerance for differences in self and others. Movement toward this goal is achieved through an unfolding process, which may be conceptualized as an interaction between other intermediary and prerequisite goals.

The initial prerequisite goal, and one that lays the foundation for all others, is self-awareness. Each participant needs to focus on, and become cognizant of, what his or her own sexual attitudes and feelings are. No reexamination process is possible without becoming aware. With increased levels of self-awareness, self-affirmation occurs. Affirmation of self may be described as both a subjective inner experience and outward verbal declaration of what one believes and feels about who one is. As increased levels of self-awareness and affirmation unfold, it becomes possible to reevaluate who one is and what attitudes one holds. Only through reevaluation and reassessment in a "psychologically safe" environment of peer interchange, involving dissimilar and conflicting value systems, does the potential exist for more tolerant and understanding attitudes to emerge.

One caveat should be given: not everyone within the group will move at the same rate or to the same degree with respect to his or her personal attitude awareness, affirmation, and reexamination. Nor will the participants necessarily experience a change in the direction of more tolerant attitudes. However, an environment should be provided that will allow and encourage each participant's involvement at his or her own readiness level.

GROUND RULES, FACILITATOR FUNCTIONS AND FACILITATOR SKILLS

One cannot become involved with human sexuality without experiencing an entire gamut of emotions. Participation in a human sexuality workshop may increase confusion, anxiety, or fear revolving around sexual issues. Such emotions, especially anxiety and fear, tend to block the participant's ability to explore and reassess his or her own attitudes and sexuality.

One might ask: what anxieties and fears exist with respect to the group experience? Predominantly, much of the anxiety revolves around being able to take the risk of self-disclosure without producing an "overexposure" in an emotional sense. Risk-taking is directly connected to one's ability to trust oneself and others. Emotional risk-taking and ability to trust are factors involved in all human encounters. However, due to the intensity of group participation, the fear of risk-taking and of trusting others may be even more magnified. One cannot be sure how others will receive and respond to one's self-disclosure, nor how one will respond to being exposed to deeper and deeper levels of self-awareness. Everything possible should be done to alleviate such negative feelings. Consequently, it becomes crucial to provide the type of environment that promotes "psychological safety."

A salient method of promoting "psychological security" is to provide some structure. One means of providing this structure is clear establishment of goals, including both the overall workshop goals and the more specific goals of the groups. Due to the short-term, intensive nature of the group experience, more is needed than merely establishing goals if a worthwhile experience is to materialize. Workshop staff do not have the luxury of having weeks of interaction for a dissipation of negative feelings to occur; thus, it becomes imperative to promote the proper total environment as quickly as possible. The use of preset, structured ground rules for group interchange has been found extremely useful for easing participants' anxieties and fears.

The ground rules are not presented for debate, but given to help create the type of safe emotional environment that will provide the potential for in-depth exploration of one's own and other's sexual attitudes and feelings. Table 9-1 lists the essential ground rules that have proved to be helpful for sexual attitude reassessment groups conducted at Sinai Hospital (also see Chapter 27).

Certainly, the establishment of clearly stated and commonly understood goals and ground rules is essential. But perhaps more essential is the function of the group facilitator. Effective facilitation of the group is a most difficult task which requires the facilitator to pursue several goals: promoting respect for the emotional integrity of each participant, promoting individual attitude awareness and reexamination, and facilitating constructive interaction among the participants.

To facilitate does not mean to direct. Often it happens that the facilitator actually leads the group in a certain direction based on a hidden agenda which might very well include "working through" personal adjustment problems of his or her own sexual life. This technique is not only ineffective for goal attainment but is potentially dangerous. On the other hand, the facilitator need not apologize for intervening to tell the participants what he or she thinks is or is not happening with the group experience and suggesting ways in which the group might move ahead.

Intervention is often useful in helping participants to overcome obstacles in their exploration of attitudes and feelings. In addition to confusion, anxiety, and fear, obstacles may be created by participants' differing motivations, hidden agendas, and emotional problems. It is crucial that the facilitator develop and promote a common direction and purpose for the group experience. This is best done by clarifying his or her function and the purpose and goals of the group at the outset.

The facilitator must also have certain knowledge, experience and skills. He or she should have a demonstrable clinical background, including knowledge of personality dynamics and the dynamics of group interaction. More specifically, he or she should possess and demonstrate qualities of warmth, genuineness, respect, and empathy essential to any effective helper. He or she must be comfortable with self and others, and

Table 9-1
Ground Rules for Sexual Attitude Reassessment Groups

BELONGING. Everyone who is here BELONGS HERE just because he is here and for no other reason. This is our top rule. It depends on nothing else. Nothing changes it.

GENUINENESS. Be yourself. Don't be phony. Don't hide behind rules and facades. We try to be expressive of our true attitudes and feelings just as much as we can. An expression of anyone's sexual attitudes or feelings is equally welcome. It is welcome and fitting because he or she believes it or feels it and for no other reason.

HELPING AND SUPPORTING. As a group, we try to help each member explore and affirm what his or her sexual attitudes are and how he or she feels about them. We do this by being attentive, by listening, and when appropriate, reiterating back to the person what we heard. If we feel that responding to the person might be helpful, then we do so.

CONCRETENESS. Be direct, concrete, and specific in your interactions. Avoid speaking about generalities, intellectualizations, or theory.

INITIATIVE. This has to do with making contact with others. Don't merely react to others' expression of attitudes and feelings. Ultimately, the responsibility for making a meaningful experience of the group lies with you as an individual. Don't hang back.

OWNING. Part of taking the initiative is "owning" the interactions of others. In a group when two people speak to each other, it is not just a private interaction. Other participants may and should "own" the interaction, not just by listening passively but by contributing their own attitudes and feelings when deemed appropriate. Being tactless is one thing. Spontaneous involvement, motivated by care is another.

LISTENING. Owning the interactions of others implies that we listen *for* the person inside. We look at both what he says and what he does, so as to get in contact with what he believes and more importantly, what he feels. Total listening is, in a sense, nonselective. It encompasses all of the cues emitted by the other, even those that the other would rather conceal and those the listener would rather not hear.

CONFIDENTIALITY. What we say here is confidential. That means no one will repeat anything said here outside the group unless it concerns only himself. This applies not just to obviously private things but to everything. To really believe this, we will have to get to know each other before we can be sure.

SILENCE. Permission not to say something helps provide a nonthreatening environment. Silence can be interpreted as being negative and therefore something to be avoided. Silence is often appropriate for it can also imply thought, attentiveness, and a concern for making an appropriate response. If you are feeling uncomfortable with silence, then say so by expressing what you are feeling at that moment.

have a clear awareness of his or her own attitudes, feelings, and sexuality. Ideally the facilitator should have been a participant in an attitude reassessment group.

In summary, then, it is not enough for the facilitator to be aware of attitudes and feelings, to have a knowledge of group process, and to have good intentions. He or she must be willing to be involved in the group experience, to be able to promote constructive group interaction within the context of group goals, and to be able to demonstrate effective skills. As Egan has put it: "He should be in touch with his own experience and the experience of others and should know something about the interaction of the two."[3]

DIFFERENTIATING ATTITUDE REASSESSMENT GROUPS

In this writer's view, sexual attitude reassessment groups differ considerably from other major "therapeutic" types such as group psychotherapy, sensitivity, or behavior contracting groups. Unlike group psychotherapy, attitude reassessment groups do not delve into the deep psychological distress of patients diagnosed as "neurotic" or "psychotic." In fact, there is a de-emphasis on disclosure of individual emotional problems. Certainly there is neither the time nor is it a goal to resolve personal emotional problems, and indeed to do so in such a limited experience might well exacerbate whatever problems may already exist.

Unlike sensitivity groups, direct interaction involving one member's opinions and feelings concerning another member is discouraged. Attitude reexamination is not intended to be confrontational. Confrontation can be dangerous to the psychological integrity of the individual as well as being antithetical to the group goals. Unlike behavior contracting groups, attitude reassessment is *not* designed to help participants develop more effective coping behaviors such as developing more assertiveness or developing better communication skills.

GROUP DYNAMICS AND DEVELOPMENT OF A BEHAVIORAL MODEL

Although there are many differences, many similarities exist with respect to the elements of group process and the stages of group experience. As Rogers has pointed out, groups initially tend to go through stages: milling around, resistance, and negative expressions.[4] Perhaps with clearer goals, the milling-around stage may be minimized. However, to some degree it always occurs. In the beginning of the experience, members may be confused or uncertain as to what will happen, and therefore little may happen. Eventually a good deal of testing may occur in the form of silence or irrelevant talk, or even in the form of negative expressions involving anxieties and fears.

Minimizing and eventually overcoming these stages requires the development of three key elements of group process: trust, openness, and cohesiveness. None of these elements is achieved completely.

Some of the behaviors which can be used to identify degree of trust, openness, cohesiveness, and goal attainment are listed in the following behavioral model, based in part on the work of Krumboltz and Potter:[5,6]

Trust and Openness Behaviors.
High Frequency of:
    Here and now statements about present experience
    Self-disclosing statements about attitudes and feelings
    Personalized expressions using "I" or "for me"
    Reinforcement of each other's self-disclosing statements
    Attentive, nondefensive listening without distorting other members' statements
    Inviting and accepting nonjudgmental and sincere questioning from others regarding previous self-disclosing statements
    Spontaneous unprompted participation
    Maintaining confidentiality
Low Frequency of:
    There and then statements about attitudes and feelings
    Statements focusing communication on previous sessions
    Statements reflecting generalizations, intellectualizations, and irrelevancies
    Depersonalized statements using "you," "people," "society does," or "one"
    Negative statements about the group experience
Group-Cohesiveness Behaviors.
High Frequency of:
    Attending:
        Physical posture suggesting a desire to be part of the group
        Facial expressions indicating an interest and active participation
        Eye contact made with each other
        Physical closeness is welcomed and encouraged
    Equal participation by all members
    "We" statements referring to the total group experience or commonalities in experience

Low Frequency of:
Distracting:
Yawning
Facial expressions of boredom and general disinterest
Joking
Little or no eye contact
Physical distancing
Time monopolized by group facilitator
Statements directed to group facilitator only
Tardiness
Absenteeism
Goal-Directed Behavior.
High Frequency of:
Expressions that disclose personal awareness of sexual attitudes
and feelings
Expressions that reflect a personal reexamination of attitudes, feelings, and value systems
Expressions that reflect an increased understanding and tolerance
of others' sexual attitudes, feelings, and sexuality
Expressions that reflect commonalities in psychosexual development
Expressions that evaluate individual progress
Low Frequency of:
Judgmental and critical comments regarding others' goal-directed
statements
Social conversation unrelated to workshop purpose and experience

There are three advantages of this operational approach: (1) it adds clarity and gives direction to the group experience; (2) it provides for an ongoing evaluation of the group process; (3) it provides the facilitator with guidelines for determining the type and extent of intervention that will be most appropriate for facilitating the discussions.

FACILITATOR INTERVENTIVE BEHAVIORS

The following is a partial list of essential behaviors which will help the facilitator to promote group process and goal attainment:
Attending:
Alert body posture
Facial expressions and body gestures that convey active involvement with the group
Ability to listen and tune-in to verbal and nonverbal cues, including tone of voice, pauses, gestures, facial expressions, and posture of group members

Modeling:
Engaging in behaviors that demonstrate trust, openness, cohesiveness, and goal-directed activity
> Facilitator:
>> I feel upset at myself for not being as tolerant of others as I would like to be.
>> I have trouble talking to someone who has a physical handicap.
>> Jane, I share your feeling that giving and receiving affection are really important to me.

Reinforcing:
Expression of support and praise of participants' statements which reflect awareness, affirmation, reexamination of sexual attitudes, feelings, and sexuality, as well as increased tolerance of others
Reinforcement of group members' support and praise of other members' attitude exploration and reassessment
> Facilitator:
>> Sue, thank you for sharing with us.
>> Bill, you seem to be becoming more aware of your attitudes and feelings about homosexuality.
>> Dick, I have noticed how attentive you have been when others have been expressing themselves.
>> It's rewarding to be aware of the number of you who are taking some risks by disclosing something of your attitudes and feelings.
>> Mary, many of your expressions indicate to me that you are developing a greater understanding of others' attitudes toward abortion.

Cueing:
Use of open-ended questions and comments as a means of stimulating greater in-depth thought and awareness of sexual attitudes and feelings
> Facilitator:
>> Sometimes it's difficult to share our attitudes and feelings about very personal areas of our lives, but I wonder if someone would share them with us.
>> What feelings are you aware of now?
>> Joe, you seem to have strong feelings. Would you like to share more of what this means to you?

Extinguishing:
Ignoring inappropriate behavior such as irrelevant intellectualized, theoretical talk or nonattending behaviors (most effective when combined with reinforcement of other appropriate goal-directed behavior)

Facilitator:

After a participant has just finished making some intellectualized comments and then personalizes, the facilitator says, Brian, your last comment seemed especially self-disclosing.

Confronting:

It sometimes becomes necessary to confront inappropriate behavior such as labeling, judgmental statements, or an attack on the emotional integrity of another participant

Facilitator:

After having one member verbally attack another for not discussing, the facilitator might say: Jim, you seem upset about John's not talking. I would like to hear from John as well, but everyone has the expressed right to talk if they choose to.

I am aware that there times when many of you are not actively listening to what others are sharing. What does this seem to be all about?

Redirecting:

Used to refocus intellectualized, impersonal statements to more goal-directed, personalized expressions, or when the participant's comments are directed mostly to the facilitator

Facilitator:

After having heard a member make an intellectualized generalization, redirect by saying: Could you personalize that? We would like to know how you feel. *Or,* You mentioned that "people have the attitude." Can you say that for yourself?

After being asked to express his attitude or feeling by a group member, the facilitator redirects: I do have feelings about that but I wonder how others in the group feel?

Reflecting:

Use of comments which summarize what has been happening in the group process (especially helpful in integrating the effects of member or facilitator comments upon the overall group experience)

Facilitator:

It seems that all of us are becoming more open.

Many of us have talked about others or people in general. I wonder if talking about self is still threatening?

Being Silent:

Effective for building trust by communicating that all members are free to express when they choose to do so and they are not pressured or coerced to disclose themselves

These behaviors are not mutually exclusive; a specific intervention may combine several. The type of intervention used, when it is used, and the extent to which it is used at any particular moment in the group experience is dependent upon the degree to which the key elements of group process and goal attainment are emerging. Certainly, if the frequency of here and now statements, spontaneous member-to-member interaction, and goal-directed expressions of attitudes and feelings has increased, the facilitator can conclude that the interventions have been appropriate and helpful. If not, the facilitator can continuously recycle the steps of diagnosing, intervening, and evaluating so as to promote trust, openness, cohesiveness, and goal attainment.

USE OF GAMES AND ACTIVITIES

Frequently, games and activities help to overcome initial anxiety and provide structure which, in turn, permits group participants to explore attitudes and feelings more freely. However, activities in and of themselves are not necessarily effective and, in fact, can be very ineffective or even destructive. Much of the efficacy of a particular activity or series of activities depends on what is presented, when it is presented, and how it is presented. Egan's observations are relevant:

> I have experienced facilitators who handled exercises so authoritatively or so awkwardly that resistances among group members were merely heightened. If the facilitator is not skilled in using exercises, or if he is uncomfortable with them then he should omit them; if they are used they should be suited to the temper and needs of the group. It also seems better to ensure that the members know why certain games are being used and to have consent to use them. The rule of thumb is simple: if exercises are helpful and suited to the group, let them be used; but they should not take the place of free interaction among participants.[3]

The facilitator's decision to use games and activities should be based on the frequency of demonstrations of the key elements of group process and goal attainment. They should never be used as a substitute for spontaneous expression of attitudes and feelings. If the activities result in an increase in initiative and constructive goal-directed behavior, they will have served their purpose.

It is beyond the purview of this chapter to describe the various activities that can be used. Those who are interested should consult Morrison and Price which is the most definitive resource available today.[7]

SUMMARY

Small discussion groups have proved to be a particularly valuable part of the attitude reassessment phase of many human sexuality education programs. If these groups are to help bring about genuine changes in attitudes toward sexuality, careful attention must be given to defining group goals and communicating these goals to members of the group, to establishing clear ground rules for facilitators and members, and to training facilitators.

REFERENCES

1. Drucker PF: The Age of Discontinuity: Guidelines to Our Changing Society. New York, Harper & Row, 1969
2. Egan G: Face to Face: The Small-Group Experience and Interpersonal Growth. Monterey, Calif, Brooks/Cole, 1973
3. Egan G (ed): Encounter Groups: Basic Readings. Belmont, Calif, Brooks/Cole, 1971
4. Rogers C: The process of the basic encounter group, in Egan G (ed): Encounter Groups: Basic Readings. Belmont, Calif, Brooks/Cole, 1971
5. Krumboltz JD: Behavioral approach to group counseling and therapy. Res Devel Educ 1:3–18, 1968
6. Krumboltz JD, Potter B: Behavioral techniques for developing trust, cohesiveness and goal accomplishment. Educ Technology 13:26–30, 1973
7. Morrison E, Price MU: Values in Sexuality: A New Approach to Sex Education. New York, Hart, 1974

Mary M. Briggs

10
The Use of Audio-Visual Materials
in Sexuality Programs

If you are reading this book you probably already teach or counsel in the area of human sexuality. You might have a collection of slides and films that you find useful in your work. The back of this book contains a list of resources for other available media. You can even attend courses on the most effective use of sex-related media. I wondered about how I might make this chapter worthwhile, and I decided to use this opportunity to share some personal experiences and observations about the use of media.

I have been doing sex counseling for four years and sex education for six. Along with Dr. Richard Chilgren, I was one of the creators of the Program in Human Sexuality at the University of Minnesota Medical School. In 1971, we were designing the first sex education course for medical students at our school. We heard of an innovative method devised by some ministers in San Francisco. Called Sex Attitude Restructuring (SAR), it was an exploration of sexual behaviors and attitudes through exposure to basic information about human sexuality, a wide range of explicit, sex-related media, and feeling-oriented small group discussions. I remember well our first pilot project. We invited Rev. Ted McIlvenna, Rev. Laird Sutton and Rev. Tom Maurer from the National Sex Forum to present a SAR for a very select group of University and Medical School officials, deans, department chairpersons, students, and religious and community leaders, all with their "significant others."

It was somehow appropriate that the seminar took place in a chapel. I remember the electricity in the room as this distinguished group of professionals watched naked bodies romping on a screen across the altar. We watched intensely, consumed with fear, anger, revulsion, arousal, joy, and boredom. A spark flew through the room as we realized that one of the naked men on the screen was the same man who was standing behind us running the projectors. The small group discussions helped us to experience our emotions more fully and to gain some understanding of our own attitudes about sex. The result was overwhelming support for SAR as a requirement for all medical students. From the beginning we sensed that the use of media was a key to the success of this educational model. We continued to pursue this sense in our investigations over the next several years.

We discovered that almost 30 years ago Alfred Kinsey had suggested the use of explicit films for sex education. However, it was not until 1967, when Ed Tyler, using materials from the archives of The Institute for Sex Research, showed sex movies to medical students, that Kinsey's suggestion was put into practice. Soon after, John Money compiled an illustrated presentation called "Pornography and the Home" which became very popular with students at Johns Hopkins Medical School. The creation of SAR in 1968 at The National Sex Forum in San Francisco was a major innovation in sex education and an introduction of a sex-positive ethic into our culture.

From 1971 to 1973, we presented many SARs and carefully evaluated every aspect of the experience. When we thought we knew what we were doing and why, we published "On Being Explicit: Sex Education for Professionals" in the May 1973 SIECUS Report. I invite you to read that if you want more detail about the SAR rationale or methodology.

Our evaluations supported our initial sense about the significance of using explicit films. The films seem to do three basic things: (1) provide information about what people do sexually; (2) elicit an emotional response, making personal feelings and attitudes more accessible to the participant; (3) make the group discussions more concrete, more specific, more personal. Our evaluation also showed that the environment of the seminar was a crucial aspect of "media." So we created the "pillow room," modeled after the space we had seen at The National Sex Forum. The living room atmosphere seemed to give people permission to confront their attitudes, beliefs, and values about sexuality.

As we developed and refined SAR, we accumulated material from many sources: explicit, educational, sensitive films from Multi Media Resource Center; explicit, educational, clinical films from EdCoa and other companies; family sex education packages from the American Lutheran Church and the Unitarian-Universalist Church; artistic films from erotic film festivals; commercial films from Grove Press; pornography from Denmark, New York, Los Angeles, and our own town; and the inevitable Cathedral filmstrip that made two statements about sex, two statements about values and twenty statements about law, order and authority.

Pornography appeared to be most useful as a part of a multi-media blitz (sometimes called the Fuck-O-Rama) which explored a broad range of sexual behavior through multiple projection of films with no emotional or relationship elements. This allowed people to saturate themselves with the physicality of sex and then move beyond that to investigate a much broader scope of sexuality.

The use of explicit films, particularly pornography, became controversial on a professional level and on a community level. Even though pornography represented only 1 of 18 hours in the seminar, it was the focus of most of the controversy. The professional debate centered on three issues: (1) the level of training of the instructors, (2) justifying the purpose for using the films, (3) the context in which the films are shown. Michael Carrera, EdD and Sharon Lieberman, MS elaborate on these issues in the July 1975 SIECUS Report ("Evaluating the Use of Explicit Media in a Human Sexuality Course").

The community controversy over these films was generated largely by people who had not seen them. The debate still continues in certain church bodies and social organizations like the John Birch Society and the Housewives' League of America.

The next step for us was to experiment with various uses of media. We hired artists to work with us. We learned to transform the pillow room into different environments. We could create a mood through visuals and sound, and we could correlate that mood with the messages we were trying to convey. Through multiple slide projections we could put people in jail, in a fern grotto, inside a body. This technique seemed to heighten the emotional impact of seminars, thereby making the learning more complete and more significant.

We started to pay more attention to the audio aspect of the seminars. Hearing "Pomp and Circumstance" while watching a porno film will do something quite different to you than acid rock, a Bach chorale, or a nursery rhyme. The difference is subtle and affective. Different emotions would rise to the surface.

As we began to train a broader range of professionals (nurses, social workers, ministers, rehabilitation counselors) we felt a need for other kinds of sex-related films, for example, explicit films of aged people or disabled people. We knew that watching a film of a quadriplegic having sex would help another quadriplegic learn more about his or her sexuality as well as help the professionals who deal with these persons to give help. Several agencies, like The National Sex Forum, are now making a broader range of films that accurately portray sexual behavior in a sensitive, personal and artistic way.

As we developed and expanded sexual health services for people with sexual problems, we saw another arena for media. Our counseling services roughly follow the PLISSIT* model developed by Jack Annon at the University of Hawaii. Within this model we are using explicit films primarily in the first three categories: providing permission, limited information, and specific suggestions. Use of video tape is the most widespread and effective use of a media tool in the last category of the PLISSIT model, intensive therapy. Clients or counselors viewing themselves on tape in a therapeutic situation can produce significant learning and change.

As we further explored the potential of various media in our educational setting, we tested the use of live theater to illustrate some issues concerning masculinity and femininity (sex roles). We wrote a script, developed a set, hired a director, rehearsed endlessly, and presented our vignettes to a special seminar for ministers. As the cast, we had a strong sense of our own creativity and this provided a charge of energy for everyone in the seminar. The audience was electric with the sense of this being something very special. The result was an important educational experience for everyone involved. The learning was on an affective level. We learned something new about ourselves, our feelings, our values, and the world around us.

Another experiment was our Seminar on Sexuality and Death (SOSAD). We wanted to see if this same educational methodology (using ''explicit'' media and group discussion) might be effective with another sensitive, deeply personal aspect of humanity—death. We also wanted to explore the relationship of sexuality and death on an emotional and spiritual level. I would like to use SOSAD as an example to illustrate some of the important aspects of developing media to supplement an educational process.

The first practical consideration is money for space, resources, equipment, films, and personnel. You do what you can do within your financial restrictions. What is important, I think, is that art and media have a place and a value at the beginning of any program or curriculum design. There must be a place for it in the initial budget or proposal. For SOSAD we had a small amount of money for film rental, photography and production.

We developed a script of the issues we wanted to address in the seminar and decided on appropriate speakers. As the script was refined, we began to see areas where we needed media to set a mood, to provide information, or to elicit an emotional response. The next step was to investigate resources. Since our budget was small, we initially looked at

*PLISSIT-Permission, Limited Information, Specific Suggestion, Intensive Therapy.

materials readily available to us from our own program, University Audio-Visual Resources, and public libraries. These sources provided us with a number of films we could use for mood setting: a film journey through a human body, time-lapse films of life and death in nature (plants, microscopic life forms), sensuous films of human bodies interacting, and a visual exploration of water (streams, rivers, the sea), depicting the process of life, death, regeneration.

We found books and magazines with photographs illustrating symbolism and relationships of life, death, and sexuality. An example is a book of photography called GRAMPS, which vividly portrays a man's process of dying. After deciding which pictures would be useful, we obtained permission from the artist or author to copy the picture. We made slides and used these visuals for environmental walls during the seminar. Occasionally you will have to pay a small royalty to reprint something from a publication. Often the publisher will waive the royalty if your intention is simply to use it in your own educational seminar.

Our next step was to explore the realm of educational, commercial and documentary films. Money was a definite limitation here as these films can be very expensive to rent. By looking through film catalogs and talking with thanatologists, we found several good films about death and dying. After previewing several of these films we decided on a few that would illustrate important concepts, provide emotional impact to stimulate group discussion, and would fit into our budget. An example was an excellent film of John Gunther's *Death Be Not Proud*. After deciding on appropriate media for SOSAD we went back to the script to coordinate the films and slides with the large group presentations and small group discussions.

This seminar was an important educational experience for most of the participants. The artist provided the motivation for us to move into an exploration of our spirituality. The media made it easier for us to move from an intellectual level to an emotional level and finally to a spiritual level of experience—getting beyond our fear of the physical reality of death so we could open ourselves to the spiritual meanings within us.

There are some other practical considerations to using media in sex education or counseling that I would like to mention. It is important to have competent, sensitive people to run the media. You do not want a projectionist; you want someone who has the brains of an electrician, the hands of a mechanic, the flexibility of a juggler, the heart of a humanist, and the spirit of an artist—someone who understands the mood you want to create and the concepts you want to teach. These people are very difficult to find; and if you do find one he or she probably will have endless battles with the more traditional academicians who believe that their lectures are all that is necessary for learning to occur. When our grants terminated and we began a long financial struggle, the artists on the staff were the first to go. We still benefit from the work they did, but I feel that the program lost an important energy when they left.

The politics of open, frank sex education are intricate and still somewhat dangerous. At this point it seems acceptable to teach doctors and ministers about sex and to counsel people with sexual problems, but community or family-oriented sex education is on shaky ground. Many parents still don't teach their kids about sex, but they don't want anyone else to teach them either. It is important to consider the dangers when making decisions about what media to use. At this point, for instance, I would never show a sexually explicit film in a public school, even if it portrayed a loving, committed, heterosexual, marital relationship. If I did, I would be risking my career and possibly my life. Human sexuality education requires a unique sensitivity; use of sex-related media demands even more.

This interdisciplinary field of human sexuality seems to be going through puberty. We are experiencing difficult changes: struggling for funding and survival, determining our beliefs and attitudes, shaping our identity. And we are going through some very creative changes. Scientists are collecting new information about human sexual function and dysfunction. Ministers are struggling with new views of meaning and ethics in the human sexual experience. Physicians are making connections between sexual health and total health care. Many competent people are teaching and counseling others to improve their sexual health. The artist must have a role in this growth and development.

It is my belief that the most effective sex educator or counselor exposes life, facilitates exploration, nurtures the meaning that evolves from the student or client, values individuality, and becomes a student so that the students become teachers, learning from each other and realizing their own potential. I also believe that as sex educators and counselors, we must use the artist to explore the realities of sexual behavior to elicit the emotional responses that will help students learn about themselves and realize the spiritual nature of the human sexual experience.

Ann Marie Williams
William R. Miller

11
The Design and Use of Assessment Instruments and Procedures for Sexuality Curricula

This chapter addresses the haunting question: "Is that sex course any good?" and the half-serious reply: "I don't know. How can you tell?" The answer to the first question obviously depends on the criteria used to define "good." The answer to the second question depends on the methods used to measure movement toward the criteria. This chapter will briefly discuss: the range of criteria used to determine the effectiveness of sexuality curricula, the "ideal" assessment instrument or procedure, the difficulties encountered in the development and application of the "ideal" method in a real program, the current state of assessment in human sexuality programs for professionals and students, and some comments and suggestions for future development of evaluation techniques.

What are the criteria used to define a "good" program? What questions should be asked about sexuality curricula at the outset to gauge the most appropriate type of program assessment? For the medical student who wants an interesting one-hour course to wedge between "Neuroanatomy lab" and "Introduction to Clinical Pathology," the most relevant question to ask may be "Do they show movies?" However, for the medical school professor or the hospital administrator concerned with the malpractice implications of permanently "deferred" pelvic and rectal examinations for colorectal, prostatic, or uterine cancer, the most important question may be "Will this medical-school course in human sexuality have *any* impact on the clinical behavior of the students when they reach house-staff level or when they go into practice?"[1,2] These questions mark two ends of the continuum of goals that sexuality programs may strive to reach. At one end are the personal goals of the individual student in medicine, nursing, social work, psychology, or pastoral counseling. Their short-term goals frequently include information about themselves, about sexual intercourse techniques, and about the opposite sex. They prefer an interesting course which is relevant to their immediate needs for information. At the other end of the continuum are the societal goals for the training of helping professionals. These goals tend to be long term and pragmatic: "Will the sexuality course affect not only the knowledge and attitudes of the students, but also their *behavior* during patient contact? How long will the effects of the course last?"

What criteria can be used to define a "good" assessment instrument or procedure for the evaluation of sex education courses for professionals? Three types of course impact can be assessed: first, beneficial/ detrimental impact on the participants' sexual attitudes, on the quantity and quality of their factual knowledge, and impact on their behavior;[3] second, both short-term and long-term effects; and third, the impact in reference to self and others, both personal and professional. In an effort to present these complex criteria in a more easily understandable format, we will now describe the "ideal" assessment instrument-procedure based on the best features of the techniques in current usage, as well as on the "if only we had" comments of our colleagues in sex education.

The "ideal" instrument would begin with basic biographical information about the participant, including age, sex, marital status, occupation, and area and extent of professional training. It would include a brief inventory of the participant's personal sexual experience, as well as his or her previous professional activities involving sexual education or counseling.

The ideal instrument would then assess the participant's baseline level of accurate information on sexual functioning and behavior. The information-assessment section would be designed for pre–post comparisons, as well as for constructive feedback to participants regarding their specific information, errors, or deficits. The factual information assessed would be standarized to allow for comparisons between classes, between programs, and between schools, and would allow measurement of trends over time.

Next, the ideal instrument would assess personal and professional attitudes regarding a variety of sexual activities. It would be important to have the participants rate their attitudes about each activity for a number of categories of people, for example, unmarried adolescents, unmarried adults, married adults, married adults engaging in secret extramarital activities, and adults over age 50.[4] Again, the assessment format would facilitate pre–post comparisons.

Another section of the ideal assessment instrument-procedure would evaluate professional competence in conveying sexual information in an interpersonal context. Both clinical skills and degree of "comfort" would be quantified by a method which was both objective and not overly anxiety-provoking for the participants involved.[5,6] Perhaps the best test of clinical skills is the measurement of the "product" of the helping-professional/client interaction, namely, the beneficial changes in the client effected by the professional.

The ideal instrument-procedure would also elicit the participants' reactions to each segment of the program (e.g., films, seminars, small group discussions, lectures, and case presentations). These "consumer reactions" would be used for the development and refinement of the sex education course in order to maintain optimal relevance and interest for the participants.

Finally, the instrument would contain rating scales for the evaluation of the participants' care/carelessness, interest/boredom in filling out the questionnaire itself. By asking for feedback on the accuracy of the responses given, the educator-researcher can estimate how much he or she can give credence to the test results ("How much faith can we put in these data?"). Suggested by Richard Cross at Rutgers in his recently compiled "Opinion Inventory,"[6a] these questions may avoid the inappropriate conclusions that can be derived from carelessly completed questionnaires.

What are the difficulties encountered in the development and application of the "ideal" instrument-procedure in a "real" program? The most obvious obstacles are time constraints in both the professional curriculum and in the faculty-staff schedules. Developing an assessment instrument or procedure is a time-consuming, tedious process. Convincing the professional school faculty to allot time for extensive course evaluation in addition to the block of time allocated for course content is difficult at best. Furthermore, the choice between two hours of evaluation (one hour each for pretest and posttest) and two hours of additional instruction may favor the more "urgent" priority—competent patient care.

Other difficulties encountered include a lack of funding for course evaluation research. One of the authors cited in this chapter admitted that "necessity was the mother of their instrument" because there were *no* department funds available to purchase a published questionnaire. This predicament is not uncommon and tends to generate a number of "home-made" questionnaires which are mimeographed for local distribution. Since time, interest, and funding may be lacking for computer analysis of the test results, many instructor-researchers have file drawers full of unanalyzed data.

What is the current state of assessment in human sexuality programs for professionals and students? What instruments are in current usage? Table 11-1 summarizes nine paper-and-pencil questionnaires which are published or have potential for widespread usage. The following paragraph begins a summary of several published articles which have used these scales and have reported quantitative data.

Table 11-1
Instructions for Assessment of Sex Education Curricula

NAME OF INSTRUMENT	AUTHOR(S) AFFILIATION; RELEVANT REFERENCE	Referent Population						Objective of Questions						Type of Questions						Length of Time	Number of Items	RELIABILITY	VALIDITY
		Med. Students	Nurses	Psychologists	Soc. Workers	Clergy	Other	Biographical Info.	Sex Attitudes	Sex Experience	Sex Information	Course Development	Other . . .	Essays	Fill-in-blank	True/False or Forced Choice	Rating Scales	Changes in Personal Behavior	Changes in Professional Behavior				
Sexual Attitudes and Behavior Inventory (SABI)	Fortmann and Mann[7] Univ. of Calif. at San Francisco 1972	X	—	—	—	—	—	X	X	X	X	*	—	—	—	X	X	X	—	30 min	250	.76–.90 test–retest	—
Test for Assessing Sexual Knowledge and Attitudes (TASKA)	Hawkins, Jr.[8] SUNY at Stonybrook	X	—	—	X	—	X	X	X	X	X	X	—	—	X	X	X	X	—	30 min	122	—	—
Minnesota Sexual Attitude Scales (MSAS)	Held, et al[4]	X	—	—	—	—	X	—	X	—	—	—	—	—	—	—	X	—	—	N.R.	35	N.R.	Construct Validity
Sexual Attitude and Behavior Survey (SABS)	Kilpatrick and Smith[9] Marcotte et al[10] Med. Univ. of S.C.	X	—	—	—	—	—	N.R.	X	X	—	—	—	—	—	—	X	—	—	N.R.	40	N.R.	Construct and Concurrent
Sex Knowledge and Attitude Test (SKAT)	Lief and Reed[1] Center for the Study of Sex Education in Medicine	X	X	X	X	X	X	X	X	X	X	—	—	—	—	X	X	X	—	30–45 min.	145	.87 test–retest	Construct Validity

140

National Sex Forum Questionnaire	McIlvenna[12] Institute for Advanced Study of Human Sexuality	N.R.	N.R.	N.R.	N.R.	N.R.	N.R.	X	X	X	–	–	–	–	–	–	X	–	–	N.R.	26	N.R.	N.R.
Harvard Sex Questionnaire	Nadelson and Shaw[13]	X	X	X	X	–	X	X	X	X	X	–	–	–	–	X		–	–	N.R.	61	—	—
Physicians' Workshop Questionnaire	Pion[5] Kapiolani Sexual Counseling Service	–	–	–	–	–	X	–	X	–	X	X	X	X	X	–	X	–	X	VARIES	40	—	—
Human Sexual Knowledge and Attitude Inventory (HSKAI)	Woods and Mandetta[14,15]	–	X	–	–	–	X	X	X	X	X	*	–	–	–	X	X	–	–	30–50 min	120	.84 test–retest	Construct Validity for Info. Content by Jury rating

N.R. = Not Reported
* = Separate questionnaire used to evaluate specific speakers and material

Numerous knowledge and attitude scales have been developed for evaluation of workshops, seminars, and courses in human sexuality for professionals and students, and a number of reports of such evaluations have been published. However, published reports with quantitative data analyses have used only a few of the available evaluation instruments. The typical evaluation design has been to administer the scales to participants or students before and immediately following the educational experience.

The Sex Knowledge and Attitude Test (SKAT) has been perhaps the most widely used instrument for evaluation of educational experiences on human sexuality.[11] The SKAT yields a single knowledge score and attitude scores on four dimensions: masturbation, sexual myths, heterosexuality, and abortion. Garrard et al administered the SKAT in a pretest-posttest design to evaluate a two-day seminar on human sexuality for medical students and faculty and for individuals from the community.[16] These authors reported that all categories of subjects showed significant change in SKAT Attitude Score in the direction of greater liberalization of attitudes. For the Knowledge section, the medical faculty groups did not increase their scores, whereas all other categories of subjects exhibited a significant increase in sexual knowledge. In contrast, Golden and Liston found no changes on the SKAT following a course for second-year medical students.[17] Both of these studies used the first version of the SKAT which entailed only one attitude scale. Subsequent studies have used Form 2 of the SKAT with its four attitude subscales.

Marcotte et al obtained pretest and posttest SKAT scores for a one-week course for first-year medical students and reported significant changes in knowledge and attitudes on all the SKAT subscales.[10] In the evaluation of a three-day workshop for health professionals on sex counseling of the physically disabled, Kreger found significant increases on the Knowledge section, but significant changes on the Attitude section were obtained only with the autoeroticism and heterosexuality subscales.[18] Mims et al reported that a five-day course resulted in significant increases on all the SKAT attitude subscales except the Abortion Scale, as well as a significant increase on the Knowledge Scale.[19]

In an experimental study comparing two different seminar formats, Vines found significant differences on the Knowledge section, but not on the attitude subscales of the SKAT, between students who had taken the seminar and control students who had not.[20] In addition to Vines' study, only one other published evaluation using the SKAT has gone beyond the simple pretest–posttest design. Garrard et al evaluated a course in human sexuality for second-year medical students.[21] The SKAT, as well as other instruments, was administered pre- and posttest and also at 6- and 12-month follow-ups. They reported similar results for both the Knowledge and Attitude sections of the SKAT: there was no significant increase in the scores from pre- to posttest, but a significant *decrease* from post- to 6 months and from 6 to 12 months. Although there was a decrease in scores over time, the scores at 12-months' follow-up were nonetheless significantly higher than the precourse scores.

Another evaluation instrument that has been used for evaluating attitudinal changes is the Minnesota Sexual Attitude Scales (MSAS).[4] The MSAS consists of 14 attitude scales, divided into two sets. In the first set, the subjects give their emotional reaction to the notion of different persons engaging in certain categories of sexual activities. Ratings are made to each of nine activities on a five-point scale (1 = I feel *great* about it; 5 = I feel *repulsed* by it). The subjects made ratings for each activity for a number of categories of people: yourself, mid-adolescents, unmarried adults, married adults, married adults engaging in this as a secret extramarital activity. Response to this second set of scales suggests how the subjects feel about different types of persons engaging in the same sexual activities.

Held et al evaluated a workshop for health professionals and spinal cord injured adults using the MSAS.[4] Participants showed significant increases on 9 of the 14 scales from pre- to posttest. They also reported on a control study with first-year medical students who completed the MSAS on two occasions with no specific educational experience intervening. These control subjects showed no significant change on the MSAS on retesting.

A third assessment device that has been used in evaluation of human sexuality programs for professionals is the Sexual Attitude and Behavior Survey (SABS).[9] On the SABS, subjects indicate under what circumstances they would find a variety of sexual behaviors or thoughts to be permissible. Six attitudinal measures are obtained: male behavior (MBS), male fantasy (MFS), female behavior (FBS), female fantasy (FFS), personal behavior (PBS), and personal fantasy (PFS) scales.

Marcotte et al, using the SABS, found more tolerant attitudes toward sexual behaviors and thoughts after a human sexuality course for medical students.[10] Marcotte and Logan similarly reported a significant increase on all six SABS subscales following a sexuality course for second-year medical students.[22] What was particularly interesting about the latter study is that subjects also showed significant changes in the Rokeach Dogmatism Scale, suggesting increased tolerance and open-mindedness in nonsexual areas also.[23]

The previously discussed studies of Garrard et al both used, in addition to other instruments, an Attitude Rating Scale or Attitude Questionnaire.[16,21] This questionnaire consists of 13 items derived from a pool of items developed by the Glide Foundation.[12] For each of the 13 items, subjects indicate their degree of agreement on a five-point scale (1 = strongly agree; 5 = strongly disagree). In the first study, Garrard et al reported a significant pre- to posttest change on 11 of the 13 items.[16] In the second study, Garrard et al found such changes on 9 of the 13 items, with significant changes from pretest to 12-month follow-up for 5 of the 13 items.[21]

A Human Sexuality Knowledge and Attitude Inventory (HSKAI) has been designed by Woods and Mandetta.[14] In a second study, Woods and Mandetta administered the HSKAI to nursing students before and after a human sexuality course and to a matched sample of students not in the course.[15] Students in the course had significantly higher knowledge scores than controls on posttest. However, no significant differences were found in students' attitudes.

An interesting questionnaire was devised by Montgomery and Singer for evaluating a brief human sexuality course for residents in obstetrics and gynecology.[6] The main part of the questionnaire presented six situations involving encounters with individuals of both sexes with varying degrees of clinical involvement and bluntness of expression. Subjects rate their degree of emotional discomfort, anxiety, or embarrassment in each situation on a seven-point scale from "acutely uncomfortable" to "completely at ease." Subjects reported significantly less anxiety in the six situations following the course.

The previously mentioned study by Vines is unique in that it included an assessment of behavior change following a human sexuality course.[20] Subjects in the course and matched controls conducted an interview with a "simulated patient" (an actress) presenting with a sexual complaint. Videotape recordings of these interviews were made and clinicians independently made "blind" ratings of the subject's degree of comfort. Vines reported that students who had been in the course were rated as less anxious in conducting the interview than controls.

In summary, several conclusions can be drawn from this review of the assessment literature. The 14 studies just reviewed were all published since 1972. Moreover, the nine instruments summarized in Table 11-1, including the revised version of the SKAT, were also all published since 1972. Thus, the evaluation of sexuality curricula for professionals has come from nonexistence to the beginnings of more sophisticated methodology in six years. The peak year for publication among these 14 articles was 1975 (five studies), although 1976 and 1977 most certainly include more publications than have been located for inclusion in this chapter.

Furthermore, it was found that the courses and instruments were available to a much wider range of professionals and students than previously found in the literature. In addition to medical students and nursing students, sexuality programs and concomitant course evaluations were made available to students in social work, pastoral counseling, psychology, and counselor education, as well as to practicing physicians and physicians' assistants. It is hoped that this trend toward increased diversity in the helping professionals introduced to sex education and counseling will be maintained and will grow to include greater numbers of these participants.

Finally, what can be suggested for future application and development of these assessment techniques? The Task Force of the Airlie Conference divided existing assessment procedures into five categories:

1. Paper-and-pencil tests, including objective short-answer and essay sections; these are usually administered before and after the course
2. Peer ratings based on small-group interactions
3. Behavioral ratings of structured tasks, including real and simulated clinical situations
4. Unobtrusive measures such as the extent of appropriate referrals and of sexual information in patient progress notes
5. Patient evaluation of medical care and patient progress.[3]

These five techniques offer a multi-method approach to program evaluation in which data from several sources can be intercorrelated. The use of a multi-method approach provides cross-validation of the data collected so that more accurate conclusions can be drawn. Moreover, this approach affords different perspectives of the impact of the sexuality program on the individual participant. This has the advantage of being sensitive to individual differences in the acquisition and application of clinical skills which the traditional questionnaires, used alone, would overlook. Moreover, the addition of control groups and follow-up evaluations is strongly recommended and would allow optimal investigation of the strengths and weaknesses of human sexuality curricula.

REFERENCES

1. Mudd JW, Siegel RJ: Sexuality. The experience and anxieties of medical students. New Engl J Med 281 (25): 1397–1403, 1969
2. Mudd JW, Fleiss JL: Physical examinations of hospitalized adults. J Med Educ 48:1140–1147, 1973
3. Task Force of the Airlie Conference: Standards and research, in Lief HI, Karlen A (eds): Sex Education in Medicine. New York, Spectrum Publications, 1976
4. Held JP, Cole TM, Held CA, et al: Sexual attitude reassessment workshops: Effect on spinal cord injured adults, their partners and rehabilitation professionals. Arch Phys Med Rehabil 56:14–18, 1975
5. Pion R: Personal communication. Kapiolani, Hawaii Sexual Counseling Service, February, 1977
6. Montgomery RB, Singer G: An experimental brief course in sexual behavior and counseling. Med J Aust 2:527–529, 1975

6a. Cross RJ: (Personal communication). Piscataway, N.J., Rutgers Medical School, February 22, 1977

7. Fortmann S, Mann J: Sexual Attitudes and Behavior Inventory. University of California at San Francisco, 1972

8. Hawkins R, Jr. Test for Assessing Sexual Knowledge and Attitudes. State University of New York at Stony Brook, 1975

9. Kilpatrick D, Smith A: The development of a sexual attitudes and behavior survey. (Unpublished manuscript) 1973

10. Marcotte DB, Geyer PR, Kilpatrick DG, et al: The effect of a spaced sex education course on medical students' sexual knowledge and attitudes. Med Educ 10:117–121, 1976

11. Lief HI, Reed DM: Sex Knowledge and Attitude Test (SKAT), 2nd ed. Center for the Study of Sex Education in Medicine, 1972

12. McIlvenna T: National Sex Forum Questionnaire. Institute for Advanced Study of Human Sexuality, 1977

13. Nadelson C, Shaw J: Harvard Sex Questionnaire. (Unpublished)

14. Woods NF, Mandetta A: Changes in students' knowledge and attitudes following a course in human sexuality: Report of a pilot study. Nurs Res 24 (1): 10–15, 1975

15. Woods NF, Mandetta A: Changes in students' knowledge and attitudes following a course in human sexuality: A case-control comparison. Sex Educ Therapy 47–59, 1975

16. Garrard J, Vaitkus A, Chilgren RA: Evaluation of a course in human sexuality. J Med Educ 47:772–778, 1972

17. Golden JS, Liston EH: Medical sex education: The world of illusion and the practical realities. J Med Educ 47:761–771, 1972

18. Kreger SM: Sexuality and disability. ARN Jour 11:8–14, 1977

19. Mims FH, Brown L, Lubow R: Human sexuality course evaluation. Nurs Res 25:187–191, 1976

20. Vines NR: Responses to Sexual Problems in Medical Counseling as a Function of Counselor Exposure to Sex Education Procedures Incorporating Erotic Film. Ph.D. dissertation, University of Pennsylvania, 1974

21. Garrard J, Vaitkus A, Held J, et al: Follow-up effects of a medical school course in human sexuality. Arch Sex Behav 5:331–340, 1976

22. Marcotte DB, Logan C: Medical sex education: Allowing attitude alteration. Arch Sex Behav 6:155–162, 1977

23. Rokeach M: The Open and Closed Mind. New York, Basic Books, 1960

PART IV

Human Sexuality Courses for Special Target Audiences

Norman Rosenzweig
F. Paul Pearsall

Introduction

For the most part the contributions up to this point have dealt with general and core issues of curriculum planning and methodology. However, it is important to keep in mind the particular purpose for which the sex education curriculum has been formulated. A different set of methodological considerations will apply if one is attempting to teach professionals to become therapists of human sexual dysfunction than if the object is to help a physician understand and feel comfortable discussing with his patients sexual aspects of conditions that are common to various aspects of medical practice. Program content for medical students need not be the same as for practicing gynecologists. Even the setting will vary according to target audiences: the teaching of specialized therapeutic skills requires an active clinical setting, which is not necessary if the object is merely to help the student feel comfortable with his or her own sexuality, to gain some new knowledge, and correct some misconceptions. Parenthetically, it is often helpful to have access to a clinical facility for treatment of sexual problems which may be uncovered among students who are taking courses in human sexuality.

This section deals with the needs of some special target audiences, and some suggestions for meeting them. Obviously it was not possible to include all conceivable special groups. Those represented here are among those for whom some special modifications are most often required. Each chapter is written by a representative of the target group who has had personal experience with the problems of articulating sexuality curriculum with practical needs of their respective group. Despite the special considerations reflected in the topics, the editors believe these chapters to be of sufficient scope to have interest and value for the general reader. Certainly an examination of the special needs of various target groups will alert the teacher to the fact that different student populations pose different educational problems, and is a step toward helping to recognize and respond to the special needs of the individual student as he or she is exposed to the sexuality curriculum.

Diane B. Watson
William L. Maurice

12
Sex Education and the Psychiatric Resident

INTRODUCTION

"Thousands of troubled marriages might be saved each year if so many physicians were not so uncomfortable about female nudity, afraid to discuss emotional problems—and more embarrassed by sex than their patients are . . . there is dismaying evidence that when it comes to the diagnostics of sex, the average doctor is an embarrassed, incompetent bungler."[1] Criticism of physicians' ability to deal with the sexual problems of their patients is not restricted to the "bad press" of women's magazines. Masters had this to say about physicians' competence: "They know no more and no less about the subject than other college graduates. They share most of the common misconceptions, taboos, and fallacies of their non-medical confreres."[2]

The last two decades have brought remarkable advances in our knowledge of human sexuality. New approaches to treatment now promise relief to many persons who were previously thought to be beyond help. With increasing emphasis on women's rights, women are now much less inclined to tolerate sexual dissatisfaction and more likely to seek professional advice. The urgent need for help with sexual problems and the great promise offered by the new therapeutic approach have resulted in a tremendous surge of interest in this field by both professionals and the general public. This explosive popularity is causing some difficulties as the widespread application of the new knowledge and techniques to general medical practice lags behind the public's expectations. Many have turned optimistically to physicians for help, and many have been disappointed.

Just as so many other "problems of living" and causes of personal unhappiness have fallen by default into the realm of psychiatry, so also has the treatment of sexual problems. The role of sexual counselor has increasingly been thrust upon the psychiatrist, who is placed in the uncomfortable, and possibly untenable, position of being considered an expert in a field for which he has had little preparation.

Inclusion of sexual problems within the bounds of psychiatry is by no means new. The intimate association between psychopathology and sexual functioning was emphasized by Freud as early as 1905: ". . . anyone who is in any way abnormal mentally is invariably abnormal also in his sexual life."[3] In the past, sexual dysfunctions were regarded as manifestations of mental disorder amenable, if at all, only to treatment based on the psychoanalytic model. The role of sexual drives in motivating behavior was considered to be of central importance in both abnormal and normal personality development. Theories of sexuality have played an important part in the evolution of basic psychiatric concepts. Considering the importance placed in the past on sexual functioning, the current lack of emphasis on understanding and treating specific sexual problems in psychiatric training seems all the more surprising.

There is considerable controversy over the extent to which sexual disability is associated with underlying neurotic or character disorders, with estimates ranging from 25 percent[4] to 100 percent.[5] While it is undoubtedly true that a sexual symptom can represent just one manifestation of an underlying psychic conflict, the obverse situation also occurs in which the primary complaint of anxiety or depression is revealed over time to be largely based on an underlying sexual problem. Although the prevalence of sexual problems in the general population is not known, it appears that sexual complaints occur with greater frequency in a population of psychiatric patients.[6]

Evidence now suggests that while many sexual problems may be manifestations of emotional disturbance or mental illness, they are often found among persons who otherwise function normally and have no overt psychopathological symptoms. Freud acknowledged this when he said that "many people are abnormal in their sexual life who in every other respect approximate the average."[3] In many cases, the sexual dysfunctions do not have their roots deep in childhood conflicts, but originate in more recent and far simpler problems. The patient may be simply misinformed on the facts of the normal sexual response, or may fail to communicate adequately to a partner. The problem might be merely one of real or imagined demands for performance with an anticipation of failure to function. Many patients with sexual problems respond rapidly and favorably to treatment methods which are designed to modify such immediate obstacles to sexual functioning.

Patients are no longer willing to suffer in silence or ignorance as were their counterparts in times gone by. The psychiatrist has been assigned increasing responsibility not only to understand the origin of the symptom, but to do something concrete toward relieving it. For many patients the new brief forms of intervention have proven far more effective than the time-consuming and possibly ineffectual approaches of traditional psychiatry.[7] Psychiatrists would, therefore, be more efficient and more effective if they had a thorough and up-to-date understanding of the nature and treatment of sexual disorders.

EVALUATION OF PSYCHIATRIC RESIDENCY TRAINING

Medical educators have recently acknowledged a deficit in the medical school training of human sexuality.[8] Perhaps overcompensating from previous neglect of the subject, the 1975 edition of the popular psychiatric textbook by Freedman, Kaplan, and Sadock devotes 250 pages to sexually related topics as compared to 130 pages on schizophrenia.[9] However, the fact remains that the majority of psychiatrists in practice today have had no special training to deal with the vast array of sexual problems which their patients bring to them. There has been to date very little comment and no objective studies on the role of sex education within psychiatric training programs. Before guidelines and goals for training in this area can be established, it is first necessary to assess the adequacy of training currently available. Do physicians, in this case psychiatric residents, acknowledge the lack of training and expertise which is ascribed to them by expert and lay press alike?

It is difficult to get objective data on physician attitudes and practices in dealing with the sexual problems of their patients, and no single method of evaluation is without significant limitations. In 1976, the author set out to assess psychiatric residency training in human sexuality in Canada by collecting information from a number of sources: (1) psychiatric residents across Canada were surveyed by means of a questionnaire; (2) samples of inpatient and outpatient records were reviewed for their sexual content in order to gain an overall impression of the history taking practices of psychiatric residents; and (3) the opinions and experiences of colleagues-in-training were solicited informally.

The questionnaire was designed to determine the extent to which information on human sexuality was included in the respondent's medical school and psychiatric residency training. Information was requested concerning residents' perceptions of their knowledge, ability, and comfort in dealing with sexually related problems. Residents were also asked to evaluate the capabilities of "other psychiatric residents" and "clinical supervisors" in terms of their knowledge of human sexuality and their ability to treat sexual problems. All items in the questionnaire were cast in a Likert five-point response format with no intervals; that is, respondents had to choose one of the five responses or not respond at all. For example, to the item "Your ability to treat sexual problems is . . ." only the following sequence of responses could be made: very adequate, fairly adequate, adequate, fairly inadequate, and very inadequate. The questionnaire was distributed by mail to 350 psychiatric residents across Canada based on the latest Canadian Psychiatric Association census. One hundred thirty-seven (40%) responded, which compares favorably with other similar surveys.[10] Twenty-six percent of the total respondents were female and the median age was 28 years. Three quarters of the respondents were in their third or later years of residency. Further details of this survey have been reported elsewhere.[11]

Residents were discovered to have a dismal impression of their medical school education. Ninety-six percent of respondents were unquestionably dissatisfied with their medical school training in the area of sexual counseling, while 81 percent felt particularly dissatisfied in the area of sexual dysfunctions. Although it is generally believed that sex education in medical school has improved in recent years, that trend was not reflected in this survey. Younger first-year residents (who are also more recent medical school graduates) did not indicate any significant improvement in the quality of their sex-related undergraduate education. It is apparent that psychiatric educators cannot simply assume that residents now entering psychiatric training do so with adequate knowledge of human sexuality.

Although residents feel that they are exposed to more sexual information during their residency than they were during medical school, it is not at all clear just when or where this information is gained. The trend toward improvement in residency training is only relative, the change being merely one from "worst" to "bad." In fact, it was discovered that fourth year residents do not feel any more knowledgeable, comfortable, or skillful in dealing with sexually related problems than their first year colleagues. The only significant change over the years of training was found to be a growing disillusionment with the ability of clinical supervisors to provide a good example. In fact, residents felt that they were considerably more capable of treating sexual problems than their clinical supervisors. Psychiatric residency training seems, then, to have remarkably little effect on physicians' ultimate competence in this field.

Another significant finding in the study was the marked difference between residents' perception of their own adequacy as compared to the adequacy of their peers, in terms of knowledge of human sexuality and ability to treat sexual problems. Fifty-five percent of the respondents ranked their colleagues' knowledge of human sexuality as "fairly" or "very" inadequate, while only 28 percent were willing to admit the same about themselves. Other studies have suggested that even though the respondents remain anonymous, they tend to be somewhat defensive and therefore less likely to indict themselves personally.[10] Given this tendency to project their own inadequacy onto others, it is likely that the correct estimate of residents' knowledge of human sexuality is less than the personal estimate and closer to the projected estimate for those "other residents."

Respondents were requested to rate the frequency of inquiry into a number of specific sexual areas during routine history-taking. They were also requested to rate their level of comfort when discussing the same topics with their patients. The assumption that there is a positive correlation between frequency of inquiry and level of comfort was borne out by the data. Those residents who claim to always inquire about a specific item were more often in the "very comfortable" category, while those who never do so were more often "very uncomfortable." A similar correlation between personal comfort of the physician and a tendency to ask routinely about sexual functioning has been previously demonstrated by Pauly in his 1970 survey of Oregon physicians.[6] The data also revealed that residents feel more comfortable discussing sexual matters with their patients when they perceive themselves as knowledgeable and competent in the subject. This finding is of educational significance, because it indicates that adequate training has the potential to help physicians overcome some of their discomfort in dealing with sexual matters.

The relationship between knowledge and comfort seems to be less clear in the case of female residents. Although women rated themselves equally as knowledgeable as their male colleagues, they felt significantly less able to treat sexual problems. More than half of the women responding felt themselves to be "fairly" or "very inadequate," whereas only one third of the men felt this way. This may indicate that female residents are, in fact, more inhibited and uncomfortable with frank sexual discussion than are male residents. On the other hand, it is possible that women are less defensive and more honest in admitting inadequacy and discomfort in the area of sex.[12] Following this line of reasoning, men would appear to avoid reporting similar difficulties, as this might threaten their masculine image. If men are in fact minimizing their own inadequacies, the women's estimate of comfort levels would more accurately reflect residents' actual comfort in dealing with sexual problems.

The chart survey clearly indicated that residents do not record or presumably take a sexual history as frequently as was suggested in the questionnaire. A total of 75 charts were reviewed using a systematic sampling method controlled for sex of the patient. The charts were equally divided between an inpatient, an outpatient and an assessment unit. Eighty percent of the inpatient charts surveyed provided no data related to the patient's sexual thoughts or functioning. In some instances the omission appeared to involve an issue of prime importance. A 58-year-old man, depressed since bypass graft surgery for arterial insufficiency, was apparently not asked about his sexual functioning, even though he was noted to have lower abdominal partial anesthesia involving the penis. A 17-year-old girl diagnosed as an "adolescent adjustment reaction" was quoted on the admission history as saying, "incest isn't wrong is it?" No sexual history had been pursued. A 54-year-old man hospitalized for "endogenous depression" spontaneously admitted that his wife was intending to leave him due to sexual dissatisfaction. No note was made of the patient's libido, nor was any apparent attempt made to explore the details of the couple's sexual problems. Neglecting to take a sexual history in all three cases seems to have been a serious omission. It is possible that the separation could have been prevented in the latter case by simply reassuring the patient and his wife that sexual dysfunction can result as a transient, secondary manifestation of depression.

The problem seems, however, to be more complex than simply neglecting to take a sexual history. In one outpatient day care facility, residents are required to take a sexual history following a structured format of intake assessment. When faced with the problem of having to acquire such information, the residents did so erratically and with no evident goal in mind. They either plunged in, in a seemingly counterphobic manner, asking blunt questions of the greatest intimacy (such as inquiries about sexual fantasies), or they deftly circumnavigated the subject while avoiding the central issues. The information they did acquire tended to be incomplete and often of only tangential importance. A 24-year-old married women assessed for a day care program was noted to complain that she felt sexually incompetent. She was quoted as saying, "I never climax unless he fondles me." No further information was included except for a detailed account of sex play she had experienced as a child. The resident noted that "she is probably sterile as she did not get pregnant during two years off birth control pills." There was no evidence presented to support this seemingly hasty conclusion and no apparent inquiry into the patient's feelings about her "sterility." The history concluded with the formulation: "The patient has longstanding psychosomatic complaints related to anxiety caused by difficulties in sexual functioning." During the course of her six-week day care therapy some emphasis was placed on her "passive-aggressive" behavior in heterosexual relationships, but no further mention was made of the sexual problems previously indicated as the core of her neurosis. Another 45-year-old man was noted in his admission history to complain of impotence and premature ejaculation. No further detail was provided. It was evident from the discharge summary that little clinical use had been made of this information. Under the heading "Course in Hospital" the following comments were made: "Problem Number Three: Sexual Difficulties—During Terry's stay in the hospital sexual intercourse was not attempted." Residents, it seems, do not know how to integrate in any meaningful way the sexual data they do unearth.

The survey of psychiatric residents revealed that residents inquire more frequently about masturbation, sexual fantasies, and homosexuality than they do about the more common sexual dysfunctions. An emphasis on the former subjects was also evident in the chart survey. The record of a 23-year-old single female day care patient indicated that the patient had masturbated regularly two or three times a week from the age of eight or nine until the present. She was also noted to have fantasized being with men who are forceful and dominating. Elsewhere in the chart it was discovered that this woman had a rectal prolapse requiring regular manual extraction of stool. It seems possible that this malady interfered with sexual functioning not only physically but emotionally. It was, however, overlooked in the psychiatric interview in favor of more esoteric inquiries. This tendency to emphasize the obscure leads one to speculate as to the rationale behind residents' sexually related questions. Residents seem to emphasize masturbation and sexual fantasies, not as they relate to sexual function and responsiveness, but rather as they pertain to theories of psychic conflict and guilt. When residents do take a sexual history, it seems to be taken for the more intellectualized purpose of a dynamic formulation than for the more practical discovery of problems in current sexual functioning. When eliciting information for the purpose of a formulation alone, residents are operating on an agenda that is very different from that of their patients.

DISCUSSION

The training of a skilled psychiatrist is a complex process which cannot be learned from books or simply acquired. It requires an apprenticeship, with the student observing an experienced supervisor in action, tediously learning the art of psychiatry through trial and error and constant feedback. Training a student to deal with sexual problems should ideally occur by the same process that training in other areas of psychiatry occurs. It should be learned through the day-to-day guidance of student by supervisor as together they evaluate and manage the myriad of problems that patients present. In sex-related issues, however, the system obviously falters. Experts in the subject are few, and open discussion of sexual problems is avoided. The student is exposed to supervisors who are themselves often embarrassed and inadequate in the face of their patients' sexual concerns. A resident treating a family together with her supervisor was instructed to "deal with the sexual problems" by herself at a later date. Other residents have complained that they have been advised to postpone dealing with their patients' sexual problems until the end of psychotherapy. The delay was suggested, it seems, with the hope that the sexual symptoms would somehow disappear in the interim. When sexual problems do emerge, they are frequently glossed over with a blanket of reassurance that as the neurosis or marriage improves so will the sexual problems. The urgency of a patient's sexual complaint frequently seems to be dissipated through intellectualized discussions of psychoanalytic theory.

It is premature to think in terms of a sexuality curriculum until there are educators available for teaching who are truly expert in the field. Clinics designed to deal specifically with patients complaining of sexual problems are gradually, however, becoming established in most major teaching centers across North America. The clinics in at least two centers in Canada initially involved only residents in obstetrics and gynecology. Residents in psychiatry do not seem to have been encouraged to venture in any major way into the sexual field. As the first psychiatric resident at the University of British Columbia to elect a rotation through the "Sex Therapy Unit," the author was warned "not to get too involved as questions on sex weren't likely to appear on the exam." At the end of the rotation she was asked by another supervisor: "You aren't going to continue in that sex business, are you?" A bias against sex education apparently exists among psychiatric faculty members despite the fact that the "Sex Therapy Unit" is an integral part of their own department.

The problem in convincing psychiatric educators of the value of training in this area seems to be that they are not aware of their own deficiencies. All of the psychiatric residents who have to date rotated through the "Sex Therapy Unit" were surprised by their initial reactions. The residents had previously considered themselves to be liberal open-minded individuals with no qualms about discussing any aspects of sexual function with any patient. It was not until an actual attempt was made to take a complete history that residents realized how very embarrassed they could become. The discomfort proved to be most acute when dealing with a patient of the opposite sex. The surprising candor with which most patients discussed their sexual problems served to convince residents that patients are not unwilling to reveal intimate aspects of their personal lives. On the contrary, it was usually the residents who found themselves hesitant or unwilling to embark on such discussion. After eliciting what they had considered to be a complete history, residents were startled to discover how much more could yet be asked. The added detail was found to be not merely an extravagance but a necessity, in order to both understand the problem and formulate a treatment plan. Observing skilled sex therapists at ease in their work guiding patients in a systematic but gentle fashion through the intimacies of their sexual experiences, and then doing it oneself under supervision, is a very effective way to learn the subject. The resident learns through modeling appropriate attitudes, interviewing skills, and treatment approaches of the supervisor.

Confusion obviously abounds regarding the role of sex education within psychiatric training programs. Psychiatry must rethink its objectives regarding training in this area. Residents recognize that sexual counseling is a significant aspect of their role as "psychotherapist" and have indicated that further training is in order. In fact, 90 percent of the residents surveyed felt that experience in sex therapy was warranted for psychiatric training.

It has been shown that it is not sufficient to simply provide residents with some facts on anatomy and physiology, nor is it sufficient to simply command them to take a sexual history. Residents require more comprehensive supervision in order to approach sexual history-taking and counseling intelligently without anxiety or discomfort. Sex education in psychiatric training seems, however, to be still considered a "soft" subject and a frill superseded by "hard-core" psychiatry.

All of the charts surveyed were not inadequate. A first year resident thoroughly explored the sexual history of his 44-year-old married, depressed male patient. The resident discovered that the patient sensed the skin on his penis to feel "different" and had become fearful and guilt-ridden about the possibility of having venereal disease. The wife confided to the resident that sex had always been for her an unpleasant duty. In conjoint sessions, the resident questioned the couple on all aspects of their sexual function, including levels of responsiveness, positions and techniques of intercourse, specific erotic areas of sexual fantasies. The resident concluded that longer standing sexual problems, not solely related to the patient's current depression, were involved and referred the couple for continuing sex therapy. It does not appear to be purely coincidental that this resident, who was obviously comfortable and thorough in his sexual inquiry, had been trained in basic psychiatric interviewing skills by one of the supervisors of the "Sex Therapy Unit."

REFERENCES

1. Fleming TJ: Why most doctors can't help women with sex problems. Redbook 132(73):130–134, 1968
2. Masters and Johnson Playboy interview. Playboy Magazine 15:67–82, 194–202, 1968

3. Freud S: Three essays on the theory of sexuality (1905). in Strachey J (ed): Standard Edition of the Complete Psychological Works of Sigmund Freud, vol 7. London, Hogarth Press, 1953
4. Maurice WL, Guze SB: Sexual dysfunction and associated psychiatric disorders. Compr Psychiatry 11:539–543, 1970
5. O'Connor JF, Stern LO: Developmental factors in functional sexual disorders. NY State J Med 72:1838–1843, 1972
6. Pauly IB, Goldstein SG: Prevalence of significant sexual problems in medical practice. Med Aspects Hum Sexuality 4:48–63, 1970
7. Kaplan HS: The New Sex Therapy. New York, Brunner/Mazel, 1974, p 435
8. Pauly IB: Human sexuality in medical education and practice. Aust NZ J Psychiatry 5:206–219, 1971
9. Freedman AM, Kaplan HI, Sadock BJ: Comprehensive Textbook of Psychiatry, 2nd ed. Baltimore, Williams & Wilkins, 1975
10. Pauly IB, Goldstein SG: Physicians' perception of their education in human sexuality. J Med Educ 45:745–753, 1970
11. Watson DB: Are they prepared? An assessment of psychiatric residency training in human sexuality. Presented at the annual meeting of the Canadian Psychiatric Association, Quebec City, October 1976
12. Greenson RR: Masculinity and femininity in our time, in Wahl CW (ed): Sexual Problems: Diagnosis and Treatment in Medical Practice. New York, Free Press, 1967, p 39–52

David M. Priver

13
Sexuality Curriculum for the Gynecologist

INTRODUCTION

It has been estimated that up to 60 percent of all patients seen by gynecologists suffer from disorders of sexual function.[1] While it may be hard to confirm such an incidence, there can be no doubt that problems of sexual dysfunction literally inundate today's practicing gynecologist. With the advent of the "sexual revolution" and the women's movement, more and more patients are confronting gynecologists with often long standing but newly perceived deficiencies of sexual satisfaction. They are often finding, to their dismay, that their physicians are sadly unequipped to deal with these problems in other than a vague, superficial fashion. Clearly, if the needs of patients are to be met, the gynecologist must address himself to the area of human sexuality. His role in this field is pivotal, because he is the person to whom women turn first with sexual problems. The gynecologist represents the "entry point" into the therapeutic system for most patients, and it is likely that this will continue to be the case.

For several reasons, the gynecologist has tended to avoid dealing with problems of sexual function. Many indicate that they simply do not have time to schedule lengthy counseling sessions. Others are, quite simply, uncomfortable dealing with other people's sexuality. They find it hard to be objective about sex practices and mores which may not be personally acceptable to them. Their lack of ability to remain non-judgmental makes any effort at therapy essentially fruitless.

While these problems are important and must be eliminated before progress can be made, they are not the major obstacle. Clearly the most critical deficit in the gynecologist's ability to deal with patients' sexual problems is the almost complete lack of education in the field of human sexuality during his training. Beginning in medical school and continuing through residency, very few practicing gynecologists are given more than a very superficial, brief exposure to sexual physiology and pathology. While efforts are now being made to remedy this problem in the medical schools, we are still left with thousands of graduate physicians for whom no formal system of sexuality education exists. These doctors will continue to practice for many years to come and, unless some system for educating practicing physicians is devised, their patients will continue to be deprived of a badly needed service.

At the outset, it will be important to carefully devise strategies for making the subject of sexuality acceptable and even desirable to the practicing physician. In this chapter, we will consider the basic elements of sexuality curricula for the gynecologist, as well as effective techniques for implementation.

OBJECTIVES

In planning such a curriculum, the first question we must address is the ultimate goal of such an educational program. For what specific role should we be attempting to equip the gynecologist? Should all gynecologists obtain the knowledge and experience sufficient to adopt sex-dysfunction therapy as an integral part of office practice? Or should it suffice to simply equip him to recognize the existence of a problem, so that he may refer the patient for actual therapy? Perhaps he should learn to diagnose dysfunctional problems, treat those which are "simple" or in which he feels he has the interest and expertise, and refer the remainder. There are vast differences in the amount of material to be presented and the educational approach used, depending upon which of these goals we hope to achieve.

There is no simple answer to this question, as there will be much individual variation among physicians in the extent to which they wish or need to become involved. Effective sex-dysfunction therapy, such as by the Masters and Johnson technique, is a very complex and time-consuming process, and it is unlikely that more than a handful of gynecologists will wish to devote the necessary time to manage all the details of therapy alone. It is also unlikely, however, that the gynecologist will want to be completely divorced from the therapeutic arena. It is in his nature to wish to retain some degree of patient contact and control, as in all other aspects of medical and surgical therapy of women. There will be some gynecologists who wish or require more in-depth involvement in sex-dysfunction therapy than others. One of the unique aspects of gynecology is the wide latitude of choice afforded the practitioner in selecting an area of special interest. He may elect to concentrate on obstetrics, surgery, endocrinology, or gynecologic cancer. Alternatively, he may wish to involve himself equally in all these areas to become a "general practitioner for women." These wide ranging choices are what have attracted many physicians, including the author, to the field of gynecology.

Therefore, it is likely that the newly emerging "specialty" of human sexuality will be viewed by some gynecologists as an area for intensive concentration based on a special interest in behavioral science. Many of these will devote their full-time efforts to its pursuit. They will require lengthy training and possibly even some form of specialty certification.

It seems likely, however, that the vast majority of gynecologists will elect to obtain a working knowledge of human sexuality for use as an addition to their armamentarium of effective clinical tools. Sexual dysfunction diagnosis and therapy will be incorporated to a limited extent into the "general practice" of gynecology. Therefore, a sexuality curriculum for the practicing gynecologist should be aimed at providing him with the ability to effectively manage the patient in accord with a system that may be summarized by five "R's": (1) recognition of the existence of a sexual problem, (2) review of the sexual history of the patient and her partner, (3) ruling-out of organic disease, (4) Rx (treatment)—to a variable extent, and (5) referral for in-depth, definitive therapy.

In order to achieve this end, there are several key elements which should be included in any basic human-sexuality curriculum. They will be discussed individually in detail in the next section.

CURRICULUM

Objectivity Training

In order to achieve successful clinical results, the physician must be able to evaluate sexual problems in an objective, nonjudgmental fashion. The initial thrust of the educational program must be designed to enable the physician to recognize and become conversant with his own attitudes and "hang-ups" about sex. This is best accomplished by presenting graphic sexually stimulating material followed by an opportunity to ventilate one's reactions and feelings in a group setting. In this way, the physician will soon realize that his own personal feelings are neither "right" nor "wrong," and that no two people in the group will react in identical ways to the material. It is important to emphasize that it is not essential, or even necessarily desirable, that the physician change his opinion about his own sexuality. The object is simply to have him "come to grips" with these views, to recognize them as uniquely personal, and to develop the ability to accept the views of others without comparing them to his own. Only in this way will he be at ease listening to his patients and able to provide them with a nonjudgmental, professional demeanor.

Review of Basic Sciences

Anatomy.   Most practicing gynecologists can be assumed to have a fairly detailed knowledge of such anatomic features as the gross morphology of the internal and external female genital organs. However, there are several sexually relevant aspects of genital anatomy which have not commonly been emphasized. An example is the pubococcygeus muscle which forms a "sling" around the outer third of the vagina. It has been found that by proper exercise techniques, the woman can easily learn to control this muscle and thus greatly enhance the pleasure of intercourse for both herself and her partner. It would be helpful for the gynecologist to familiarize himself with the normal location, shape, and tone of this muscle in order to better evaluate patients with various dysfunctional complaints.

A better working knowledge of the neuroanatomy of the pelvis would help with such problems as dyspareunia. Also, advising and counseling patients on effective techniques for erotic tactile stimulation would be enhanced by more detailed knowledge of this area. The curriculum should also include a brief but thorough review of male sexual anatomy.

Physiology.   Until recently very little was known about sexual physiology. The recent work by Masters and Johnson has shed much light on this area, and these findings should be brought to the attention of all gynecologists who deal with sexual dysfunction.[2] The physiologic changes that accompany the various phases of the sexual excitation cycle should be emphasized, as well as the physical and emotional effects of female hormones. Another important area is the physiologic changes of the menopause, as this is a time of great sexual conflict in many women. Male sexual physiology should also be reviewed.

Pharmacology.   As our knowledge of the side effects of drugs increases, we are finding more and more drugs which have significant effects on sexual function. It is important that gynecologists, as well as all physicians, familiarize themselves with these effects, as they may be devastating to the unsuspecting patient. A classic example is the impotence that is often a side effect of some of the antihypertensive drugs. This effect has long been known, but many physicians have failed to warn patients about it, often with catastrophic results. Other examples include birth-control pills, which occasionally depress libido, and several psychotropic drugs which, while not affecting sexual function directly, may do so indirectly by causing amenorrhea and occasional galactorrhea. It would probably be best not to speculate on the possible side effects of the hallucinogens such as marijuana. Studies that have purported to show decreased testosterone levels in male marijuana smokers are of somewhat questionable validity. To date there has been no consistent pattern of effect of these drugs.

Review of Clinical Sciences

Psychiatry. A basic working knowledge of psychiatric illnesses and methods is most important for the gynecologist. Many obtain this in medical school or residency, but the subject should be thoroughly reviewed in a curriculum for the practicing gynecologist. Interviewing techniques which enhance rapport and properly elicit clinical information are important contributions of this field. In addition, the gynecologist should become adept at recognizing and dealing with the emotional problems of patients, as these may have a direct bearing on the problem at hand. It is not at all uncommon for sexual dysfunction and moderate degrees of depression to be closely interrelated. Similarly, dysfunctional complaints may be a manifestation of serious psychiatric disturbance, calling for an entirely different therapeutic approach.

Sexual practices commonly referred to as "abnormal," such as homosexuality, sadism and masochism, and fetishism, often fall into the province of the psychiatrist. These important aspects of sexuality are crucial to any such educational program.

Internal Medicine. Several critical areas exist here. Two of the most important are the cardiac patient and the stroke patient. Due largely to ignorance of their sexual needs and abilities, these patients have often become sexual, as well as physical, cripples. The patient recuperating from a heart attack is rarely given helpful, meaningful advice from his doctor regarding sexual limitations. Both he and his wife may have great fear and guilt feelings if the heart attack occurred during sexual activity, as is often the case. Clearly, the large majority of cardiac patients may resume sexual relations safely at some point of recuperation. It is important that the doctor be aware of these needs and the deleterious effect, both physical and mental, of his failure to address them.

An equally tragic situation confronts the stroke or spinal injury patient. Doctors have usually assumed that sexual activity must cease for such patients. In the vast majority of instances, this is not so. It is up to the physician to acquaint himself with his patient's limitations and counsel him or her as to specific feasible sexual techniques.

Surgery. About 1 out of 15 women in the United States will develop breast cancer at some point in their lives. A much higher number will develop benign conditions requiring surgical evaluation. One of the biggest problems in the management of breast diseases is the fears of cancer that may prevent many women from seeking early detection. Large numbers of women actually avoid reporting the presence of a breast lump to their physicians because of fear of the possible loss of a breast. The fears center around the woman's perception of a loss of sexual attraction and femininity that she feels must occur when a breast is removed. While these fears cannot (and probably should not) be entirely removed, it is possible and desirable for the gynecologist to instruct his patients not only in the importance of self-examination, but also in the fact that their sexuality relates to more than the presence or absence of a breast. The gynecologist should be in a position not only to assist in management of breast conditions, but also to provide support and guidance for the continuing sexuality of both the patient and her partner.

Similarly, gynecologists are often approached by patients who wish to have plastic surgery done to enlarge their breasts. While such surgery may occasionally be of true benefit, such a request is commonly indicative of other types of sexual conflict. It is important to review with such patients their sexual history in an effort to elicit evidence which may indicate sexual counseling rather than surgery.

Prostate surgery in men is fraught with sexual side effects, and it is important that both the patient and his partner be aware of them. Transperineal prostatectomy almost always results in impotence, and transurethral prostatectomy often causes retrograde ejaculation. The latter need not be a devastating problem if the patient is forewarned. The gynecologist should have a working knowledge of these effects, as the problems will often be brought to his attention by wives of men who have had prostate surgery.

Obstetrics. Pregnancy, despite its joyous connotations, may be a time of great sexual tension. It is commonly believed that sexual activity during pregnancy may be harmful, despite the complete lack of evidence for this view. Sexual abstinence during pregnancy is not only unnecessary, but also may cause resentment of the baby by the couple. More study is required in the area of the physiologic effects of orgasm in pregnancy. The findings by Masters and Johnson that orgasm causes a uterine contraction has been taken by some to suggest a possible hazard of orgasm causing premature labor. It seems doubtful that this would be valid, as uterine contractions normally occur throughout pregnancy. Generally speaking, patients may be told that, in the absence of pregnancy complications such as abnormal bleeding, infection, and possibly cervical incompetence, no alteration of sexual habits should be necessary.

Gynecology. Even in the gynecologist's own field there are areas in which aspects of sexuality have been ignored in his training. One of the most important of these is the area of gynecologic surgery. The hysterectomy, although a common operation, creates many irrational fears in women relating to the loss of femininity and other imagined side effects. When combined with removal of the ovaries, the patient commonly experiences "menopausal" symptoms which may further exacerbate these fears. It is important that the gynecologist familiarize himself with these fears and work to reassure his surgical patients that their capacity for sexual fulfillment will remain intact postsurgery. A common problem is the apparent shortening and narrowing of the vagina which patients often experience when vaginal hysterectomy is combined with bladder or rectal repair. The gynecologist must point out to the patient that this sensation is only temporary, and that under normal circumstances the vagina will accommodate itself to whatever dimensions are required.

The complex emotional patterns of menopause require great insight for proper management. The patient is often troubled by a declining feminine self-image and may develop doubts about her sexual attractiveness. These women require reassurance and support. It is often helpful to point out that she will no longer be burdened by fluctuating hormone levels and that she can thus count on a more steady, even emotional level. Properly prepared, there is no reason why today's menopausal woman should not feel liberated and contented with herself as a sexual being.

Multidisciplinary Approach

The gynecologist should be made aware of the resources which are available to him in managing sexual dysfunction patients. Unique and valuable therapeutic contributions can be made by a wide range of professional therapists. Among these are psychiatrists, clinical psychologists, social workers, marriage counselors, and rehabilitation therapists. Each of these should have input into an educational program for the gynecologist, so that he may become aware of their functions and may more efficiently utilize their services.

APPROACH TO RESIDENT EDUCATION

The obstetrics-gynecology resident should be relatively easy to educate in the realm of human sexuality. His role is essentially that of a student, and he functions in an already established educational structure, the hospital residency program. In addition, he is younger and thus presumably, more receptive to new concepts. There are, however, two problem areas that must be addressed in order to effectively institute such a program.

First, the resident tends to be procedure-oriented. From his limited viewpoint, his most important objective is to learn to "do" things, such as operations, deliveries, and diagnostic examinations. He can be expected to be resistant to a series of didactic lectures which he may view as a return to the drudgery of medical school. Thus, a sexuality curriculum must include a substantial amount of "practical" experience, such as learning to perform a sex-oriented pelvic exam in which the patient and her partner view and participate in the exam and are instructed in sexual anatomy and physiology.

Second, the hospital-based resident rarely comes in contact with sexual-dysfunction patients, as such patients are infrequently hospitalized. This problem has been expressed by Lief:

> The teaching of sex education cannot be left to an accidental kind of clinical experience where a student's learning depends entirely upon the types of cases he encounters; this leaves too much to chance. And the minor types of sexual maladjustments—of major importance in the lives of people having them—are not commonly seen in a teaching hospital unless they are secondary to other illnesses (e.g., frigidity in a woman with fibroids, premature ejaculation in a patient with angina pectoris).[3]

Thus, the curriculum should provide opportunity for selected patient contact, possibly on a preceptorship basis with interested members of the attending gynecology staff. Hopefully, this would include some exposure to actual sex-dysfunction therapy in the active role of co-therapist.

APPROACH TO EDUCATING THE PRACTICING GYNECOLOGIST

Unlike the resident, the gynecologist in private practice is oriented to such matters as time and money, rather than procedures. In addition, he has quite adequate amounts of patient contact and follow-up. For these reasons, it is best to approach sexuality from an office-practice viewpoint.

The inclusion of practice-management consultants into the curriculum will help provide the logistical means of incorporating sexuality evaluation and therapy into daily office practice in a smooth efficient manner. Problems which must be addressed include the proper techniques of scheduling counseling sessions. Office receptionists tend to try to find out the nature of the patient's needs when an appointment is scheduled. Many patients may be reluctant to discuss these matters with the receptionist. The doctor and his office should arrange a communication system by which the patient may schedule "consultation" time without going into detail with office personnel.

Also included should be input from representatives of third party carriers, so that billing for the service may be facilitated and patients may know at the outset what their costs will be and what, if anything, will be covered by insurance policies.

There is a tendency for professional meetings and courses to be conducted in resort facilities in a semivacation atmosphere. With emphasis upon minimal course hours and maximum recreation and parties, it is unlikely that the doctor will return with anything substantial beyond a suntan and a hangover! If true education is to be the objective, the course should be held in surroundings which are conducive to intensive study such as a convention center in a Northern city. Also, physicians should be encouraged to arrange for adequate coverage of their practices so as not to be "on call" during the meeting. It is extremely helpful to provide each participant with reading material well in advance so that he may be presumed to have a certain basic understanding of the fundamental aspects of the course.

The maximum amount of time devoted to such a course should be two-and-a-half days, preferably over a weekend. One evening should feature a dinner with guest speaker, otherwise non-course time should be left unscheduled. If it is determined that this does not provide adequate time, the concept of a separate "advanced" course may be instituted.

SUMMARY

As the person to whom most sexual dysfunction complaints are initially brought, the gynecologist should play a pivotal role in providing entry into the system for sex-dysfunction therapy. Unfortunately, his lack of education in the field of human sexuality has left him largely unable and unwilling to do this. In this chapter, we have examined the essentials of course content designed to remedy this deficit. We have assumed an objective of preparing the gynecologist to recognize, evaluate, and, to a limited extent, treat the patient with dysfunctional problems. In addition to reviewing sexual aspects of basic and clinical sciences, the curriculum includes objectivity training and the use of a multidisciplinary approach. Emphasis is placed upon the differing needs and interests of the obstetrics-gynecology resident and the practicing gynecologist. Recommendations are made for the most effective means of presenting a sexuality curriculum to each of these groups.

The opportunity presently exists to expand our knowledge of sexual function and to provide meaningful patient services in the process. It is hoped that those interested in establishing a sexuality curriculum for the gynecologist will view this as a starting point from which additions and alterations can be made, depending upon perceived needs and desires. With the eventual incorporation of sexuality training into obstetrics-gynecology residencies, the gynecologist of the future will be better able to fulfill his role of counselor, teacher, and healer.

REFERENCES

1. Burnap DW, Golden JS: Sexual problems in medical practice, in Vincent C(ed): Human Sexuality in Medical Education and Practice. Springfield, Ill., C. Thomas, 1968, p 47–59
2. Masters WH, Johnson VE: Human Sexual Response. Boston, Little, Brown, 1966
3. Lief HI: Sex education in medical students and doctors, in Vincent C(ed): Human Sexuality in Medical Education and Practice, Springfield, Ill., C. Thomas, 1968, p 19–33

Sheldon Fellman

14
Sexuality Curriculum for the Urologist

The urologist has traditionally considered himself the protector and authority on the function of the urinary tree and the male genital system. He is likely to consider the male genitals in their role as an organ for the transport of urine, occasionally in a reproductive functional sense, but infrequently in their sexual-function role. However, this accident of anatomy would seem to make it mandatory that the urologist be knowledgeable about the physiology of male sexuality, an authority in the diagnosis of male sexual dysfunction, and an effective instrument in the therapy of such dysfunctions. The urologist is certainly not alone among his physician and surgeon colleagues in his reticence to discuss, diagnose, and treat matters of sexual function and dysfunction. Like his colleagues, he probably grew up in an era when sexual matters were considered private, taboo, and not suitable for open discussion except in a jocular sense. The medical school curriculum and residency programs provided no instruction in this area from either the physiologic, dysfunctional, diagnostic, or therapeutic approaches. This cultural background, coupled with a lack of knowledge, produced many physicians who did not feel comfortable discussing sexual concerns with their patients.

Most urologists understood that the majority of sexual disorders were functional, nonorganic problems, and did not fall into the scope of a genitourinary surgeon. Prior to the publication of Masters and Johnson's *Human Sexual Inadequacy,* the urologist was not alone in his view that these dysfunctions were essentially nontreatable entities. This attitude produced a sort of therapeutic nihilism: "Why bother to expend the necessary time and interest when the bottom line would produce an absence of benefit to the patient?'' One cannot help but wonder if this is a reason or an excuse.

Certainly, significant numbers of sexual problems can be solved or alleviated in one or two hours time, particularly those involving sexual misinformation, or where a patient experiences a transient or intermittent dysfunction. Included in this group are patients whose dysfunction is drug-related.

The illogic of the typical urologist's position can be pointed out in two ways. First, the urologist continues to treat many diseases such as malignancies of the testes where the "bottom line" is even more often not a good result. Second, the urologist may well expend more than two hours in treating a patient's hydrocele when one considers the initial visit, history-taking, physical examination, laboratory data, performance of an operative procedure, dictation of an operative note, dictation of a case summary, and postoperative visits with the attendant note-taking. Were the urologist the patient, he would certainly be much more concerned about the inability to obtain an erection than the presence of fluid within the scrotum. This logic may be irrefutable, but it is still difficult to convince urologists that sexuality properly belongs within their province when they possess cultural discomforture and lack the academic background in sexual physiology, behavior, and function.

While the popularly depicted sexual revolution of the last generation may not indeed have been a revolution, there has unquestionably been a far greater volume of material regarding sexual behavior in the popular media and a far greater willingness to discuss sexual behavior among our youth. In addition, many primary and secondary schools provide some modicum of sexual education which, while the course content may not be all that professional sex educators would desire, at least has taken sexuality out of the closet and made the discussion of it part of an open and public forum. All medical schools in the United States currently offer courses in human sexuality. These vary widely in the hours devoted to this subject and in the scope of the various curricula. Nonetheless, they again reinforce the concept that sexuality is a fit and suitable matter for open discussion, and most certainly suitable for discussion between doctor and patient. It is unlikely, however, that these general courses will provide sufficient background to make the urologist of the future an expert in sexual physiology, human sexual behavior, the diagnosis of sexual dysfunction, and sex therapy.

Inasmuch as the urology resident of today spends a minimum of five years of postgraduate training, including at least three years in a department of urology, it seems appropriate that such expertness be acquired in this portion of his education and training. It is unlikely that this change will occur spontaneously in urology residency programs in the United

States. Those in charge of such programs, while unquestionably of great skill as genitourinary surgeons, researchers, and teachers, almost universally do not possess the background, and, for reasons mentioned previously, they are not interested in providing knowledge about human sexuality to their residents. It appears that the impetus to include sexuality content in postgraduate residency programs must come from the American Board of Urology. If the Board were to make it known that henceforth its examinations for certification would encompass those matters pertaining to sexuality which might reasonably be considered within the ken of the urologist, there would be an immediate inclusion of this content in the residency programs, since the goal of all residency programs must be the achievement of diplomate status for its graduates.

It is unlikely that the current faculties of the various residency programs could accomplish the appropriate instruction. However, guest instructors with suitable expertise and teaching experience are certainly available, and affiliations with recognized sexual dysfunction centers and clinics could be arranged. In addition, residents could be sent on a sponsored basis to approved sexuality workshops and seminars.

The American Urologic Association could also have a significant role in the education of practicing and teaching urologists. Undoubtedly with the impetus provided by the American Board of Urology, national and sectional meetings and postgraduate seminars sponsored by the American Urologic Association would devote more time to sexuality in their programs. Both urologists and non-urologists who have the requisite knowledge and teaching ability could be encouraged to provide suitable teaching in the field of human sexuality.

Historically the specialty of urology has been one of instrument and gadget orientation. Urologists have been pioneers in exact and precise diagnostic instruments. Perhaps the advent and easy commercial availability of such instruments as the nocturnal penile tumescence monitor will stimulate urologists' interest. In addition to making one facet of the treatment of male sexual dysfunction a surgical exercise, the availability and practicality of penile prosthesis will accelerate interest in the full spectrum of sexual dysfunction. The use of audio-visual devices for the training of urologists and as an adjunct in patient therapy should further assist in this regard.

It is unlikely that most urologists can function practically in a full sexual counseling role. The cost of payroll for an office staff which may include surgical technicians, laboratory technicians and nurses, rental of an office suite with several consultation and examining rooms, the acquisition of many complex and costly diagnostic and therapeutic instruments, as well as the burden of sky-rocketing professional liability insurance payments, make the urologist noncompetitive economically in a long-term counseling situation. The psychologist, social worker, and psychiatrist can all provide such counseling at a lower fee to the patient because they have a vastly lower overhead. Regardless of their skill in diagnosing and treating sexual problems, these other specialists cannot provide the physical examinations, laboratory studies, and possible x-ray examinations that may be a necessary part of the patient's evaluation. In addition, the fact that many urologic disorders are directly related to sexual dysfunction makes the urologist the appropriate physician to make diagnostic judgments in many cases of sexual dysfunction. He should, as already mentioned, be able to treat simple sexual dysfunctions which can be handled well in brief counseling sessions, and he should have a thorough knowledge of referral sources for those patients who require more extensive therapy.

George Szasz

15
Sexuality Curriculum for the Physiatrist, Physiotherapist, and Occupational Therapist

INTRODUCTION

There is a growing recognition that sexual disturbances represent a major problem in the rehabilitation of disabled individuals, in the preservation of marriages following disability, and in overcoming devastating concepts of self-worth. To date sexual disturbances of the handicapped have been generally ignored. One important reason for this has been because physicians and paramedical personnel did not receive any training in this area of rehabilitation.

In this chapter a "sexuality curriculum" for physiotherapists and occupational therapists will be presented. This curriculum arose out of daily clinical experiences within the context of a sexual rehabilitation program for spinal injured and other chronically ill patients. Therefore the sexual rehabilitation program will be described first, and then examples of the involvement of physiotherapists and occupational therapists in such a program will be presented. A description of the objectives which arose as the result of these involvements and the content of the "sexuality curriculum" will follow. Finally, the dilemmas related to the development of such a program will be considered.

SEXUAL REHABILITATION PROGRAM

In 1975 a program of sexual rehabilitation was established in an acute spinal injury unit and later broadened to include adult patients in a rehabilitation center. This program consists of work by a physician and specially trained sexual counselors on three levels. First, it entails aiding disabled persons to identify the degree of sexual disability and to recognize and realize their potential. Second, it is concerned with aiding the disabled individual and the significant partner in the development of acceptable alternatives. Third, it includes moving professional and public attitudes toward greater acceptance of the disabled as a person with sexual functioning capabilities. Sexual rehabilitation can be followed through these steps:

1. *On admission.* The patient's assigned nurse takes a nursing history and, in the course of obtaining data from the patient, inquires about concerns the patient may have about sexual functioning. The nurse offers reassurance that such concerns are common and explains to the patient that a sexual counselor works on the ward.

2. *Introductory visits.* The sex counselor with the patient and members of the family acknowledge the existence of sex-related concerns, if any, to help the patient to organize these concerns, to obtain evidence of sexual capabilities, and to outline future steps in the rehabilitation program. By the second month most patients are over the acute phase of their injury and are usually ready for the major assessment of their sexual potential.

3. *Assessment.* Seven categories have proved to be useful in establishing both the patient's and the partner's sexual functioning status.

   a. Sexual response status reflects the ability of the patient to experience the normal cycle of physiological events in sexual response.

   b. Sexual activity status gives indication of the available motor functions which might be used for embracing, intercourse and the like.

   c. Sexual interest status reveals the patient's preoccupation with sex-related issues.

   d. Sexual behavior status gives information about the patient's skills for social interaction and sexual activities.

   e. Sex organ status gives evidence of the anatomical integrity of the genitalia and the effect on it of urinary drainage apparatus, genitourinary infections, surgery, etc.

   f. Fertility status reveals the patient's need and ability to procreate or the nature of contraception desired.

   g. Sexuality status describes the ways and means the patient uses sex activities to indicate that he is a man or she is a woman.

During the assessment, each category of the patient's sexual functioning status is discussed. Specific alternatives are then explored, and on occasion demonstrated. For example, the partner may want to witness how a reflex erection can be brought on, or both may want to know what position in intercourse may be most feasible. Some patients may want to know about sexual aids. If the patient and the partner agree, a summary of the findings is placed on the chart.

4. *Follow-up visits.* The purpose of the follow-up is three-fold. First, to correct areas of confusion and misinformation; second, to prepare the patient for home visits and discharge from hospital; third, to encourage experimentation with alternate styles of sex-related activities. A private room is made available to the couple for unobserved use at their convenience. Some patients wish to delay experimentation until in their home environment. Patients who have no partners may be encouraged to experiment by themselves.

On occasions the experimentations or even their prospects may raise various defenses because of fears of failure or rejection by the partner, or because of a tendency to overprotect each other. Sometimes these issues are settled by using the approaches of sex therapy, psychotherapy, and marital therapy; more often, however, problems are settled through a clarification of the couple's sex-related objectives, through continuous reassurance and encouragement, and some technical advice in the course of follow-up visits.

EXAMPLES OF SEX-RELATED INVOLVEMENT OF THE PHYSIOTHERAPIST AND OCCUPATIONAL THERAPIST

As the clinical services became organized, sexual rehabilitation emerged as a specialized dimension of the overall rehabilitation program in the acute spinal injury unit. Similarly, as the services were extended to patients in the long-term rehabilitation facilities, the services became identified both by patients and by staff as a legitimate specialty area. This, however, did not mean that sex-related conversations between patients and rehabilitation therapists stopped. In fact, some staff members felt more at ease in discussing these issues with the patients, because, as one physiotherapist stated: "The conversation could always be closed by me telling the patient: why don't you go see the sex counselor?" Several of the nurses, orderlies, as well as the rehabilitation therapists, started to refer patients to the sex counselor. The counselor began to approach the physiotherapist and occupational therapist for information about patients' motor-functioning status or description of the home environment in which romantic interaction or lovemaking might take place. In some instances the patients' sex-related approaches to the staff were discussed at the regular team meetings, where each of the team members had a chance to express their own feelings and share their experiences.

The following case examples illustrate specific occasions in which

various types of sex-related interactions occurred between the sex counselor and the rehabilitation therapists, between the patients and the
therapists, and between the therapists and the other members of the team.

Case example 1: A 47-year-old divorced woman suffering from the effects of
an incomplete C 6–7 lesion requested assistance from the sex counselor. She
wished to have intercourse with a male friend but was afraid that ''I won't be able
to move my hips and clasp my legs around him.'' The sex counselor approached
the physio- and occupational therapist for specific information on this woman's hip
movement capabilities, for possible assistance with pillow supports under her
pelvis and legs, and for some method of holding her ankles together to clasp the
male.

Case example 2: A 49-year-old paraplegic man and his 37-year-old wife expressed great concern about involuntary urinary and bowel discharge during sex
play. The patient's wife approached the occupational therapist for suggestions
regarding management of urinary drainage apparatus in bed, for advice about the
best and most economic types of sheet covers and deodorants, and for methods of
washing stained sheets and safeguarding the mattresses. The therapist turned to
the sexual counselor for verification of the patient's sexual-functioning status and
to work out how best to discuss these issues with the couple.

Case example 3: An 18-year-old woman patient was engaged in a lighthearted
conversation with a male nurse about fashions and clothing styles while doing her
exercises in the physiotherapy room. Discussion focused on the differences between ''sexy'' and ''sensuous'' clothing, and the patient turned to the
physiotherapist for her opinion.

Case example 4: A 28-year-old single male quadriplegic with limited hand
motion and grip asked the male physiotherapist for advice about a way to stimulate himself to see if he still had the ability to ejaculate.

Case example 5: A 22-year-old single paraplegic woman was upset about the
sex-physical assessment. Upon her return to her room, she said to the
physiotherapist: ''Why can't they leave me alone? I don't want to know all about
that down there.''

Case example 6: A 21-year-old single male quadriplegic turned to the female
physiotherapist to express his embarrassment over his constant erections, which
are particularly noticeable while doing floor exercises.

The first two examples identify the rehabilitation therapist as a consultant to the sex counselor. In these consultations the sex counselor
expects that the rehabilitation professional will put aside his or her personal behavior code and will accept the patient's needs and concerns as
legitimate. In the first example, the professionals have to accept that a
woman, who is 47 years old, a divorcee, and a quadriplegic, may desire a
physical relationship and intercourse in a special position. In the second
example, the rehabilitation therapists are called upon to deal with the

physical realities of lovemaking with a spinal injured person. In both these instances the therapists' acceptance of the patient's needs led first to the assessment of the patient's sexual-functioning status and then to the resolution of some of the problems.

Cases 3 and 4 identify the rehabilitation therapists as consultants to the patient. In Case 3, the therapist finds herself in an informal setting and drawn into a sex-related conversation. Few professionals would identify this verbal exchange as a consultation, yet an analysis of the situation suggests that this patient may have been asking for a professional opinion: "Am I attractive enough for a man to have interest in me sitting in a wheelchair?" or "Could I wear more attractive clothing?" or perhaps, "How can I come across as a sensuous person in a wheelchair?" Of course, the patient may have only been trying to get the attention of a significant male around her, or indeed may have just wanted to clarify the dictionary definition of "sexy" and "sensuous." The fact remains, however, that few if any conversations in the milieu of a hospital unit can be looked upon as merely idle chatter. Indeed, the therapist's casual statement may have more significance to the patient than the official conclusions of the attending physician.

In Case 4, the situation is more formal in that the therapist is being asked for specific technical advice about masturbation. The professional's understanding of the physiological principle of seminal fluid formation and ejaculation, and the physical activities involved in this sex act is of importance. Yet again, without an accepting attitude the therapist is not likely to be a valuable source of information to the patient.

The incidents presented in Cases 5 and 6 portray the rehabilitation therapist in a preventive role. Appropriate intervention offered at the right moment may defuse difficult situations. Although in Case 5 the patient's complaint about the sex counselor's physical examination may be valid, it could be also a way of expressing anger and frustration over her disabilities. The situation in this case becomes more complex because the complaining patient may also create anxiety among the other patients about the value of the sex rehabilitation service. To be effective in such a situation, the physiotherapist and the occupational therapist need to recognize the patient's usual way of reacting to the disability, to have some information about the findings of the sex counselor, to know what procedures constitute the sex physical examination, and to have some understanding of the reactions of the other patients in the room. Having this information, the rehabilitation therapist can offer reassurance and clarification in such a way that she may prevent further agony for the patient and, at the same time, support the professional services offered by the sexual counselor. If the rehabilitation therapist discovers that the patient inadvertently suffered in the process of the physical examination, then the therapist may wish to approach the sex counselor and other team members about this, so that they may formulate another way to assist the patient in her turmoil.

In Case 6, the patient has uncontrollable reflex erections. The therapist knows about that, but what is she to do? Explaining to the patient the physiology of this reflex, and providing a special underwear to accommodate his bulging penis, could well prevent an embarrassing experience for all.

EDUCATIONAL OBJECTIVES

These clinical examples suggest that the rehabilitation therapists may have to act as consultants to the sex counselor, as teachers and consultants to the patients and their family, as supporters of the therapeutic milieu, and as practitioners of preventive intervention. To fulfill these roles the therapists need to become more secure and experienced in three areas. First, they require knowledge of sexual and reproductive physiology and of contemporary sexual practices. Second, they have to acquire those behaviors which show acceptance of the patient's concerns. Thirdly, they have to acquire skills, both to discover the patients' sex-related concerns and to give appropriate reassurance and education to the patients and their families.

Each of these case examples indicates the need for knowledge of some aspect of sexual functioning: the appropriate management of Cases 1, 2, and 6 demand understanding of basic sexual physiology and the related motor, bowel, and bladder functioning processes; Case 3 requires understanding of sexual growth and development, including some of the factors that might influence the patient's self-image; Case 4 requires knowledge about one particular sex act; while Case 5 indicates the need for information about the method of sexual rehabilitation specific to that particular unit.

The behavior by which a therapist can demonstrate acceptance of the patient's sexual concerns is more difficult to document. In Case 1, after being informed of the 47-year-old woman's concerns by the sex counselor, the rehabilitation therapist demonstrated her "acceptance" by first reviewing the reports on the patient's motor abilities. Then she further demonstrated her acceptance by asking specific questions: "What position does she prefer?"; "Does she like her hip on the bed or elevated on a pillow?"; "Is the bed firm?"; "How much help can she expect from her partner?" The occupational therapist then actually lay on a bed to measure the thickness of the foam rubber support that might be of value, and after considering various alternatives she suggested a simple pillow support for the patient's buttocks, and a soft anklet to hold the ankles together. The sex counselor transmitted these recommendations to the patient and to her partner. As it turned out, the anklet was not needed, but the pillow helped the upper body movement to the satisfaction of both.

Demonstration of acceptance is more difficult when the interaction takes place between rehabilitation therapists and patients. For example, in Case 3 the rehabilitation therapist demonstrated her acceptance in the following ways: she did not tell the male nurse to leave the physiotherapy room when the conversation moved to the discussion of sexuality and sensuality; instead, she joined in the conversation, and later planned a shopping trip with the patient for fashionable clothing, and also brought the patient a fashion magazine.

There are two types of skill requirements: one, to clarify information, and the other, to give information. In Case 5, the rehabilitation therapist helped the patient to express her sex-related concerns: "You look upset . . . can you tell me what bothers you? . . . by 'down there' do you mean the vulva and the vagina?" Had she not asked for clarification, the therapist might have mistakenly said to the complaining patient: "You are right, I don't think that anyone should meddle in your private business." However, this would have been contrary to the patient's interest and the objectives of sexual rehabilitation.

In Case 4, information would be required about the patient's customary way of masturbation before appropriate alternatives could be offered: ". . . there are many ways to masturbate . . . what are some of the ways you have heard of? . . . have you thought of doing it that way? . . . which way would you prefer? . . . well, with your grasp being weak, perhaps that would not work out quite as well . . . have you thought of using a small pillow?"

UNDERGRADUATE "SEXUALITY CURRICULUM"

An attempt has been made to translate these educational requirements into an undergraduate "sexuality curriculum" in one School of Rehabilitation Medicine. The rehabilitation medicine course at this school consists of the combined training in physical and occupational therapy. The first year may be taken in the faculty of arts or science at a college or at another university; the second, third, and fourth years are taken in the School of Rehabilitation Medicine. During the summer sessions and in the fourth year, increasing amounts of clinical experience and instructions are obtained at various hospitals and institutions under the guidance of university-appointed instructors. At the termination of the program, the students are eligible for membership in the Canadian Physiotherapy Association, and they possess a Bachelor of Science degree in Rehabilitation. In this school the vast majority of students are women in their early 20s.

The "sexuality curriculum" is part of the regular program and starts in the second year with a consideration of the relationship between reproductive and other uses of sexual activities. The physiology of the male and female sexual response is then outlined, and the motor activities required for the different sexual practices are analyzed. The concepts of sexual norms are discussed, and the sexual behavior practices of the 1970s are portrayed. In the third year, sexual problems of able-bodied and handicapped patients are contrasted under the categories of sexual-response difficulties, sexual disinterest, and sexual-activity problems. In the fourth year, sexual growth and development patterns are related to physical, mental, and social functioning. The sexual problems caused by developmental handicaps and chronic illness are illustrated.

To document the clinical relevance of the lectures, videotaped interview segments are used to portray the sexual life patterns of able-bodied and handicapped men and women. Small group presentations are utilized to encourage expression of the student's own personal feelings. In the relative intimacy of these groups some of the students felt free enough to bring up their own sex-related experiences and personal experiences with patients in their clinical rotation. A few students discussed their dilemmas about dating handicapped persons.

Sex-related questions are included in the regular examination. The following is an example of one question:

> A 32-year-old former airline stewardess, married for six years and having a three-year-old son, has been referred to the physiotherapy and occupational therapy department. She had been suffering from rheumatoid arthritis for five years, with some visible deformities of her hands and periodic painful swelling of her fingers and wrists. In the course of physiotherapy the patient reveals some of her difficulties at home and expresses concerns to the therapist about her loss of sexual interest. Discuss the potential sex-related difficulties of this couple under the headings of: Sexual Response, Interest, Activities, Behavior, Fertility, Genital Hygiene, and Self-Image.

Examination results indicate that the students do their homework diligently. However, when students arrive at the Spinal Injury Unit for their clinical rotation, they cannot transfer the knowledge into clinical practice without further instruction. Therefore, those students who are assigned to the Spinal Injury Unit receive a practical "in-service education," in which they learn about the sexual rehabilitation process from the sex counselor, and they hear about the sex-related concerns of their assigned patients. The sex counselor gives examples of the "consulting role," the "teaching role," the "preventive role," and illustrates how the patient–therapist conversation may influence the therapeutic climate of the ward. The counselor also explains how to chart relevant sex information. When the students participate in team meetings, the sexual counselor tries to review with them those sex-related issues which may have surfaced in the course of these meetings.

DILEMMAS

The "sexuality curriculum" outlined in this chapter is weak in many respects. For example, hardly considered were the sex-related problems of the developmentally handicapped and the aged, the issues related to birth control for the handicapped, or the problems associated with institutionalization. Also, hardly any clinical experiences were provided for the students.

These insufficiencies could be ascribed to the limited curriculum time (five hours in each of three years) allocated to this area. However, it is not at all certain how much time needs to be allocated to a "sexuality curriculum." In fact, before this type of program is expanded at all, some solutions must be found to the following problems: first, it must be determined if there is really a need for "sexual rehabilitation;" second, if there is, the roles the rehabilitation therapists should assume in that area must be defined; and third, one must ask whether it is possible to train students of rehabilitation therapy for roles that are not yet demonstrated by their teachers or the practitioners of the profession.

Sex-related social and cultural changes of the 1970s demand an affirmative answer to the first question. Practicing rehabilitation therapists know that patients are begging for help. Many young handicapped, who suffer the effects of such conditions as meningo-myelocele, cerebral palsy, or deafness are requesting "sex talks" from their therapists. A wife whose husband lost his penis in an accident turns to the physiotherapist for a "stuffed sock which he could wear in his pants instead of the penis." An older man asks the occupational therapist who is working with his spinal injured wife: "Do you think my wife will have sex again?" A 26-year-old patient, who is suffering from muscular dystrophy (and who has been kept alive with the support of an iron lung for ten years), hesitantly inquires from the physiotherapist if somehow his penis could be massaged. The wife of a spinal injured patient asks the physiotherapist: "Where could I buy a rubber penis?"

So there is a need for sexual rehabilitation. What role should the rehabilitation therapist assume? That of a sex counselor? To fulfill that role, the rehabilitation therapist would have to possess an understanding of the physiology of sexual functioning and of the relationship between sexual functioning and various forms of physical and emotional difficulties, interviewing skills in the sex-related areas, and the know-how of sex physical examination. In addition, as a sexual counselor she would have to be adept at the management of personal and marital crises related to sexual frustrations.

The rehabilitation therapist could become qualified as a sexual counselor, but immersion in such a specific area represents too much specialization for most rehabilitation therapists. Therefore, the combined consulting-teaching-preventive roles outlined in this chapter would appear to be the more natural extension of the rehabilitation therapist's present role. The well-trained and experienced occupational and physiotherapist is already fulfilling a consulting role to orthopedic and neurosurgeons, as well as to family physicians, respiratory specialists, the nursing staff, the social worker, and others on the team. Also, rehabilitation professionals are active practitioners of preventive medicine and much of their work has to do with teaching. Thus, with some additional training the traditional roles could be expanded to include the management of sex-related rehabilitation issues.

Unfortunately, however, the consideration of sexual disabilities has been so specifically ignored in the past that the expansion of the traditional activities of rehabilitation therapists may have to be looked upon as the assumption of a new role. This brings up the third question: can students be trained for such a new role without role models? The answer is no. Professional training is, to a great extent, a form of rehearsal for a role. Students require role models, that is, professionals whose behavior they can imitate. If their teachers do not portray the behavior related to the desired role, then, at best, the students will become confused. Some will consider the "sexuality curriculum" as an attack on their established moral views; others will perceive it as an additional burden in an already heavy educational program. To be sure, some students will derive personal benefit from these sex-related presentations. But the thoughtful students will see through the hypocrisy of a professional educational program in which the students are asked to experiment and to take professional and personal risks, yet their teachers are permitted to shy away from assuming the necessary leadership in this exploration of professional boundaries.

For these reasons a "sexuality in-service education" of the teachers in a school of rehabilitation medicine may have to assume priority over the expansion of undergraduate "sexuality curriculum." The faculty in-service educational program could be conducted as an ongoing seminar, consisting of sex-related clinical case presentations, demonstrations of various ways of responding to sex-related professional and patient inquiries, and discussions. Such a program might assist faculty members to identify and experiment with various levels of sexual rehabilitation.

Who will teach the teacher? The ideal "sex" teacher would be a physiotherapist or occupational therapist who, after some years of clinical practice, obtained extensive clinical experience as a sex therapist. Teachers with such qualifications are few. A reasonable alternative might be teaching by a group of professionals. One member of such a team of "sex teachers" might be a medical professional whose specialty area is in the sex field. This person could supply the knowledge, demonstrate some of the necessary assessment and management skills, and reinforce the legitimacy of the subject area. A desirable second member of the team would be a nonmedical professional who has specialized as a sex counselor. As long as rehabilitation therapists are not available to fulfill this role, a nurse trained in sexual counseling of the handicapped would do well. She could demonstrate how a non-physician practitioner works in this field or how her basic training can be used as a foundation for her expanded role. The third member of a teaching team would be a senior faculty member of the school of rehabilitation medicine. This teacher and practitioner would serve as the coordinator of the program and as the interpreter of the faculty members' sex-educational needs to the sex therapist and counselor. When the sex-related dimension of the rehabilitation therapists' work becomes clarified, the administrator of the school will be able to allocate appropriate personnel, curriculum time, and funds for the provision of a "sexuality curriculum" which might properly equip the student professional for the work that is expected of him and her.

E. Ingvarda Hanson

16
Sexuality Curriculum and the Nurse

INTRODUCTION

Historically, the nursing profession has addressed the health care needs of the overall person. Such a broad commitment to the promotion and restitution of health has necessitated that nurses consider all aspects of health including sexual health. In fact, for decades, nurses have contributed to the improvement of maternal-child care, to promotion of emotional and physical health for families, to reduction of contagious diseases including those which are sexually transmitted, to family planning and related sterility/fertility problems, to health education, including sex education for the school-age child, and to improvement of working conditions and child care facilities which attract women into the work force. Such leadership, although laudable, is just a beginning, for it touches only selected aspects of sexual health care. The potential contribution of the nursing profession to sexual health promotion and care is unlimited when one considers that in most nurse–patient interaction, there is a need for sexual health assessment; likewise, nursing intervention as related to sexual health is frequently indicated. Such extensive involvement in sexual health care requires knowledge about and sensitivity to the sexuality of both patient and nurse. Nursing curriculum must build toward that goal;[1,2,3] therefore, the purpose of this chapter is twofold: (1) to delineate broad concepts of sexuality and sexual health care which suggest significant aspects of nursing practice, and thereby essential components of nursing education; and (2) to suggest a means by which such concepts can become a viable aspect of the nursing curriculum.

CONCEPTS OF SEXUALITY AND SEXUAL HEALTH CARE
ESSENTIAL TO NURSING PRACTICE

Nine concepts of sexuality and sexual health care which are significant for nursing practice are stated below. Each is briefly discussed. These concepts may be used as guides for content related to sexuality and sexual health care within a nursing curriculum.

Concept I: All people are sexual.   The nurse must recognize intellectually and emotionally that he or she is a sexual person and that sexuality permeates all aspects of his or her life—physical, emotional, social, cultural, and even professional life. The nurse must recognize that all health personnel are sexual; moreover, the nurse must recognize that all persons in her care are sexual, including children, aged persons, physically and mentally disadvantaged, critically ill persons, dying persons, persons with contagious diseases, unconscious persons, those out of contact with reality, healthy persons, malingering persons, black persons, white persons, religious persons, sexually free persons, and sexually inhibited persons. An appreciation of sexuality as being ever present in spite of personal, cultural, or health variations is the basis from which nursing practice, which includes sexual health care, must build.

Concept II: The physiological component of sexuality is greater than the reproductive system and, in fact, permeates the entire body.[4,5]   It is essential for the nurse to consider the anatomical and physiological characteristics of people from several perspectives related to sexuality: What embryonic events determine sexuality? What genetic factors are in evidence in body size, shape, and function? What body configurations determine the sex of assignment and which systems contribute to the development of sexual identity? How does the endocrine and neurological system influence sexual role behavior? What does each body system contribute to the physical sexual response cycle? How does the sexual response cycle influence each body system? What is the relationship between the reproductive system and total body functioning? How do males and females differentiate physiologically from conception until death? What effect does each successive chronological year have on the physical sexual functions of the body? What are common sexual dysfunctions? What is the preferred mode of therapeutic intervention?

Concept III: The sexual self evolves as an integral component of total physiological, psychological, and sociological development; indeed, sexual differentiation/development begins at conception and continues until death.[6-9] With the assignment of sex at birth, a lifelong pattern by which people relate to each other according to gender is instituted. Patterns of interpersonal interactions are modified by the expectations society places on the behavior of males as compared with the behavior of females. The child cognitively and affectively must learn identification, that is, relating to persons of the same sex as opposed to complementation, that is, relating to persons of the opposite sex.[10] This cognitive/affective process continues throughout life, ever influencing behavior including the nurse–patient relationship, the individual response to stresses such as illness, and the patient's receptivity to therapeutic interventions for sexual problems.

The nurse must clearly recognize that in each society and within family units, behaviors are coded as appropriate for one sex or for the other.[10a] Not infrequently, illness necessitates a sex-coded role behavior change, thus threatening the sense of sexual security in the ill person; furthermore, in some situations, family members must alter their sex-coded behavior patterns in order to compensate for the altered capacities of the ill person.

Sexual identity, although apparently influenced by biological factors, develops very early in life through learning experiences with significant others. Sexual identity, that is, knowing who one is as a sexual person, is frequently threatened at crisis points in life such as during adolescence, retirement, and illness. Through each stage of life, the focus of sexual differentiation/development is altered. The child focuses on developing sexual identity, along with a trust and tenderness relationship in which attachments to significant others are formed. As the child grows, he takes on the sexual role characteristics of his family and society and he codes behavior as appropriate for one or both sexes. During school age, the child focuses on defining the rules of society regarding sexual behavior and expanding his concept of the sexual world. In adolescence, his physical sexual feelings erupt and he becomes preoccupied with his value to himself and to others. Gradually, responsibility for sexual behavior develops which eventually frees the adult and older person to enjoy sexual expression within their value system and to find pleasure in seeing the continuity of man through children. In summary, psychological and sociological aspects of sexual differentiation/development must be understood by the nurse as an integral aspect of the whole person. In addition, the nurse must recognize appropriate therapeutic interventions when sexual health problems, associated with differentiation/development, are identified.

Concept IV: A person's state of health/illness will affect that individual's sexuality, biologically, psychologically, or sociologically.[11-13] The nurse must be aware of the potential effects which physical symptoms of illness have on different aspects of sexuality. For example, does the symptom threaten the person's sense of sexual identity, that is, how he or she feels as a man or woman? Does the symptom interfere with activities which are important to sexual role behavior? Do the symptoms force an individual to give up or alter behaviors which have been coded as appropriate only for his or her sex? Does the symptom affect the person's sexual relationship with others? Does the symptom affect sexual expression, either as it is experienced through creative work or recreational efforts, or through interaction with another person? Does the symptom alter sexual interest or desires? Does it become a barrier to physical sexual expression because of fatigue, undesirable appearance, odors, or dysfunctional body parts? Does the symptom directly affect the sexual response cycle by slowing or preventing vasocongestion and related physiological changes? Does the symptom interfere with pleasurable sensations or emotions associated with sexual expression? Does the symptom interfere with sexual self-pleasuring?

The person's mental health also directly affects sexual functioning. Symptoms associated with mental illness may distort a person's sexual self-concept, interfere with social/sexual relationships, alter the physiological sexual response cycle, and infringe on feelings of sexual pleasure. Even emotional changes within the range of normal behavior will have an effect. For example, anticipatory grief associated with reduced life expectancy can interfere with a person's capacity to experience sexual pleasure. Preoccupation with health, or life and death issues, is likely to reduce sexual desire and pleasure; on the other hand, such concerns may prompt some persons to pursue and enjoy sexual pleasure, at least while overt physical symptoms of the underlying illness are negligible.

Concept V: The physical sexual response cycle affects each body system and therefore has potential to affect symptoms of some illnesses.[4,12] An example of this effect is evidenced by some persons who have cardiovascular or respiratory illnesses. The increased blood pressure, pulse, and respiration associated with the physical sexual response add strain on a malfunctioning respiratory or circulatory system. What, if any, precautions need to be taken? What effect will love play and intercourse have on the body in general? Will the body tolerate the weight of another person, or the positions and movements of intercourse? What sexual health education, if any, will the person need in order to safely and pleasurably pursue physical sexual activity?

Concept VI: Therapeutic modalities, including hospitalization, may affect the sexuality of the patient and his family. Such effect may be perceived as either positive or negative.[12] Hospitalization usually is a deterrent to sexual expression. The lack of privacy practically prevents self-pleasuring, intimate conversation, and physical contact between the patient and a significant person. Some drug therapies are now recognized as interfering with libido or the physical sexual response cycle. Other therapies such as x-ray, surgery, orthopedic devices, and even rest therapy either directly interfere with sexual role behavior and sexual expression or indirectly alter the person's perception of self as a sexual being. At times, the therapeutic modalities do not directly affect the patient, but rather deter the significant other from expressing sexual feelings or from viewing the patient as a sexual person. On the other hand, therapeutic modalities at times reduce pain, enhance body image and sexual self-concept, and promote sexual communication and expression. For example, drugs which reduce pain, corrective surgery, mental health care, and any therapy which increases a person's energy level are frequently a positive influence on sexuality.

Concept VII: Conception, pregnancy, pubescence, and menopause are physiological and psychological events which affect aspects of sexuality, particularly sexual identity, sexual role behavior, and sexual expression.[14-16] Pubescence triggers intense feelings of sexual excitement and the desire for physical sexual expression. In the maternity-parenting cycle, both mother and father are confronted with temporary alterations in love play and intercourse, as well as with the permanent changes in sexual role functioning associated with parenthood. Like pubescence, the menopausal years may threaten sexual identity and roles in women; men may experience a similar phenomenon. Should a physical or mental illness occur at these critical times, additional stress is not only placed on sexual functioning per se, but also on sexual maturation.

Concept VIII: An individual or family unit, although sexually independent, is very much affected by the sexual milieu of the community and society.[17,18] Nursing, which is concerned with community health, must be concerned with the sexual health component of a community. Is the community informed about sexual health as it pertains to human development, to the maternity experience, to sexually transmitted diseases, to congenital and acquired anomalies which interfere with sexuality, to the genetic transfer of health problems, to variations in people's choice of sexual love object and means of sexual expression, and to sexual crimes against other persons? What contribution can nursing make to the health interventions needed for each of these community concerns? What is the local, national, and international feeling toward nursing, a predominantly women's profession? What is the effect of women's and men's liberation movements, and what can the nurse do in order to be a positive influence in these areas?

Concept IX: The nursing process is the means through which the nurse provides sexual health care.[19] The nurse must make an assessment of the patient's sexual health status and needs; this assessment should be incorporated into the total nursing assessment. Although specific sexual data pertaining to a particular patient's health-care needs and goal is pertinent, sexual assessment must also include changes in the patient's total life functioning which are usually significant threats to gender identity and sexual role, sexual life-style preferences, sexual maturity level, and modes of sexual expression. The nurse must plan for intervention based on the data, with the primary focus on facilitating communication about sexuality, correcting myths or misinformation, providing education about sexuality and the sexual implications of the illness, encouraging the patient to explore his or her feelings and resources for assistance with sexual concerns, and referring the patient to other therapeutic modalities as indicated. Ongoing evaluation of sexual health care by patient and nurse is essential if effective sexual health care is to be provided.

Summary. The above nine concepts related to sexuality and sexual health care are suggested as guides to areas of content for nursing curriculum. Content related to each is viewed by this author as essential to nursing practice and therefore, is indicated in nursing curriculum.

INCORPORATION OF SEXUALITY AND SEXUAL HEALTH CARE CONCEPTS INTO A NURSING CURRICULUM

Developing a nursing curriculum which addresses the nine sexual concepts presented above is a complex multi-faceted task. Perhaps no component of nursing curriculum is as vulnerable to ridicule, neglect, or misunderstanding from nursing educators themselves, as that of sexuality and sexual health care. Understandably so. Nursing educators come from the same fabric of life as do patients with similar misinformation and intense feelings about sexuality.[20] For those educators whose nursing education occurred more than five years ago, it is unlikely that they received extensive information on sexuality other than as part of reproduction. A slightly larger group of recently graduated nurse educators have studied aspects of sexual health care. However, the need for sexuality and sexual health education is recognized by many, and a variety of curriculum approaches are being tried. Whatever approach is used in sexual curriculum development, two major obstacles appear to surface: the lack of prepared faculty to delineate the content, and of more significance, the lack of faculty prepared to teach and reinforce the learning throughout the total curriculum, particularly in clinical experiences.[21,22] In order to minimize these obstacles, the following plan is submitted for those faculty who identify a need for such content in a nursing curriculum but who are without a plan of action.

From the perspective of this author, it appears that sexuality content reflected by the concepts presented earlier in this chapter, might best be incorporated throughout the theoretical and clinical curriculum, rather than presented only in intensive workshops or courses. However, the latter are not negated and may be a most effective way to promote learning on selected aspects of sexuality, particularly for reappraisal of attitudes toward sexuality. Intensive workshops on sexuality for nurses only or interdisciplinary workshops might be excellent supplements to the basic content taught throughout the curriculum;[23,24] likewise, separate courses on human sexuality could enhance the depth of learning.[25,26]

If the intent of a faculty is to incorporate content throughout the curriculum, it is recommended that as many faculty as possible be involved in the process. However, the right to not be involved in planning must be respected for those who feel uncomfortable with the topic. The overall purpose of this approach is to promote as broad dissemination of information on sexuality to faculty as possible. This means that faculty will need opportunities to gain a theoretical knowledge about sexuality, to discuss and reflect on their attitudes and feelings concerning sexuality, and to incorporate sexual health care into their own practice of nursing and clinical teaching. Such faculty experiences need to be instigated before curriculum change is begun; likewise, ongoing faculty education on sexuality and sexual health care is essential.

When an introduction to sexuality and sexual health care for faculty is indicated, it might be presented as a one or two-day workshop or a short series of seminars. The purpose of this faculty education program is to introduce faculty to concepts of sexual development as a basis for their learning, as well as to introduce them to content on the nurse's role in sexual health care. In addition, faculty must be introduced to guidelines for providing sexual health care throughout each aspect of the nursing process—assessment, planning, intervention, and evaluation. Faculty need time to explore their feelings about sexuality content in general and about sexual health care in particular, or to express any doubts they may have concerning nursing's responsibility in this area. If this initial program is conducted by a nurse sex educator from outside the school of nursing, the faculty might be free to disclose their feelings and to question the opinions of a "specialist" with whom they have no close personal or professional association.

In four schools of nursing, where the author has served as resource person for initial faculty education on sexuality and sexual health care, a small group of faculty have volunteered to plan the subsequent process of incorporating such concepts into the curriculum. Their task is to lead the faculty through the sequential events as follows:

1. Review of the school's philosophy, purpose and objectives is paramount. Although it is likely that the introduction of content on sexuality will be compatible with a school's philosophy of nursing education, faculty discussion of this matter serves to confirm the appropriateness of including such content. Some faculty may be surprised to find a mandate in the philosophy *for* content on sexuality. Certainly any reference to concern for the total patient demands that sexual health care be expanded well beyond the realm of reproduction or venereal diseases. Should faculty find sexuality content incompatible with the school's philosophy, further study and possible revision is indicated. When program objectives are reviewed, faculty must be concerned with the explicitness of the sexual health component in the objectives. The more explicitly the sexual health care component is stated, the more accountable faculty and students must be for its viability. Program objectives referring to the physical, psychological, and sociological aspects of care might well be revised to directly include sexuality.

2. Review of course objectives and specific content is the next step of the incorporation process. Keeping the previously stated nine concepts of sexuality and sexual health care in mind, the faculty must identify the sexuality and sexual health care content included and gaps in that content. At this point, consultation might be indicated from persons well-versed in sexual health care. For example, faculty may need assistance to recognize the sexual implications associated with various illnesses. A course which focuses on the nursing care of persons with acute and chronic diseases of the cardiovascular system, for example, should reflect content related to all nine concepts of sexuality and sexual health care. The following content related to cardiovascular symptomology and sexuality is delineated as a sample of the content which would be expanded and included in one course on the nursing care of persons with cardiovascular illnesses:

Concept I. Cardiovascular patients, even those who are seriously ill, retain their sexuality, sexual role behaviors, and preferences for specific modes of sexual expression.

Concept II. The nurse must recognize the patient's state of physical sexual development and sexual health. Such understanding must build on knowledge of sexual differentiation/development presented in courses on anatomy, physiology, and growth and development, which usually are taught early in the nursing curriculum.

Concept III. Considering the patient's age and cardiovascular symptoms, what effect might there be on the person's total sexual development? If the patient is a small child, debilitating cardiovascular illness can interfere with the usual patterns of sexual identity development, identification and complementation experiences, and related sexual role development. Such interference obviously does not come from the direct effect of the cardiovascular pathology, rather it comes from the altered social milieu of a child who has a low energy level and who requires a protective environment. Such a child does not have the same freedom to interact vigorously with adults or peers in experiences crucial to sexual differentiation. Adults with cardiovascular disease who must alter their activity level are subject to changes in the usual adult sexual development related to sexual role behavior and physical sexual expression. Examples of and effects of such changes on individuals must be explored, as well as the effects of the illness on childbearing and rearing—a responsibility of the adult. Cardiovascular illness in the elderly can adversely interfere with those activities which the individual views as socially/sexually rewarding.

Concept IV. With the stress of cardiovascular disease, the body may have less cardiovascular reserve to expend in the sexual response cycle. Fatigue, fear of a heart attack, fear of death, pain, and shortness of breath, all may interfere through psychological mechanisms with the sexual response cycle. Some men experience difficulty in achieving an erection or ejaculation. Women may have inadequate vaginal lubrication or unsatisfying sexual encounters. In addition, persons of either sex are vulnerable to a lower libido when seriously ill. The stress of cardiovascular disease in some persons also affects their ability to carry out sex-coded role behaviors which may have been significant, such as work, housekeeping, social activities, and child-rearing.

Concept V. Love play and intercourse place an increased workload on the cardiovascular system. The safety of the cardiac, coronary, or hypertensive person engaging in physical sexual activity must be explored and guidelines to sexual education for the cardiovascular patient, as delineated in the literature, must be included in the curriculum.

Concept VI. The cardiovascular patient is vulnerable to adverse sexual effects from hospitalization and drug therapy. Obviously, these therapies are not to be negated, rather the nurse must be educated to minimize their potential trauma. Hospitalization, even intensive care settings, may be made less threatening to the sexual self when privacy needs, flexible visiting hours, and respect for the patient's dignity are maintained. Some drugs used in cardiovascular illness adversely affect sexuality. These must be identified, the information shared with the patient as appropriate, and when feasible, alterations made in the drug therapy program.

Concept VII. The nurse must identify those cardiovascular patients who are in crises concurrent with one of the natural life crises. Any acute cardiovascular illness during pubescence, pregnancy, or menopause, for example, will certainly deter individual sexual maturation which normally occurs in that period of time.

Concept VIII. A discussion of the community's view toward chronic illness, such as heart disease, and sexuality is indicated. Has the patient been conditioned to think of heart patients as asexual persons, or is the community milieu open to discussion of the sexual implications of illness?

Concept IX. In-depth discussion and clinical practice in the sexual health assessment specific to persons with heart disease is imperative. Sexual health intervention must emphasize education on sexuality. One aspect of that education may be to help the patient understand that sexual expression can be safely compatible with heart disease. The nurse must learn to evaluate with the patient his or her own sexual health care, so that the nurse can be responsive to additional or changing needs of the patient.

After content has been delineated, evaluation tools must be appropriately revised. Students, like faculty, must be held accountable for content on sexuality and sexual health care, which may otherwise be perceived as "interesting" but nonessential content.

3. Incorporation of sexual health care concepts into clinical nursing experiences is the next step. It is a more difficult process. Not only must clinical objectives and evaluation reflect such concepts, but also guides for nursing assessment, for nursing care plans, for interactional analysis, and for recording must be revised to incorporate sexual health care. It becomes readily apparent that those faculty who feel comfortable with their own sexuality and who have a knowledge of sexual health care will more likely select patient care assignments that clearly demonstrate the sexual health component of nursing care. Likewise, such faculty will promote student learning in this area from most patient-care situations. Student experiences, needless to say, are influenced by the faculty perception of sexuality and sexual health care. However, when objectives, evaluation, and learning tools specifically include the sexual health care component, faculty peer review and student questions will promote accountability and may be the catalyst to faculty requests for more education in this area. Library and media resources on sexuality and sexual health care must be reviewed, expanded, and readily available to faculty and students.

4. Repeated ongoing faculty learning experiences as related to sexuality and sexual health care are essential. Faculty turnover alone necessitates a continuing educational program, for it cannot be assumed that new faculty, even recent graduates, have knowledge in this area. Faculty who previously saw no need for such education may alter their view and participate in educational opportunities at a later time. Even those faculty who participated from the inception of the sexuality program return to learn from a new perspective; many times they move from an intellectual learning to reappraisal of their attitudes.

Incorporation of sexual health concepts into the nursing curriculum is a perpetual process. Monitoring and evaluation of the content by the faculty themselves in theory and in clinical supervision is essential for its viability. Careful rechecking against the basic concepts and with updated research and theories is indicated. As faculty gain comfort and confidence in this area, they may instigate intensive affective learning experiences for students such as two- or three-day attitudinal reappraisal experiences to supplement, but not replace, the content incorporated throughout the curriculum. Elective courses which permit in-depth study of a selected aspect of sexual health care with related clinical experiences should be made available to those students who wish to pursue this aspect of nursing care.

REFERENCES

1. Mims FH: Sexual health education and counseling. Nurs Clin North Am 10:519–528, 1975
2. Megenity J: A plea for sex education in nursing curriculums. Am J Nurs 75:1171, 1975
3. Education in Human Sexuality for Health Practitioners. WHO Chron 29:49–54, 1975
4. Masters WH, Johnson VE: Human Sexual Response. Boston, Little, Brown, 1966
5. Money J, Ehrhardt AA: Man and Woman, Boy and Girl. New York, New American Library, 1974
6. Green R: Sexual Identity Conflict in Children and Adults. New York, Basic Books, 1974
7. Zubin, J, Money J (eds): Contemporary Sexual Behavior: Critical Issues in the 1970s. Baltimore, Johns Hopkins University Press, 1973
8. Wagner NN: Perspectives on Human Sexuality. New York, Behavioral Publications, 1974
9. Offer D, Simon W: Stages of sexual development, in Kaplan HI, Freedman AM (eds): The Sexual Experience. Baltimore, Williams & Wilkins, 1976, p 128–141
10. Money J, Ehrhardt AA: Man and Woman, Boy and Girl. New York, New American Library, 1974, p 14
10a. Money J: Sex roles and sex-coded roles. Written for the Sixth Annual Award, American Association of Sex Educators and Counselors, Washington, D.C., 1976
11. Kaplan HS: The New Sex Therapy. New York, Brunner/Mazel, 1974, p 75–85
12. Woods NF:Human Sexuality in Health and Illness. St. Louis, CV Mosby, 1975
13. Tyler EA: Sex and medical illness, in Sadock BJ, Kaplan HI (eds): The Sexual Experience. Baltimore, Williams & Wilkins, 1976, p 313–318
14. Masters WH, Johnson VE: Human Sexual Response. Boston, Little, Brown, 1966, p 141–168
15. McCary JL: Human Sexuality. New York, D VanNostrand, 1973, p 92–100
16. Sadock BJ, Kaplan HI, Freedman AM (eds): The Sexual Experience. Baltimore, Williams & Wilkins, 1976, p 128–181
17. Athanasiou R. A review of public attitudes on sexual issues, in Zubin J, Money J (eds): Contemporary Sexual Behavior: Critical Issues in the 1970s. Baltimore, The Johns Hopkins University Press, 1973, p 361–390
18. McCary JL: Human Sexuality. New York, D VanNostrand, 1973, p 271–325
19. Hanson EI: Sexual Health Care in the Nursing Process. A film produced by Directions for Education in Nursing Via Technology. Detroit, Wayne State University, 1976
20. Lief HI, Payne T: Sexuality—knowledge and attitudes. Am J Nurs 75:2026–2029, 1975
21. Fontaine KL: Human sexuality: Faculty knowledge and attitudes. Nurs Outlook 24:174–176, 1976

22. Renshaw DC: Nurses need formal sex education. J Nurs Educ 12:16–19, 1975
23. Woods NF, Mandetta A: Changes in students' knowledge and attitudes following a course in human sexuality: Report of a pilot study. Nursing Research 24:10–15, 1975
24. Yeaworth R, Mims F: Interdisciplinary education as an influence system. Nursing Outlook 21:696–699, 1973
25. Mims FH, Brown L, Lubow R: Human sexuality course evaluation. Nurs Res 25:187–191, 1976
26. Mandetta AF, Woods NF: Learning about human sexuality—a course model. Nurs Outlook 22:525–527, 1974

PART V

Some Sample Programs

Norman Rosenzweig
F. Paul Pearsall

Introduction

This section contains much more than some samples of representative programs of education in human sexuality. It presents the historical evolution of human sexuality programs, the pedagogical problems encountered, the philosophical objectives, the search for successful methodologies, the trials, errors, and successes, and how each learned from the others. Here are the original pioneers: The Institute for Sex Research, the Reproductive Biology Institute, the National Sex Forum. Here are the early innovators and trend setters: Johns Hopkins, the University of California at San Francisco, the University of Minnesota. Here are the programs that modified, adapted, and learned from the others, and added their own special contributions: Northwestern, Loyola, Vancouver, Stony Brook, and our own program at Sinai Hospital of Detroit.

While the programs differ in setting, format, content, methodology, style, target audiences, and in other respects, the reader will be impressed by the common elements. The editors believe that no educator should attempt to develop a sexuality program without first attending other programs as a participant. This section should help the reader to decide which programs would most suit his or her own needs.

The section concludes with an outline of our program in the Department of Psychiatry at Sinai Hospital of Detroit. Our chapter is offered as an illustration of several suggestions made in the book, and is designed not only to describe our program but to illustrate some sample steps we feel important in establishing a program. It is our sincere hope that the reader may benefit from our experience, as we have so benefited from the experience of others.

Ruth Beasley

17
Training the Educator in Human Sexuality: Eight Years of Human Sexuality Programs for Professionals

INTRODUCTION

The Institute for Sex Research, founded by Alfred C. Kinsey and currently directed by Paul H. Gebhard, has been conducting a program in human sexuality each summer since 1970. In the course of those eight years, we have seen professional attitudes, educational opportunities, and the public demand for trained personnel change and grow rapidly.

Our experience has been with designing and evaluating an intensive, short (usually 10-day) educational experience which is geared toward the individual who has already achieved a working degree. There will be some differences, therefore, between the Institute's program and those which are part of an ongoing academic curriculum. Because our program attempts to provide broad coverage of basic topics as well as sociosexual issues and attitudes, there will also be differences from those short programs which focus on only one topic or area.

BACKGROUND

From 1970 until 1972 the program was designed to provide training for medical educators, primarily psychiatrists, in order to facilitate the introduction of the subject of human sexuality into medical school curricula. Other professionals were admitted to the program, but attended separate sessions which took a more general approach to sex education.

In 1973 the program goals and sessions were completely integrated for all participants, and individuals from the fields of social work, nursing, psychology, and related service professions were actively encouraged to attend. However, until 1976 the focus of the program was still to train individuals who were teaching faculty in medical or graduate schools with the long-term goal of curriculum change.

Paralleling the societal changes and increased public demand for information and service, the goals of the program have now been expanded to include the training of individuals currently employed in a service capacity, such as a community mental health center or a physical rehabilitation hospital, rather than only in an academic setting. Obviously, as the program itself has changed, so have the content and the types of individuals who attend.

By the end of the 1976 program we had trained 745 individuals from nearly every academic discipline, widely varying work settings, and from many foreign countries. Due to the reputation of the program, we are now forced to limit enrollment to a maximum of 135 participants and can be selective about admitting a highly involved multidisciplinary group which helps to promote an active information exchange.

Although our program consists of only a few days, participants continue their contact with the Institute via the Information Service which provides a long-distance access to the extensive research collections. Through our follow-up surveys we are gratified to discover that a great deal of information can be compressed into a short time span and be translated into a measurable impact on the participants' professional skills. The Institute continues to feel, therefore, that there is a definite need for continuing education programs such as ours which supplement other educational approaches in the area of human sexuality.

FORMAT

Although some of the subjects covered have changed over the years, the basic format of the program has remained much the same since 1970.

One of the early planning decisions was to use the best speakers available for each subject area. In looking back over various elements which have contributed to the success of the program, this one must be given great credit. For the Institute staff to admit that they did not have in-depth knowledge of all aspects of sexual behavior required both courage and a commitment to a level of quality which persists to this day.

The program schedule is quite full and can be exhausting. Each of the week days begins at 9 A.M. and consists of at least three two-hour presentations, with most days also having a two-hour evening session. The sessions themselves are deliberately varied between traditional lectures and panel discussions, supplemented with the use of audio-visual materials as appropriate. All presenters are encouraged to allow a significant amount of time for audience questions. For the last five years we have not scheduled more than one presentation at the same time to avoid forcing participants to choose between two lectures of potential value. Even with morning and afternoon coffee breaks, the general effect of sitting in a meeting room 8 hours a day for 10 days can be physically tiring.

Due to the dual emphasis on admitting participants with widely varying interests and the provision of time for question and answer sessions, few of the sessions consist of simply an uninterrupted didactic lecture. Each year the audience has quickly absorbed the concept that it enhances the program experience to have participants raise questions relevant to their current interests or practices. In addition to promoting an atmosphere of free exchange with presenters, the program format is also designed to encourage an extensive exchange of information among the participants themselves.

In evaluating the early programs, we noted that a question dealing with the value of exchanging problems and solutions with peers was one of the highest rated aspects of the program; but we also observed that some people experienced difficulty entering informal discussion groups or joining groups during meal time—the periods of greatest exchange. In 1975 we began to schedule a concrete period late each afternoon which we labelled a "hospitality hour." Institute staff and visiting lecturers attend and deliberately attempt to draw individuals into discussion groups and promote dinner groupings which will include any individuals who appear to be simply too shy to invite themselves. After the first few days, nearly all participants actively engage in this exchange behavior without assistance.

Even though many of the lectures are given by guest experts, the Institute staff attends as many of the program sessions as possible. In evaluation comments, the ready accessibility of the staff seems to be very important in urging participants to raise questions not being covered in the formal program. Visiting lecturers are also asked to attend all social functions and to make themselves available for informal discussions. Some time is also built into the schedule for participants to visit the Institute's research collections during their stay. Many past participants have subsequently designed research projects and returned to work in the collections after their attendance at a training program.

The final integral part of the program format is a sexual attitude workshop which is conducted in small groups (no more than eight people per group) and led by facilitators skilled in both small group processes and dealing with sexual topics. Unlike some other attitude workshops with a focus on discovering or expanding one's own sexuality, these groups are charged with focusing on how the individual participant's sexual attitudes carry over into their professional performance. Until 1973, these small groups met each evening and discussed the topics covered that day. After investigating the format of similar workshops, however, the small group sessions were condensed into an intensive two-day program conducted on the weekend six days after the beginning of the workshop. Evaluations indicated that the small groups were needed earlier in the program in order to deal more promptly with emerging concerns and problems, and consequently the entire schedule was changed in 1975 so that the attitude reassessment workshop now begins on the third day of the total program.

PROGRAM DEVELOPMENT

Surely after eight years of experience with a program, one would expect to be able to state succinctly exactly how to go about designing an adequate continuing education program in human sexuality. For an excellent review of the "state-of-the-art" in continuing education, and for an acceptable reason of why such a simple formula for success is not yet possible, I refer you to Armand Lauffer's recent book.[1] The following sections will follow the eminently sensible procedural steps proposed by Lauffer; we will then discuss the Institute's experience with each procedure.

Problem Identification and Needs Assessment

Prior to 1970, the Institute staff and others in the fields of sex research and sex education had discussed the need for more adequately trained health professionals. At that period, most concern was focused on physicians, particularly psychiatrists, who had educational responsibilities in medical schools. Fortunately, this need was also recognized by the National Institute of Mental Health which awarded contracts to the Institute to conduct such training programs in 1970, 1971, and 1972. At this stage, no formal survey or needs assessment investigation was undertaken.

By 1973 the interests of NIMH and the concerns of active leaders had begun to include teachers of social work, nursing, counseling, and other related health-delivery services among those groups needing training. This shift in focus has now gone further to emphasize training for personnel actually working with the public, especially with populations who rarely have access to highly-skilled professionals such as psychiatrists.

During this gradual change in problem focus and needs, the primary sources of information were individuals active in the field of sex, health and mental health agency officials, and our own program participants via their evaluations and suggestions. The problem statement was also expanded to include a research component which would conduct follow-up surveys and assess program impact; at this stage, funding was put on a grant basis to allow for more continuity and flexibility to respond to changing needs.

Building a Structure of Relationships

Depending on the institution about to embark upon a continuing education program, varying formal and informal structures can be established. In the case of the Institute, most of our external relationships already existed and mainly needed only to be expanded to include conducting training programs in addition to our existing functions. Obviously, we formalized new contacts within the training branch of our research funding agency. Since our Institute is affiliated with Indiana University, it was necessary to consult with all relevant offices in that structure well before any public announcements were made. Due to the Institute's stature in the subject area and our constant communication with other researchers and centers, contacting potential guest lecturers and soliciting valuable suggestions have posed no problem.

However, little thought was given initially to any change in internal structure. For the first two years, responsibility for the program was assigned to one of the research staff; then, until 1976, primary responsibility was assigned to the head of the Information Service. In both cases these were individuals who were already carrying heavy commitments for other important projects. We tried various solutions, such as assigning extra clerical assistance and creating a committee of senior staff to participate in decision making, but the magnitude of the work involved and the spread of the work throughout the entire year, eventually led to a revision of the internal structure. Currently, the program is directed by a year round part-time administrative staff member, with adequate clerical support, who serves as chairperson of the summer program committee composed of senior staff. The training program function has evolved into a separate element within the Institute with clearly delineated relationships with other units.

Formulating Objectives, Means, and Strategies

The Institute has never gone through a formal exercise of listing specific objectives, means, or strategies clearly separate from other planning processes; these steps have always been subsumed within statements of needs or program goals. All of these elements have been discussed at length, however, both internally and with external individuals.

These elements of the planning process have also been affected by the gradual changes inherent in the total program. For example, as the focus changed from training academics to training individuals in applied settings, we investigated possible new avenues for advertising the program to attract a different group of participants. This resulted in placing announcements in a greatly expanded list of journals plus acquiring different mailing lists. Concurrently, guest lecturers were also selected from individuals in applied settings rather than from strictly research settings.

The emphasis in this step should be on the consumer, both before and after the program. Make the program description as clear and honest as you can so that participants arrive with a set of goals which match the program goals as closely as possible. During the program itself, make yourself receptive to informal discussions which may allow for minor corrections or additions while participants are still in residence. After the program, take both solicited and unsolicited evaluations and suggestions seriously if you plan to offer another program.

Implementation

The implementation of program development is the one step that truly does become easier with experience. Basically, one should be realistic about all resources available, including staff, equipment, finances, facilities, and other concrete items that will carry your program plans to fruition and result in glowing evaluations.

Actual implementation begins months in advance, with reserving meeting facilities, discussing housing arrangements with local hotels, and compiling information that participants will need to survive for ten days in a small college community. The Institute quickly learned that we did not have the staff to make housing reservations for individual participants or to provide transportation from the airport; when one promises such services and does not carry them out efficiently, participants begin the program with a disappointed attitude which rarely improves. Our solution is to provide extensive information on transportation, housing, restaurants, local entertainment, or sports facilities, and other local vagaries such as weather, and to let participants make their own arrangements.

Attention to operational details are noticed and appreciated by participants. From the registration process to the final evaluation, the goal should be smooth efficiency that intrudes upon the training process as little as possible. Obviously, if the convention center's air conditioning breaks down in July, there is little you can do; but you can make sure that extra bulbs for various audio-visual projectors are readily available.

The Institute's program depends heavily on guest lecturers, skilled small-group facilitators, and adequate staffing. Salaries, travel expenses, and honoraria add up quickly. We charge a registration fee which covers our program costs, but we are aware that not all programs can assess fees high enough to provide renowned lecturers. Therefore, it is imperative to be realistic in all of the implementation areas throughout the planning process in order to provide the best program possible with the available resources.

CHANGES IN CURRICULUM CONTENT

Some changes in subject coverage are readily apparent from a review of the topics presented at each of the eight programs since 1970. Lectures on anatomy, reproduction, and contraception are no longer being offered. Sessions devoted to sociosexual issues or controversies emerged in the fourth program and continue through the current program. Highly specific presentations about the sexual problems of special populations began in the sixth program utilizing 25 separate sessions; in the current program the number of sessions devoted to these topics has been reduced, but each session has been expanded to cover a broader range of problems.

Other changes are less obvious from simply reading the list of titles, for example, the many entries listed as heterosexual behavior. In early programs, heterosexual behavior was covered in separate sessions (e.g., solitary sexual behavior, petting, and coitus). In 1973, all the relevant behaviors were combined into one general lecture which basically summarized the more extensive data review of preceding years. By 1974, however, the heterosexual behavior lecture changed dramatically by dropping the previous emphasis on reading data summaries and moving toward an emphasis on the implications of existing sexual behavior for professionals. Entirely new subtopics, such as sexuality of the elderly, were also added.

The use of films and other audio-visual materials has also changed. During the first several programs, films were usually integrated into lectures at the end of the didactic presentation and preceding the question and answer portion of the session. For the past three years, however, many of the participants have already seen most of the films and other materials available to the field of sex education, and we have stopped showing such materials during lecture sessions in order to maintain audience interest and to use the time saved for further discussion. We still integrate unique or recently produced materials into lecture sessions, but the more common materials are shown in long time-blocks and considered as optional sessions provided mainly for those participants who have not yet seen the materials.

What forces have generated such changes over the course of eight years? Some external factors, such as changes in the emphasis of funding agencies and general public demands for services, have been discussed earlier. Change generated by formal evaluation processes will be covered in the next section of this chapter.

Less obvious sources of change also exist, although they can rarely be directly documented. The individuals who now attend the program are different from those who attended in the early 1970s. Although a cursory review of educational levels would lead one to assume that having more Masters-level participants than MDs and PhDs, as in the past, would necessitate providing more general coverage of topics; the reverse is actually true. Most current participants demonstrate a solid background in the basic literature of the field, and some have had either college courses or attended other workshops before arriving at our program. They definitely do not need to hear reviews of research findings, unless the studies are very recent or not yet published.

The majority of those who attend now are not in academic settings with goals related to curriculum development. Even though they hold degrees from many different disciplines, most have a crucial element in common: they are employed in jobs which are literally "on the firing line." Their major goals in attending the program are related to gaining information and skills which will help them answer the questions of their clients, patients, cases, parishioners, or peer group. Most do not attend under the illusion that they can become skilled sex therapists in ten days; they simply know that they must add competency in order to provide adequate service within their current job setting.

Another source of change is internally generated. Staff members are exposed to new publications, research in progress, and trends throughout the year. Suggestions for new topics and speakers flow to the summer program committee constantly. An infrequently mentioned factor is also staff boredom; frankly, we like to experiment with new topics and lecturers related to our own interests and projects. Since staff participation and enthusiasm is communicated to the participants, this source of change can also be valid.

Although the previous eight years of training programs reveal enormous ranges in topics, I have no doubt that a review eight years hence will document further changes in content, format, participants, materials, and approaches. Successful planners will, in fact, expect and welcome these future changes in the field.

Monitoring, Feedback, and Evaluation

The Institute program has progressed from a single, anonymous final evaluation to a more sophisticated evaluation process which actually begins with the initial application form. As we now have participants from many backgrounds and job settings, we currently ask each person to code their evaluations so that we can investigate any differences between educational or occupational groups. Each applicant supplies the usual demographic information and completes an extensive scale of goals for attending the program. Each program event is also evaluated for content, style, and contribution toward individual program goals. A final extensive overall evaluation is given to each participant for return after a month. Although most of the forms are constructed with set scales, each section includes at least one open-ended question. Follow-up surveys are conducted by mail.

Formal evaluation procedures are necessary, but not at the exclusion of informal feedback opportunities. For this reason, the senior staff should be readily available for informal discussions throughout the program. Unsolicited letters, both favorable and unfavorable, should be reviewed by all staff. It has been our recent practice to forward summaries of evaluation data and comments to guest lecturers as well.

The key concept is that the staff must demonstrate to participants that their evaluation efforts will be taken seriously and will result in actual program change whenever possible. One technique the Institute employs is to send the schedule for forthcoming programs to past participants so that they can see substantive changes. In addition, all letters, phone calls, or other communications are acknowledged and full information is supplied regarding the individual's suggestions or complaints.

Evaluation by all levels of internal staff is important to program development as well. A formal "debriefing session" is held immediately after each program so that problems can be discussed and detailed notes made for planning the following year's program. These sessions range from input on subject content and lecturers to suggestions on minute administrative details that program participants would not even notice. Again, the program staff must convey that changes are being actively solicited and welcomed.

PROBLEMS

Regardless of the preceding neat categories of program development and overview of how the Institute has dealt with the process over the course of eight years, problems still occur. Participants arrive with goals widely divergent from the stated program goals and become disgruntled. Guest lecturers miss planes. A lecturer propounds a radical departure from accepted theory, and the audience reacts strongly without careful listening. A running argument develops between differing schools of thought and consumes several question and answer sessions. One speaker runs over the time allotment and puts the whole day's schedule behind.

The only advice is simply to plan carefully, allocate resources realistically, monitor constantly, be available to hear complaints, evaluate as thoroughly as possible, and be highly receptive to change. In effect, the program process represents a full cycle when it is offered on a regular basis. Many of our most lasting decisions have been made during one program in reaction to a problem, even though it could not be implemented until the following year.

A problem not yet raised in this chapter and only recently faced by many of the educators in this field is that the subject of human sexuality itself generates an atmosphere conducive to tensions, fears, concerns, and behaviors that simply do not occur in continuing education programs for other subject areas. This must be recognized and given serious attention by the program staff, even though they themselves may have become enured to the very normal reactions to being suddenly immersed in lectures, films, slides, and other materials rarely seen by most professionals. These reactions must not only be accepted; they should be expected and openly discussed with the participants. Because the Institute program is intensive and most of the participants are from out of town, the atmosphere here is perhaps more obvious than in programs which are part of a curriculum offered over a semester within the trainee's home setting.

BENEFITS

Why would an established research institution plunge into a continuing education program and then invest extensive effort in it for eight years if all the above problems exist? Because there are appreciable benefits that outweigh the expenditure of resources. Although the Institute wished to continue to consider its research projects as its primary contribution to the field of human sexual behavior, the field itself demanded an expanded role.

Now that the staff has survived eight programs, we are beginning to appreciate the benefits of continuing education activities for our own staff. The opportunity to interact with people in applied settings adds a further dimension to our research. Hearing informational needs articulated generates new research ideas. Visiting with guest lecturers allows us to exchange prepublication information. Listening to audience questions gives us insight into how research findings are being disseminated and interpreted.

Not all of the benefits are reactive or passive. We now have an additional avenue for expressing and acting upon new research trends or up-coming problems we see facing the field as a whole. To be able to participate creatively in activities such as these, permits the Institute to make a much richer and more diversified contribution to the development of sex research.

REFERENCES

1. Lauffer A: The Practice of Continuing Education in the Human Services. New York, McGraw-Hill, 1977

Raymond W. Waggoner

18
Training and Ethics of the Sexual Therapist: The Education Program at the Reproductive Biology Research Foundation

In the early 1950s William Masters began his hegemonic study of sexual physiology, and as a result of this very important research, he published a book with Virginia Johnson entitled *Human Sexual Response*. This work in turn led to the development of a carefully designed treatment approach for sexual dysfunction. As the treatment program developed, descriptions of it were published in a number of carefully written papers, and eventually appeared in Masters' and Johnson's second book, *Human Sexual Inadequacy*.

Largely as a result of the pioneering work of Freud, Kinsey, and Masters and Johnson, sex is no longer a forbidden discussion topic. During the last few years, what has been called a sexual revolution has produced significant changes in our cultural pattern, with various aspects of sex discussed freely in the public media.

Kinsey's work has proven to be very valuable, largely from a statistical point of view, and also because it brought into the open many of the problems associated with various kinds of sexual activity. His information was obtained entirely by specially trained interviewers and his findings revealed the disparity between the way people actually behaved sexually and the social mythology surrounding sexual conduct. Masters' and Johnson's work is based on factual research including direct observation and measurement of sexual activities, so that their book, *Human Sexual Response,* contains information which dispels many old myths about sexual function found in the literature, such as the differentiation between vaginal and clitoral orgasm.

The Masters and Johnson approach to the treatment of sexual dysfunction demonstrated that long periods of treatment were not necessary to achieve good results, and that most cases could, in fact, be treated in a relatively brief period of time. Subsequently, numerous clinics for the treatment of sexual dysfunction were established. (Masters has estimated that perhaps as many as 5000 sex therapy clinics are in existence.) Unfortunately a number of these programs are staffed by untrained personnel. Obviously, in the few years since publication of *Human Sexual Inadequacy,* it would be impossible for such a large number of clinics to be staffed by well trained personnel. However, from the first, Masters and Johnson were concerned about proper training of sexual therapists, and they initiated their own educational program.

PILOT TRAINING PROGRAM

A pilot program was established at the Reproductive Biology Research Foundation (RBRF) in 1971 to train dual sex teams in the rapid treatment of sexual dysfunction.[1] Since Masters and Johnson were not certain that their techniques could successfully be learned by others, the pilot training program sought to determine whether results obtained by trained teams were in the same range of success as those obtained by Masters and Johnson. If comparable success could be demonstrated, treatment of sexual inadequacy and marital conflict could become more readily available, and the training of additional sex therapy teams would be definitely indicated.

Emily Mudd and I were asked to serve as consultants in setting up this program. At first, we felt that a male–female team could be trained in a month. We soon discovered, however, that this was inadequate. The training period was increased to six weeks, which also proved to be too short a time for a satisfactory understanding of the Masters and Johnson method, and this type of training program was then discontinued.

To understand the complexity of training a team in the treatment of sexual dysfunction, one must realize that at the RBRF single individuals are not treated. Since Masters and Johnson are convinced that sexual dysfunction is the product of an interaction and there is no uninvolved partner, treatment is conducted only with couples, because inevitably the attitude and behavior of one partner has a significant effect upon the other. The treatment program thus involves four people: the dual sex-therapy team and the couple who are being treated.

Criteria for accepting trainees were based on the initial team approach of Masters and Johnson. One team member must be a physician who would be willing and able to undertake the complete physical examination of both patients. The other team member should have a degree in nursing or one of the behavioral sciences such as psychology or social work. In the initial screening, candidates were selected from diverse geographical areas, from both academic settings and private practice, with special preference given to those who had an academic appointment. Potential candidates were then asked to complete an information form and to send this form and a curriculum vitae to the Foundation's Review Committee, consisting of the Director and Co-Director of Training, the Foundation Director, and a selected staff member. Applicants whose credentials appeared satisfactory were invited to visit the Foundation to become familiar with its format and to enable the training staff to interview the team as individuals and as a working unit. The interviewers' impressions of each applicant's attitude, values, goals, and personality, as well as the interaction of the team, were recorded.

Of those interviewed, six teams were selected. Males in the six teams included four board-certified psychiatrists and two board-certified obstetricians-gynecologists. Female team members included three nurses, one anthropologist, one social worker, and one psychiatrist. Four of the trainee teams were husband and wife and two were not.

Since the co-directors could be present only part-time, it was necessary to have permanent staff constantly responsible for the trainees, and we felt it was important that this staff represent both the female and male points of view. Virginia Johnson and Marshall Shearer, a staff psychiatrist, accepted this responsibility, and other members of the permanent staff gave significant assistance.

Trainees were expected to have a thorough knowledge of both *Human Sexual Response* and *Human Sexual Inadequacy* prior to starting their training. Invariably, we found that the trainees' knowledge of sexual physiology was limited, and additional attention had to be given to teaching sexual physiology.

With the patient's written permission, all interviews are tape recorded. Trainees were oriented to the treatment method by listening for a day or two to recorded staff interviews at various stages of the treatment process. Then each trainee was assigned to work with a permanent staff member of the opposite sex, and after they had treated two or more patient units, two trainees were assigned as a team to treat a patient unit. Every interview by a trainee was recorded and also monitored from another room by staff supervisors. This method provided material for later supervision discussion, and protected the patients by permitting interruption of the interview by office phone if necessary.

RESPONSE TO THE TRAINING PROGRAM

We found that there were both advantages and disadvantages if the trainee team were husband and wife. The number of teams was obviously too small to come to definite conclusions concerning the value of married versus unmarried teams. Training of dual sex teams, especially husband and wife, is incredibly more difficult than training a single individual, because of the inevitable complexity of interacting factors. With the positive interrelationship of husband and wife, there was a tendency for one or the other, usually the wife, to retreat from a true peer relationship and to assume a secondary role, which is not consonant with the concept of a dual sex team in which each member has equal status and responsibility. On the other hand, there appeared to be certain positive advantages to the husband-wife team whose previously established forms of communication were helpful in the therapeutic situation.

All trainees had some difficulty with the two initial history interviews. Those with a nursing or behavioral sciences background seemed to have greater difficulty than those whose training and experience included the concept of a structured but open-ended interview. Trainees with a background in obstetrics-gynecology, social work, or psychiatry had no difficulty with this concept. Gynecologists tended to elicit a great deal of factual material with little or no information about how the patient reacted emotionally to life experiences, whether sexual or nonsexual in nature. On the other hand, the psychiatrists tended to ask questions about the meaning of historical events in many areas in a patient's life, but not in sexual areas. For example, if a man reported that he was unable to have an erection the first time he attempted intercourse, it was unusual if the patient was asked how he felt, or what explanation he gave himself, or how he perceived the reaction of his female partner.

All trainees had a great deal of difficulty following the development and progression of the sexual distress. This was unexpected in view of the fact that candidates had been screened to determine that they were able to deal comfortably with sexual problems, and in most instances, their professional background embodied the concept that, to be understood, the course of an illness must be traced from its onset. They did not pursue material in the sexual area with the kind of professional curiosity that physicians use daily in regard to other disabilities. They seemed content to establish the fact that sex in the beginning of marriage may or may not have been adequate and that now a sexual dysfunction existed, without establishing when the difficulty began, what explanation the patient himself gave, or what he and his wife had done to attempt to correct the situation. The trainees naturally are a product of our society, and as such, evidence some of its sexual conditioning. This was a contributing factor to their anxiety early in training. Anxiety about the topic of sex seemed to be relatively nonexistent by the third week.

The treatment process is specific to each type of sexual distress and is tailored to the individual needs of the patients. Trainees tended to overgeneralize their learning experience from one disorder to another or from one patient to another. The concept of pacing a patient through the course of treatment was one that seemed entirely new to the trainees, and no one grasped more than an appreciation of this concept during the training period. For example, the concept of pacing the patient's physiological sexual appetite was new to the trainees.

Almost all couples seen in treatment at the Foundation have a communication problem of varying degree. Certain couples would not have had sexual difficulty if their communication had been adequate. Consequently, it was important to teach trainees how to encourage patients to communicate at all levels, both verbal and nonverbal.

All trainees had difficulty with the concept of the role of the therapist vis-a-vis the co-therapist. The psychiatrist understandably had more trouble in sorting out these roles than any of the other trainees. Most of the psychiatrists had experience in treating couples as the sole therapist. It was difficult for trainees to understand that they must adhere to the basic concept of the male therapist representing and being responsible to the male patient, while the female therapist had a similar relationship to the female patient. If these roles become blurred, major transference difficulties, misunderstandings by both patient and therapist, and lack of communication may result. As these roles are adhered to, transference difficulties can be handled or, in large part, avoided.

The overriding trainee response was anxiety. It is understandable and to be expected that these professionally equipped men and women, many of whom had been engaged in active clinical practice for several years, would find their role of learner both new and difficult. The experience of having each interview monitored inevitably provoked anxiety. Feelings of resistance and irritation produce ambivalence toward the program.

The psychiatrists experienced anxiety when they recognized that they had to unlearn some psychiatric patterns, particularly with regard to the co-therapist role, and that they also had to provide specific education about the nature of sexual functions to their patients. Other trainees experienced anxiety when they realized that they were dealing with feelings and emotions and using psychotherapeutic principles with which they were unfamiliar. This was especially true for female trainees whose anxiety might focus on their relationship with the male co-therapist. Some female trainees tried to deal with the inequality between team members by assuming equality, others by denying their skills and withdrawing, and others by taking on a gross air of superiority. Such struggles sometimes resulted in depression, but the most common reaction was anxiety. Such anxiety was undoubtedly augmented by the phenomenon of information overload which occurred in the initial brief training courses.

It is a recognized tenet in both medicine and the behavioral sciences that a trainee will take longer to treat a patient or accomplish a given procedure than an experienced expert. However, patients coming to the Foundation had agreed on a two-week period for treatment, and frequently the extra time needed was not available. This problem created additional anxiety in both trainees and supervisors.

During the last phase of their training when trainees began to work with each other as co-therapists, the anxiety associated with problems of working with a co-therapist resurfaced with renewed intensity. In addition, the dynamics of the relationship between co-therapist trainees and between trainees and staff supervisors were thrown into bold relief. The interactional dynamics between co-therapists reflected the dynamics of their overall relationship, including the relationship of their marriage in those instances where the trainees were husband and wife. Anxiety was generated as trainees became aware of these new relationships or attempted to avoid such awareness. These interactional dynamics were sometimes detrimental to the progress of therapy.

It is important to try to analyze the factors involved. Much of the difficulty is associated with anxiety in both trainees and training staff. Staff anxiety tended to accentuate trainee anxiety. Furthermore, during the last two weeks of training when trainees functioned as a treatment unit, small problems in the treatment program could not be immediately corrected. Discussion of these with the trainees following the therapy session further accentuated anxiety in the trainee couple.

As a result of experience with this pilot training program, and because of the significant expense involved, short-term training of four to six weeks was abandoned and a new system was instituted in which a trainee couple spends at least a year, and preferably two or three years, at the Foundation, where they function as junior staff members.

ETHICAL CONSIDERATIONS

The remarkable proliferation of therapy programs in the United States has caused concern about the ethics of treatment among many well qualified practitioners in the sex therapy field. An important consideration is the proper qualifications of therapists who treat sexual dysfunction. In January 1976 the Reproductive Biology Research Foundation held a very valuable and successful meeting on the history and ethics of the treatment of sexual dysfunction. Noted psychiatrists and sex therapists discussed various aspects of the problem, and their presentations will be published.

A number of organizations have been formed to develop standards for therapy and to emphasize the ethical standards which must be part of the training of sex therapists. In 1975 the President of the Michigan Psychiatric Society appointed a committee to study this problem. Their recommendations were presented to the Council of the Society, and copies were then sent to the American Psychiatric Association and the

Michigan State Medical Society. The Michigan State Medical Society's Committee on Scientific Educational Affairs suggested some changes which were incorporated in the report. In its final form, the following standards were proposed:

1. The therapist should possess knowledge of and experience in the application of basic psychotherapy treatment programs and principles of human learning. This knowledge should be demonstrated by the possession of a degree in a health care field.
2. In those instances where a physician serves as one member of a dual team, the co-therapist should have had supervised therapy training, and the therapists should be certified or licensed or both by the State in their respective health care fields.
3. It is important for the therapist to be personally secure and confident of his or her knowledge of sexual physiology and cognizant of current research findings in the field. This means that the therapist should be able to assume an authoritative role in counseling with patients in order to obtain the best results.
4. It is essential that therapists have knowledge of emotional disorders and appropriate treatment, combined with the ability to determine appropriate referral and to recognize the limits of his or her own range of interventive competence.
5. The therapist's background should include sufficient knowledge of and ability to work with various aspects of sexual distress including communication difficulties, metabolic limitations, neurological, gynecological, urological, and other physically based incapacities, as well as the consequences of the aging process.
6. The therapist should conduct or require a physical examination of patients to be treated for sexual distress and be able to interpret the results of this examination to the patient.
7. Physical sexual intimacy should be limited to the interaction between the patient and his or her partner of choice in private. There should be no physical interaction between the therapist and his or her patients at any time during the treatment program or in the follow-up period.
8. The therapist should be available to the patient for help following the intensive phase of the treatment program.
9. The therapist should very carefully protect the privacy and confidentiality of patients at all times.[2]

An obvious conclusion from this discussion of training and ethical considerations is that the sex counselor and sex educator must have many characteristics in common. Knowledge of sexual physiology and psychology is vitally important for both. It is to be hoped that it may be possible in the not too distant future to develop educational programs which will aid in the prevention of sexual dysfunction.

REFERENCES

1. Waggoner RW, Mudd E, Shearer M: Pilot program in the training of dual sex teams for the rapid treatment of sexual dysfunction: A pilot program. Psychiatric Annals, 3:61–76, 1973
2. Michigan Psychiatric Society Position Statement: On qualifications for therapists in the treatment of sexual dysfunction, MPS Newsletter, 19(4):4, 1977

Ted McIlvenna

19
The National Sex Forum Model

INTRODUCTION

The National Sex Forum model, known as the Sexual Attitude Restructuring (SAR) Process, was developed over a period of seven years in response to the need for objective, factual, and relevant information for persons in the helping professions. The initial funding and sponsorship came from the Glide Urban Center, an agency of the United Methodist Church, in cooperation with several charitable foundations.

THREE FACTS IN EVIDENCE

The National Sex Forum program began with three facts in evidence:

1. That sex was managed better than ever before in history, due to the increase of knowledge, the freedom of interchange of information, and finally, the focus of energy toward sexuality.
2. The spreading convictions among sex professionals that it was time to radically rethink the uses of sexuality apart from the procreation of children; that sexuality was a positive and enriching experience for people making commitments to their own sexuality, to socio-sexuality, and to sexuality as part of the creative life of the community.
3. A discernible need for sex programs focusing on teaching people how to have a better and more fulfilling sex life and sexual proficiency, not constraint.

IMMEDIATE PROBLEMS

The immediate problems in the 1960s were what to teach, who teaches, and how to teach.

What to Teach? Most sex education fell into the categories of reproductive biology and social etiquette. Noble sperms crawling up to mate with eggs was something that simply happened, and not something that was experienced or thought about and had little to do with a 14-year-old boy masturbating seven to nine times a week, or a young girl making commitments to her body and her sexual pleasures. The social etiquette approach often turned out to be misinformed good advice reflecting no emphasis on individual differences.

Who Teaches? Most persons teaching about sex were people claiming sex expertise based on their knowledge of other fields somehow related to physical or psychological functioning or to social behavior. Thus, it became the doctors, ministers, nurses, school health science teachers, and newspaper advice columnists who were the "givers of information." These persons taking the mantle of authority were not to blame—they simply became experts by default and made the most of it.

How to Teach? The majority of sex education courses had several things in common: they were dull, often inaccurate, and woefully lacking in either resource materials or creative educational methodologies.

FIRST EXPERIMENTS OF THE NATIONAL SEX FORUM

The first National Sex Forum courses for persons in the helping professions were good examples of a group of sophomore sex educators combining their new-found knowledge and liberal social views in 12 hours of serious lectures aimed at setting people straight. It didn't take long to learn that people don't care how smart you are; they only cared if the information passed on to them was such as to help them understand their own sexuality better and so enable them to help those with whom they worked.

Other methodologies were tried, ranging from marathon encounters, Army-character guidance programs, San Francisco Mixed Media (a light show format) to the Bell System's programmed learning methods. By 1968, the National Sex Forum had arrived at three assumptions for testing and by 1971 had tested these assumptions as follows:

1. The most significant factor in sex education is that sex can be talked about casually and nonjudgmentally.

		Agree	*Disagree*	*Don't Know*
Asked of:	300 females	98.0%	0.7%	1.3%
	600 males	98.5%	1.5%	
	900 Total	98.3%	1.2%	1.3%

2. Individuals should be allowed meaningful exposure to a realistic objectification of the range of behavior into which their own experiences and those of others fall.

		Agree	*Disagree*	*Don't Know*
Asked of:	300 females	98.0%	1.0%	1.0%
	600 males	99.3%	0.5%	0.2%
	900 Total	98.9%	0.7%	0.4%

3. The person who teaches, counsels, or gives advice (regardless of professional qualifications) should have a low burden of sexual guilt feelings so as to be of service to others rather than serving his or her own needs.

		Agree	*Disagree*	*Don't Know*
Asked of:	300 females	98.7%		1.3%
	600 males	99.2%		0.8%
	900 Total	99.0%		1.0%

NSF SECOND EXPERIMENTS

The second group of experiments had to do with specific types of materials. The NSF chose seven categories of material and procedures to test:

1. Books of photographs and drawings. Twenty books were put together containing 400 photographs and drawings drawn from historic sex literature and the contemporary marketplace. These books were placed for easy accessibility during the entire session and people were invited to look at them whenever they wanted.
2. Tapes of music, erotic poetry, light humor and comedy monologues (e.g., Lenny Bruce tapes), and recorded sounds of people engaging in sexual activities.
3. Five-hundred slides of erotic art objects and famous erotic paintings and drawings drawn mostly from the Kronhausen Collection.
4. Fifteen historic and 15 current sex action films drawn from private collections and the contemporary marketplace. Later, as many as 60 films were tested.

5. Eight fantasy films carefully chosen to give a positive and value-oriented view of sexual thoughts and dreams and desires.
6. Talking about sex in small groups, in the larger group, and in encouraged voluntary groupings around meals. We found that there was no difference between organized small groups with leaders and spontaneous groupings talking about their reactions to the materials presented.
7. The controlled environment setting of the training space using special lighting, pillows, variable and alternate sound sources, and projected color combinations to create mood.

A total of 460 persons were asked to evaluate the courses. The following question was asked: "You have just been through a course using several categories of materials and educational procedures. Please evaluate as to whether or not each of these categories helped you better understand your sexuality and the sexuality of others." Results are reported in Table 19-1.

THE SAR PROCESS

Even though we are still experimenting, the National Sex Forum has formulated a plan based on the 11 units of the SAR Process. What follows is a step-by-step script of the SAR Process as given over a two-day period.

Day One

(About one half hour before the course is to begin, as people are arriving, show the World Erotica slides and play the first part of the Montage tape which features Don Warden.)

Unit: Introduction and Endorsement. This includes making the participants feel comfortable with the whole idea of seeing films and talking about sexuality, as well as a brief overview of the history of sex research, the movement for psychosexual understanding, some of the more important findings of Kinsey, Masters and Johnson, and other sex researchers, and the reasons and history behind the National Sex Forum and the SAR Process (40 minutes). *Media:* "Genesis" (Slide Set II) 5 minutes, "National Sex Forum Assumptions" (Slide Set II) 5 minutes.

Unit: Fantasy. Films depicting fantasy and discussion of the role of fantasy in sexuality (40 minutes). *Media:* "River Body" (8 minutes), "Love Toad" (2 minutes, 30 seconds), "I Change I am the Same" (40

Table 19-1
Evaluation by Participants of Forum Courses

	Greatly helped	Helped	Neutral	Detracted	Greatly detracted	Don't know
1. Books of photographs and drawings						
Asked of: 204 females	23(11.2%)	96(49.1%)	65(31.9%)	20(9.8%)		
256 males	41(16.0%)	170(66.4%)	38(14.8%)	17(6.6%)		
460 Total	64(13.9%)	266(57.8%)	103(22.4%)	37(8.0%)		
2. Tapes of music, etc.						
Asked of: 204 females	38(18.6%)	126(61.3%)	36(17.6%)	2(0.9%)	2(0.9%)	
256 males	44(17.2%)	128(50.0%)	74(28.9%)	7(2.7%)	3(1.2%)	
460 Total	82(17.8%)	254(55.2%)	110(23.9%)	9(1.9%)	5(1.1%)	
3. Slides of erotic art objects						
Asked of: 204 females	50(24.5%)	108(52.9%)	44(21.6%)	2(0.8%)	3(1.2%)	
256 males	41(16.0%)	181(70.7%)	30(11.7%)	2(0.5%)	3(0.7%)	
460 Total	91(19.8%)	289(62.8%)	74(16.1%)			
4. Historic and current sex action films						
Asked of: 204 females	114(55.9%)	87(42.6%)	3(1.4%)			
256 males	191(74.6%)	62(24.2%)	2(0.8%)	1(0.4%)		
460 Total	305(66.3%)	149(32.3%)	5(1.1%)	1(0.2%)		
5. Fantasy films						
Asked of: 204 females	115(56.4%)	86(42.2%)	3(1.4%)			
256 males	180(70.3%)	69(26.9%)	7(2.7%)			
460 Total	295(64.1%)	155(33.7%)	10(2.2%)			
6. Talking about sex						
Asked of: 204 females	178(87.3%)	25(12.3%)	1(0.5%)			
256 males	101(39.5%)	141(55.1%)	7(2.7%)	7(2.7%)		
460 Total	279(60.6%)	166(36.1%)	8(1.7%)	7(1.5%)		
7. Setting of the room						
Asked of: 204 females	103(50.5%)	99(48.6%)				
256 males	92(34.6%)	138(53.9%)	24(9.4%)	2(0.8%)		
460 Total	195(42.4%)	237(51.5%)	24(5.2%)	2(0.8%)		

seconds), "Jump Cut" (1 minute, 30 seconds), "Orange" (2 minutes, 40 seconds), "A Quickie" (1 minute, 45 seconds), and "Unfolding" (17 minutes) or "The Bed," (20 minutes).

Break for 10 Minutes.

Unit: Masturbation.   Brief discussion of the myths and realities of masturbation (50 minutes). *Media:* "Susan" (16 minutes), "Soma Touch" (12 minutes), "Handvoice" (7 minutes), "Margo" (11 minutes), "Shirley" (13 minutes), "Feeling Good" (25 minutes), and "One on One" (10 minutes).

Break for 20 Minutes.

Unit: Male Homosexuality.   Discussion of facts and myths about homosexuality, where the gay man fits into society today, victories and defeats of the gay movements, etc. If at all possible, it is important to have a male homosexual do this lecture. If it is not possible to get a speaker, the film "A Gay View/Male" (17 minutes) can be used (80 minutes). *Media:* "Vir Amat" (15 minutes) and "Stamen" (15 minutes) may be shown before or after the discussion and may be shown one at a time or at the same time.

Break for Dinner for 1½–2 Hours.

Unit: Desensitization.   This unit demythologizes sex by showing that there are only so many things that human beings can do sexually; it is a barrage of films shown simultaneously and planned to get past the intellectual level to the gut level. There should be an introduction to this unit so that people understand the reasons for it (75 minutes). *Media:* The Forum has a four-reel set which may be rented, or you can make your own set through use of commercial, historical, and current sex action films and NSF films. Usually begins with showing "Titles Available," which is five minutes long. The entire desensitization unit should run for at least 40 minutes.

Break for 10 Minutes.

Discussion.   The group should be given an opportunity to discuss their feelings and reactions to the desensitization set. People may or may not wish to do so, and they should not be forced. Finish Day One with one or two films from the Resensitization Unit.

Day Two

(About one half hour before the course is to begin again, as people are arriving, play all of the "Orgasm" tape, or parts of that and the "Sexual Reflections" tape, along with soft music, then into "Near the Big Chakra," which is 15 minutes long. The tape sections are part of the three-part series, "Two Women's Attitudes Towards Sex").

Unit: Female Sexuality. Discussion, including a question and answer period, about women as heterosexual, bisexual, and lesbian; about women's sexuality physiologically and historically, and about the feminist movement and its impact on sexuality. It is important to have at least two women of different sexual preferences in this section. If this is not possible, the film "Self Loving" (35 minutes), may be used (120 minutes). *Media:* "We Are Ourselves" (15 minutes), "In Winterlight" (18 minutes), and "Both/And" (25 minutes) may be shown before or after the discussion.

Break for Lunch for 1½ Hours.

Unit: Information Giving About Our Bodies. A discussion, using slides, about the sexual response cycle in women and men (30 minutes). *Media:* "Sexual Response Cycle" slides.

Unit: Resensitization (or Sexual Patterns). This includes a number of films showing various persons' patterns of sexuality (50 minutes). *Media:* "Rich & Judy" (12 minutes), "Free" (12 minutes), "Fullness" (13 minutes), "Sun Brushed" (14 minutes), "Sun Children" (14 minutes), "Joy in Her Pleasure" (11 minutes), "A Ripple of Time" (24 minutes). Two other NSF films, "A Quiet Afternoon" and "Reflections," each 20 minutes in length, may be used in addition to the above or in lieu of them.

Unit: Sex and the Disabled. A look at the reality that disabled persons are sexual beings too (45 minutes). *Media:* "Just What Can You Do?" (23 minutes), "Touching" (16 minutes), and "If Ever Two Were One" (14 minutes).

Break for 10 Minutes.

Unit: Sexual Therapy and Sexual Enrichment. A discussion of sex therapy and sexual enrichment (90 minutes). *Media:* "Squeeze Technique" (10 minutes), "The Erogenists" and "Give to Get" (11 minutes each), and "Looking for Me" (29 minutes).

Notes

1. By expanding the time involved, small group discussions can be inter-jected. Such discussions fall naturally at the end of the Masturbation Unit, the Desensitization Unit, and the Female Sexuality Unit. Another option is to omit small groups, but give those participants who wish a chance to bring in lunch and have a group discussion at that time.

2. The time for each unit can vary more or less, but the order of the units is vitally important to the process.

3. All media listed (except the desensitization reels) are available from Multi Media Resource Center, 1525 Franklin Street, San Francisco, California 94109, and are fully described in their catalog.

4. To fit into the times indicated, it is sometimes necessary to show more than one film at a time.

James P. Held

20
The Minnesota Program*

BEGINNINGS

By mid-1970, curriculum planners in the University of Minnesota Medical School had accumulated extensive evidence of need for education and training in the area of human sexuality for both patients and health care professionals. A review of available training resources revealed a deficit in methods and materials to explore attitudes toward sexuality. The planners also learned that the Reverend Ted McIlvenna and his colleagues at the National Sex Forum (NSF) had developed a two-day seminar on human sexuality that focused on feelings and attitudes. Following a preview of the NSF process by a subcommittee on human sexuality, the University of Minnesota began to develop its attitudinal approach to sex education for medical students. The Educational Policy Committee of the Medical School approved a two-day pilot program based on the NSF model to be attended by key faculty, administrators, students, and community leaders. After the pilot program, all participants recommended that the program become part of the school's curriculum.[1]

*The program in Human Sexuality has been supported in part by grants from the Commonwealth Fund, the Bush Foundation, the Playboy Foundation, the American Lutheran Church Division of Social Service, United Methodist Board of Christian Social Concerns, the National Institute of Mental Health, the Rehabilitation and Training Center Grant No. RT-2 Social and Rehabilitation Services, Department of Health Education and Welfare, and the University of Minnesota Medical School.

229

In spring 1971, three such two-day Sexual Attitude Reassessment (SAR) seminars were offered to self-selected medical students. They too reported personal and professional benefit and recommended it become part of the curriculum. Since then the SAR seminar has become part of a course in human sexuality required for all second-year medical students.[2-4] As this course developed, interest in a broader effort in the field also grew.

In December 1971, the Program in Human Sexuality (PHS) was formed as a new academic and administrative unit responsible to the Dean of the Medical School. Its organizational place within the Medical School shifted in March 1977, when the Program came under the academic and administrative jurisdiction of the Department of Family Practice and Community Health. The Program is charged with developing educational programs, providing services, and conducting research to improve sexual health. An interdisciplinary approach is taken, drawing faculty from medicine, sociology, social work, education, counseling, physical medicine and rehabilitation, family studies, and psychology. Program activities have expanded to include undergraduate and graduate medical education, continuing education for health care professionals, clinical services, evaluation, and physiological research. The next section describes the educational and training opportunities offered by the Program in Human Sexuality for health care professionals and highlights the Program's research and service components.

AREAS OF FOCUS

Medical Students. A continuing priority of the Program is undergraduate medical education. The course in human sexuality which began as an option for senior students was later approved as a required second-year course. As the course has evolved, increasing emphasis has been placed on building clinical skills and developing student awareness of the consequences of their sexual attitudes in dealing with patients. Considerable attention has been given to the formation of specific learning objectives and the development of appropriate ways to evaluate clinical competencies.

The current program for first-year students includes several hours of lectures on sex-related material, a two-day SAR seminar, and optional experiences in human sexuality. The second-year students take a six-week course in human sexuality which features individual learning packages, patient management problems, and didactic presentations. Third-year students are offered an elective which provides patient contact for those students who are interested in more intense work in sexual counseling.

Residents and Physicians. The overall goal of programs for residents and physicians is not to train a small number of specialized sex therapists but to prepare medical professionals to deliver sexual health care in their own practice settings.[6,7] Under a grant awarded in 1974 by the National Institute for Mental Health, graduate and continuing medical education offerings now include full-time and part-time resident rotations, skill-oriented and attitudinal workshops, and a formal graduate seminar for residents who cannot take a rotation in this field.

Training is currently focused in three areas: (1) sexual counseling of couples, (2) sexual counseling of individual men or women, and (3) medical aspects of sexual health care. Participation requires a minimum of 16–20 hours per week for 12 weeks. Under the supervision of a staff member, trainees may work as co-therapists (one-to-one and conjoint) with individuals and couples experiencing sexual difficulty or dysfunction, co-lead same-sex and couples groups, and seek clients in the Sexual Health Services medical clinic. All trainees are required to attend a SAR seminar and a weekend seminar, "Introduction to Sexual Health Care," to conduct intake or assessment interviews, and to participate in a regular group supervision seminar that includes case presentations, role-playing, and lectures. All trainees are assigned to a permanent supervisor during their rotations.

Rehabilitation Professionals. Beginning with a pilot SAR seminar in December 1971, the Program in Human Sexuality has pioneered work in the area of sexual adjustment of the physically disabled. A series of skill-building seminars for rehabilitation practitioners followed, with specially trained staff which included many disabled persons. Because of the special needs of this audience, an extensive library of audio-visual media on sex and disability was created. After the successful development of the three-day skill-building SAR seminar in sexuality and physical disability, a curriculum manual was written, audio-visual materials were packaged, and a five-day seminar was designed under a contract with a regional HEW rehabilitation training center to teach rehabilitation trainers how to use the complete curriculum.

In addition to developing the basic three-day seminars and the five-day rehabilitation trainer training seminars, Program staff active in the field have established a National Task Force on Sexuality of the Physically Disabled and have prepared a book for health care professionals and the disabled entitled *Sexual Options for Paraplegics and Quadriplegics.* Numerous articles have appeared in professional journals and texts.[7-11] Rehabilitation centers in California, Texas, Colorado, Illinois, New York, Pennsylvania, and Canada now provide three-day seminars based on the Minnesota model for rehabilitation practitioners. What is known as the Disability Section of the Program continues to serve as a consultant and as a national clearinghouse for institutions, agencies, and rehabilitation personnel, providing educational methods, media, and models for learning about sexuality and physical disability.

Social Workers. A recognition of the potential for social service personnel to deliver primary care in sexual health prompted the Program to explore training of these personnel through a contract with the Minnesota State Department of Public Welfare. The first program worked with staff trainers from state hospitals. A second project offered three-day workshops (including a two-day SAR) for county social workers from the Minneapolis–St. Paul metropolitan area and developed a resource center for use by the previously trained trainers. The success of this project led to another contract to extend the three-day seminars to social workers throughout the state, to design and present two-day advanced seminars for those previously trained, and to offer one-day workshops on special issues such as rape, sex education for the mentally retarded, and incest. Clinical internships are also supported by this contract in order to prepare various state employees to serve as trainers or as sex counselors in connection with their regular job duties. Finally, the contract also provides for expansion of the resource center and the creation of certain original materials for it.

Clergy and Seminarians. Since its inception, the Program has had continuing contact with the religious community. Staff of the local Lutheran Social Service agency introduced the Medical School to the SAR model (the SAR itself was designed by the National Sex Forum which was part of the Glide Methodist Church). Because theologians, seminarians, and clergy are key providers of sexual health care, their involvement with the Program has been important. Input from this group has also proven helpful in wrestling with the value issues raised during attitudinal workshops. Interaction between the religious community and the program has taken two principal forms. When the course in human sexuality for second-year medical students was first developed, seminary students from three local seminaries were included in the SAR seminars and other activities. However, scheduling problems forced cancellation of this joint participation. A week-long workshop has been offered as an elective to the seminarians each year. The Program has collaborated with the American Lutheran Church to develop and run similar "Weeks of Enrichment" for the Church's professional staff. Another form of involvement with the religious community is through an advisory group called the Committee on Religion and Ethics. The group is composed of persons working in various capacities with churches, synagogues, and religious educational institutions who contribute their philosophical comments and critical observations.[12]

Special-Interest Groups.   Meeting the education and training needs of special-interest groups has prompted much applied research within the Program, particularly to adapt the SAR process to new areas of emphasis. One adaptation of the SAR has been developed for families.[13,14] The seminar is similar to that used with medical students, with the addition of material about birth control and venereal disease and an increased emphasis on values. This SAR seems to have an impact on families far beyond that of conventional sex education, increasing communication and lowering intergenerational barriers. This activity has been one of the most satisfying and exciting endeavors for PHS, but also one of the most difficult.

Other programs have also been piloted. A SAR for chemically dependent persons, exploring such issues as emotional highs, intimacy, and dependency needs, proved to be a powerful experience. Similarly, a SAR was designed for sex offenders, victims, and state corrections personnel as part of an experimental treatment program in a state security hospital.[15]

Physiological Research.   A PHS project was funded in 1976 to study human sexual physiology. Standardized methods for quantifying physiological responses associated with sexual functioning are currently being developed. Laboratory results will help define and establish standards for sexual health. Research includes quantifying sexual response and its variability with age, particular medication, method of contraception, and certain disease processes. Another area of investigation is metabolic expenditure and cardiac load associated with sexual activity. With this data, persons with a high risk of cardiac failure and persons who have had coronary malfunctions can be better counseled. The Program also has undertaken a project to evaluate potential recipients of an implanted penile prosthesis and to assess the impact of this surgery upon the patient's sexual behavior.

Sexual Health Services.   In 1973, a clinical arm of the Program began to offer counseling for sexual dysfunction to the general public, and thereby to provide a training arena for health professionals. Sexual Health Services (SHS) today offers treatment programs for persons with a wide variety of sex-related concerns and problems.[11]

A fundamental aspect of SHS treatment philosophy is the recognition that sexual concerns and problems are not synonymous with psychopathology. SHS also reflects the conviction that health is more than simply the absence of disease. The treatment programs are based on concepts of responsibility for self, permission to be sexual, the use of re-education, the facilitation of increased awareness in clients, and structured behavior change.

SHS offers individual, conjoint, and group counseling and therapy as well as a variety of enrichment programs. Sexual health consultants see individuals and couples with specific sexual dysfunctions and also those with more complicated and diffuse problems of personal sexual concern, conflict, or sexual incompatibilities in a relationship. Sexual enrichment and therapy programs are time-limited but flexible.[16] They combine basic education, communication training, self-awareness and insight therapies, Gestalt techniques, small group processes, and behavioral "homework" assignments. Programs last approximately 10–60 hours, spanning a time period of anywhere from 3–12 weeks. Services include counseling in same-sex groups for sexually dysfunctional men or women, conjoint or group therapy for sexual dysfunction or relationship problems, individual counseling for sexual concerns, and a special education and enrichment sequence aimed at increasing the sexual satisfaction and enjoyment of clients with no identified sex-related problems. The programs have been evaluated using subjective measures (the extent to which the program satisfied client's pretreatment goals) and using objective instruments (pre- and posttests). Results of immediate and one-year posttreatment evaluation have shown positive change in a majority of cases.[17]

PROBLEMS

Goals and Objectives.   A major problem for the Program throughout its history has been the development of programmatic objectives. Translating the Program's original charge (education, research, and service to improve sexual health) into more specific objectives required agreement on certain assumptions (a search for consensus) which has required continuous struggle. What should be the scope of its programs: A broad context such as improving and "humanizing" the health care system? A focused context such as incorporating study of human sexuality into the curriculum of the Medical School? Or should there be some balance of the two? Should a new unit develop a strong foundation, reputation, and power base locally, then move into the national arena, or vice versa? Should the Program emphasize education, research, or service? What percent of effort should go to each? To what extent do research or service exist to make education possible? Conflicts among staff members over differences in philosophy made it difficult to maintain a general mission statement that was programmatically meaningful. Instead, concrete objectives were developed for individual projects. Evaluating prospective projects and resolving the inevitable competition for resources within the Program thus became a matter of subjective judgment on the part of the director. These decisions generated discussion, debate, and struggle over the determination of relative contribution of these projects to commonly acknowledged objectives. The vagueness of the mission statement allowed for too broad a diversity in interpretation among the staff joining the organization. The continuing difficulty in this area has been squarely faced by the Program since becoming a part of the Department of Family Practice and Community Health. Developing program-wide specific objectives is a top priority.

Credentials. Another issue for PHS (not unexpected) was that of devising standards to evaluate the credentials of staff and faculty for personnel or programs in human sexuality. Recognized credentials in related fields were no guarantee of competence, because the traditional training of health care professionals has not included study of human sexuality. In the absence of licensing or appropriate academic or professional degrees in the subject area, paraprofessional staff wrestled with real or imagined (often self-imposed) feelings of being "one-down" in comparison to staff members with conventional credentials from recognized disciplines in the helping professions. This tension was especially exacerbated whenever work in sexuality overlapped traditional helping professions (e.g., sexual therapy for persons with related psychological problems). In response to this difficulty, the skills of each sexual health worker have been specified, and competency-based job descriptions written. Identifying skills available and skills required enables an appropriate match of person and function. Forthright interpersonal communication among all staff also has been fostered to alleviate these areas of real concern.

Funding. Finding sources of funding is a continuing battle for programs in sexuality as it is for other health fields. When the Program began, sex was seen as a new field of study. Thus research and development funds were relatively available. But after four years, the study of sex is less dramatic and controversial. Initial grants are ending, and the Program must look to other sources of funding. The Program is currently being supported by funds generated by the Sexual Health Service unit, grants for training and physiologic research, and medical school contributions.

SUMMARY

The enumeration of concerns ought not to overshadow the context in which the problems occurred. The accomplishments of the Minnesota Program are significant. Among the first programs of its kind in the country, the Program in Human Sexuality remains one of the few with so comprehensive an approach to sexual health care. It has pioneered projects in physical disability and sexuality, training for medical residents and social workers, physiological research, family sex education, and chemical dependency and sexuality, many of which have served as models for other centers around the country. In teaching undergraduate medical students, the Program's efforts continue to reflect the most innovative approaches in the field. The Minnesota Program has now entered a new phase, with the opportunity for increasing maturity and stability as an organization, following its formation and initial rapid growth. Re-evaluation of initial objectives and the search for a new director, coincident with becoming part of the Department of Family Practice and Community Health, promise new perspectives of continued growth and opportunity in the field of sexual health.

REFERENCES

1. Chilgren R, Briggs M: On being explicit: Sex education for professionals. SEICUS Report 5:1–3, 1973
2. Rosenberg P, Chilgren R: Sex education discussion groups in a medical setting. Int J Group Psychother 23:23–41, 1973
3. Held JP, Cournoyer CR, Held CA, et al: Sexual attitude reassessment: A training seminar for health professionals. Minn Med 57:925–928, 1974
4. Garrard J, Vaitkus A, Held J, et al: Follow-up effects of a medical school course in human sexuality. Arch Sex Behav 5:331–340, 1976
5. Held JP, Marcotte DB: Lectureless medical education: A new model. J Psychiatric Educ (in press)
6. Maddock JW: Sex education in professional schools. Res Devel Educ 1:73–78, 1976
7. Maddock JW: Sexual health and health care. Postgrad Med 58:52–58, 1975
8. Cole, TM, Chilgren RA, Rosenberg P: New program of sex education and counseling for spinal cord injured adults and health care professionals. Int J Para 11:111–124, 1973
9. Cole TM: Sexuality and the physically handicapped, in Green R (ed) Human Sexuality: A Health Practitioner's Text. Baltimore, Williams & Wilkins, 1975
10. Held JP, Cole TM, Held CA, et al: Sexual attitude reassessment workshops: Effect on spinal cord injured adults, their partners and rehabilitation professionals. Arch Phys Med Rehabil 56:14–18, 1975
11. Anderson, TP, Cole TM: Sexual counseling of the physically disabled. Postgrad Med 58:117–123, 1975
12. Yates W: The role of the theological ethical task force in the University of Minnesota program in human sexuality. J Counseling and Values 7:190–197, 1976
13. Rosenberg PP, Rosenberg, LM: Sex education for adolescents and their families. J Sex and Marital Ther 1:53–67, 1976
14. Held J, Rosenberg P: Evaluation of the effects of family sex education seminars on adolescent sexual awareness. Presented to American Orthopsychiatric Association March, 1975
15. Macindoe I, Pengelly E: The Behavioral, Emotional and Attitudinal Development Program (mimeographed booklet). St Peter, Minnesota Security Hospital, 1974
16. Maddock J: Sexual Health: An Enrichment and Treatment Program. Washington, D.C., Graphics Press, 1976
17. Held JP, Logan CA, Maddock JW, et al: The evaluation of sex health services in a medical setting. J Sex Marital Ther 4:256–264, 1977

John Money

21
The Johns Hopkins Program

HISTORY AND PRINCIPLES

Human sexuality was first taught as part of the official medical school curriculum at Johns Hopkins in 1969–70. The person who asked me to teach this subject was Richard Allen Chase, MD, who had been charged by the then Chairman of Psychiatry, Joel Elkes, to redesign the freshman course in psychiatry and behavioral sciences. I designed the human sexuality section of this course without knowledge of what was being taught in medical sex education elsewhere, though I did know that the teaching of human sexuality in medical schools was newly the "in" thing.

With history as a guide, I now know that Johns Hopkins was one of the first half dozen medical schools in the United States to offer a course in human sexuality, and the second, after Indiana, to make extensive use of erotically explicit slides and movies. Ed Tyler at Indiana drew on the extensive film library of confiscated pornography given to the Kinsey Institute for Sex Research by the police in Chicago and New York. I used materials loaned or given to me by commercial pornography distributors for whom I had been an expert witness in court. In those days, there were no established educational distributors of explicit erotica.

Academically, the late 1960s were the era of student protest and demand for social relevance in the curriculum. That is why I decided to include a lecture on "Pornography in the Home" in the human sexuality curriculum. The illustrative slides and movies were relevant to child and adolescent psychiatry, to the sexology of the paraphilias, and above all to medical sociology in general, as the old taboo against the explicit portrayal of sexuality (at that time no medical text contained a photograph of an actual delivery!) was being challenged in the courts. Moreover, it confirmed for students the full range of sexual normalcy in the two phases of sex, namely proception and acception, that precede the possibility of conception, pregnancy, and childbirth. The latter three, at that time, were the only respectable aspects of sexuality in medical practice and research.

It is not feasible for a medical student to become a surgeon if the sight of blood appalls him and forever makes him nauseous and sick in the operating room. Likewise, it is not feasible for a student to become a sexologist, or even to include sexual medicine in his professional practice, if the diverse and varied manifestations of sexuality in human beings appall or repulse him. A student will not ascertain the degree to which he or she is or is not appalled or repulsed unless he or she is tested by being confronted with these manifestations, including some of the more gross and atypical unorthodoxies and pathologies.

It is conceivable that didactic confrontation could take place exclusively in the clinic, in personal contact with patients. This ideal can be met in individual, apprentice-type, postdoctoral training. However, the logistics of clinical rotations preclude it as the sole method of teaching a large medical school class; it is too difficult to synchronize patient appointments with each student's rotation so as to guarantee adequate coverage of syndromes and topics. Therefore, it is necessary to prepare the student in the classroom for his or her encounters in the clinic.

All good classroom teaching combines lectures with audio-visual supplements and demonstrations, live or filmed. Thus, at Johns Hopkins, the teaching of human sexology (or sexuality, if you prefer that term) relies on films depicting explicit sexual practices and on classroom interviews with volunteer patients who exemplify a given syndrome or life style.

The combined content of the lectures, movies, and interview-demonstrations challenges a student's impartiality and professional non-judgmentalism in the context of human sexual phenomena. This challenge is rather special with respect to the sexological curriculum, for at the present time there is no premedical folklore in high school and college that prepares the premedical student to be sexually nonjudgmental, even when his image of romantic love and idealized heterosexuality is shattered by what his patients say and do. There is a parallel challenge when he is first confronted with the pathological malevolence of parents who, as child abusers, shatter his uncritical image of the sanctity of motherhood. He encounters similar difficulty with being nonjudgmental when he first encounters medical imposters, patients with Munchausen's syndrome, whose symptoms are self-induced. Nonjudgmentalism also does not come easily to him in his dealings with dying patients. Otherwise, for the most part, he enters medical school knowing that doctors don't chide, chastise, blame, or punish; they treat. Nonetheless, it is difficult for some medical students not to pass judgment when the behavior of his or her patient, as in certain categories of sexual behavior, is socially stigmatized as a sin, a deviancy, an abomination, or a crime against nature.

The ideology of medical education is sometimes prescribed by special committee. Mostly, however, it is simply a phenomenon of the zeitgeist, the spirit of the era. The ideology of medical sex education, though in the zeitgeist, is still rather diffuse. In consequence, medical sex educators have acquiesced to having their specialty judged on the criterion of its value, not only for nonjudgmental professional application, but also for restructuring the personal sexual attitudes of their students and for improving society. Neither mathematicians, physicists, physiologists, nor other hard scientists acquiesce to justifying their teaching this way. For them, the function of education is to transmit knowledge, controversial or otherwise.

Knowledge transmitted certainly changes the information content of the student's mind. It may lie there dormant, as if in computer storage. More likely, it enters into dynamic interaction with information already there. The dynamic outcome may be that the newly transferred knowledge is assimilated and then disqualified from further use; or it may be assimilated and used by rote, unmodified; or it may be assimilated, but used only after having been modulated by what was already there.

A teacher can scarcely feign indifference to the ultimate outcome of the transfer of information from him to his students. As an examiner, however, the ultimate outcome is not his business. The function of the examination is simply to ascertain whether the information did or did not get transmitted.

I have no objection to a workshop for personal, private, and nonprofessional attitude restructuring except that, insofar as it applies to a student's own sex life, it should be an elective requiring the student's informed consent and volunteer enrollment. Not all medical students are ready or able to be personally remade sexually. Their expectancy and preparedness as students is simply to be made into doctors. In sexuality, it is enough for them to become better informed doctors. The authority of the professor is to pass or fail them, not to convert or reform their private, nonprofessional ideology.

Some medical students will have achieved, before entering medical school, the degree of nonjudgmentalism requisite to effective case management in even the most personally offensive sexual cases. Others achieve it in the course of their instruction in human sexuality, while still others are dependent on a delayed-action effect. Some are unable to achieve it at all. For them, nonjudgmentalism with patients threatens their own privacy of self-judgmentalism. They apply nonjudgmentalism personally, and reject it as a hedonistic philosophy equated with promiscuity, looseness, and indifference to moral standards. They will never be able to cope with sexuality in their patients. They will either circumvent it or, more wisely, go into a specialty that does not require them to cope with sexuality.

The synopsis of what they will be required to learn in psychiatry and behavioral sciences is given to the Johns Hopkins medical students at the beginning of the academic year in a bound volume, the Course Outline. The following material is taken from Section 4 of the Outline, entitled Human Sexual Behavior.

COURSE INTRODUCTION AND OBJECTIVES

Whereas the law is judgmental, medicine is nonjudgmental. The physician in training needs to develop a moral stance of nonjudgmentalism toward the patient. In matters of human conduct, sexual conduct included, the doctor treats all comers. In matters of sexual conduct, the doctor's nonjudgmental impartiality with respect to the patient is essential to therapeutic success as it is in, say, temporal lobe epileptic behavior, suicidal behavior, self-inflicted injury, or carelessly contracted venereal disease. Nonjudgmentalism toward the patient as the person manifesting a syndrome is not synonymous with absence of judgment regarding the syndrome, specifically with respect to its etiology, diagnosis, prognosis, and treatment. Nor is nonjudgmentalism toward the patient synonymous with lack of judgment regarding one's own personal conduct and morality. Nonjudgmentalism toward the patient is professional nonjudgmentalism. It is as essential to one's medical professionalism as is technological competence.

It is easier to be professionally nonjudgmental with respect to etiology and diagnosis than with prognosis, and least easy with respect to treatment. The doctor must make a decision regarding the disposition or treatment of a case, and in so doing must have recourse to his own judgment as to what to do. Judgments related to sex and death are among the most difficult with which the medical student is confronted, and on which he must ultimately take a stand, for they involve not only technical choices regarding what to do, but also one's own personal moral and religious values or both. In matters of sex, to take a few examples, a medical student needs to formulate his point of view regarding early teenaged sex and accessibility of contraception, abortion, school and community sex education programs, erotic entertainment and pornography, homosexual law reform, conjugal visits in prison, and so forth—all of which will, sooner or later, require decisions forced upon him by, or on behalf of his patients. Some sexual decisions that have a direct and intimate personal reference for many students pertain to a broken love affair, the acceptability of a premarital housekeeping arrangement, the timing of marriage, the timing of pregnancies, the absentee spouse or parent, professional careers for both spouses, and youthful divorce.

In five teaching sessions, it is manifestly impossible to cover everything pertaining to the psychology and behaviorology of sex, even in abbreviated form. Moreover, in sexology as in the rest of medicine, today's facts become tomorrow's history as knowledge advances, so that it is better to learn principles than catalogs of how-to-do-it. Your aim should be to attain the same professional nonjudgmentalism and alertness to the sexual system in human health and disease as you will to the alimentary, respiratory, or other systems. Learn to recognize when there is a sexual component to your patients' ills; and learn to maintain the sexual health component of their total health and well-being.

The sexual system, supremely an example of the unity of body-mind, comprises both imagery and action, as manifested in romance, love, eroticism, copulation, reproduction, and parenthood. There is no manifestation of health and disease in which the sexual system is not, in some degree, primarily or secondarily affected.

Your goal is to feel as much at ease in examining and inquiring about the relevance of sexual, as of any other functioning, to the complaints of any and all of your patients. Then, in your future clinic assignments, you will be able to apply and expand your knowledge of the clinical relevance of sex over and beyond the restrictions of what can be covered didactically in five sessions. You will become sophisticated in deciphering the relevance of sexuality and its malfunction to any and all symptoms you may encounter.

Sexual symptoms can, in some instances, be traced etiologically to a chromosomal error; or to a neural, vascular, or endocrine lesion or deficit; or to infection; or neoplasm. Some medications also affect sexual functioning. In the absence of a department of sexology in American medical schools and hospitals, patients with such complaints are distributed through various specialty clinics, in some cases to more than one clinic. In consequence, the delivery of sexual health care is frequently poorly coordinated. This situation is not helped by reason of the fact that there is no acceptable textbook of sexology yet in existence. You are, therefore, confronted with the task of assembling your own compendium of knowledge as you work in the various clinics in which are likely to be found sexual dysfunctions with the above etiologies. Otherwise, you will be unable to formulate a differential diagnosis and establish a correct diagnosis.

The majority of cases of sexual dysfunction do not have one of the above etiologies. They are, therefore, classified simply as dysfunctions, and subclassified as hypophiliac, hyperphiliac, or paraphiliac. In the most general sense, and by inference, they represent a dysfunction of sexual pathways in the brain. The etiology of such dysfunction is usually considered to be developmental in origin and related to, though not necessarily the exclusive product of error of learning, especially learning as applied to the dynamics of human relationships. For this reason, and because the dysfunctional symptoms manifest themselves in the dynamics of human relationships, they are commonly referred to as psychodynamic in origin.

In sexology, as in any other branch of medicine, the etiology as well as the prognosis governs whether one treats the laboratory results, the organ system, or the person. The good physician never forgets the person in the forefront of the laboratory results and organ system. No physician, however, can neglect the person when the symptom or syndrome is one in which laboratory results are noncontributory and there is no known specific treatment of the organ system per se. Care then takes the form of amelioration of suffering and rehabilitation of the person or both.

The medical philosophy of amelioration or rehabilitation is frequently the only practicable one in sexual medicine. In some instances the prognosis can be good, as for example in couple counseling for anorgasmia, impotence, or related hypophilias. That is why excellence in the art of dialogue, based on astuteness in behavioral psychodynamic diagnostics, can be of great practical value in therapeutics.

The lecture titles show that you are expected in this course to learn about gender identity and its differentiation, with special reference to intersexuality. This material will have direct correlation with what you learn about intersexuality in endocrine and genetics courses, but its more general value will be in giving you an understanding of gender identity/role differentiation and development in normal childhood.

The material on sex education has direct bearing on your future function as sex educators for your patients and your community. With its use of explicit visual erotica it serves also the purpose, however, of prying open your minds and attitudes from the taboo and repression with which you have been indoctrinated since infancy. Without this mind-opening, you will not be able to be a good doctor. Various examples of visual erotica also introduce you to some of the paraphilias.

If you are interested in being more specific, and if you augment your lectures with assigned reading, you can prepare yourself for clinical counseling of patients and of their parents in, for example, the following:

1. Hermaphroditism and related birth defects of the sex organs, beginning at birth with deciding on the sex of assignment in which habilitation will be most complete.

2. Sex chromosome anomalies, including Turner's (45,X) syndrome, Klinefelter's (47,XXY) syndrome, the triple-X (47,XXX) syndrome, the XYY (47,XYY) syndrome, and their mosaic and other variants.
3. Pubertal precocity, idiopathic or of other etiology.
4. Pubertal delay or failure of onset, as in agonadism (anorchia in boys, Turner's syndrome in girls); prepubertal castration; hypopituitary syndromes including Kallmann's syndrome of hypogonadotropinism and anosmia in males; and so-called constitutional delay of adolescence.
5. Discrepancies and variants of gender identity differentiation, including bisexualism, homosexualism, transsexualism, transvestism, and the paraphilias.
6. Dysfunctions of the sexual partnership, as in sexual apathy, anorgasmia, hyperorgasmia, premature ejaculation, impotence, genital anesthesia, painful coitus (termed dyspareunia in women), vaginismus, and vaginal dryness.
7. Pubertal and adolescent sexual ignorance (often accompanied by anxiety) concerning masturbation, recreational sex, parenthood, contraception, abortion, and venereal disease.
8. Problems of childhood, adolescence, and adulthood related to incest, rape, pedophilia, gerontophilia, and other socially unsanctioned sexual relationships.

In addition, you will know something also of the medical sociology and cultural anthropology of sex as it affects your practice of medicine. Otherwise you will be "culture blind," and unable to perceive either the chronological or ethnographical relativities that are, and have always been, characteristic of human sexual expression. In our own society you will be aware of how sexual taboo affects us all, professionally as well as personally.

The lectures and demonstration interviews will show you that most sexual symptoms (though not all) are indications of a sick relationship, not simply of a sick urogenital system. That is why there are no quick nostrums for impotence and such complaints, and why the new dual-sex-team therapies have more modest success than is sometimes claimed for them. Erotic gymnastics are not a cure for an ailing relationship; and an ailing relationship is usually the product of long-term disillusionment, not simply of inadequate love-making techniques.

To understand the errors of a relationship, and to become privy to them, you need to know how to be the master of the interview as effectively as you know how to be the master of the physical examination. To do a good interview, you have to know how to decipher the significance of covert signs and propositions, which is what behavioral psychodynamics is all about.

If you leave the course with a new sense of nonjudgmentalism and new skill as an interviewer, you will readily be able to fit what you learn from your lectures and readings with what you will learn in later clinical courses about, for example, techniques of birth control, abortion, infertility treatment, and treatment of venereal diseases, which are closely related to, but not the focus of a course in human sexual behavior.

The material on interviewing and behavioral psychodymamics will have carry-over value to other aspects of psychiatry and, indeed, to every interview, including medical history-taking, that you ever conduct.

CLASS MEETINGS

For their freshman course in psychiatry and behavioral sciences, the medical students meet 35 times, in three-hour sessions. Five of these meetings are allocated to the section on human sexual behavior. This is their only formal course work in human sexuality, though clinical electives can be arranged in subsequent years for the few who request them.

The synopses of the first three topics on human sexual behavior, as given in the course outline, are reproduced below. Each of the three topics is illustrated with 50 or 60 slides. The fourth and fifth topics are, respectively, Principles of Interviewing, and Dynamics of Behavioral Interaction. Though the didactic content is generalized, attention is given in both instances to the applicability of the instruction to the sexual interview and sex therapy. These two topics also provide the opportunity to add more case illustrations, more demonstration movies, and more live interviews.

Synopsis of Topics

Topic 1. Gender Identity/Role: Differentiation, Development and Dysfunction.

- Introduction and course objectives
- Movie: "Our Birth Film"
- From chromosomes to adult gender identity; sequential development (Fig. 21-1)
- Definition: gender identity/role
- Prenatal and postnatal phases: continuity versus dichotomy
- The "Adam" and the "Eve" principles in sexual differentiation
- Sex-shared, threshold-dimorphic traits (Table 21-1)
- Analogy with native language
- Matched-pair method in hermaphrodite studies; case illustrations from the adrenogenital syndrome and the androgen-insensitivity syndrome

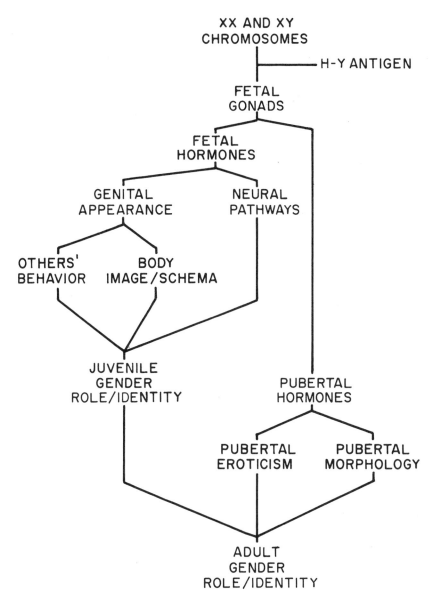

Fig. 21-1. Sequential components of the differentiation of gender identity/role.

Table 21-1
Sex-Shared, Threshold-Dimorphic Behavior

General kinesis
Dominance assertion and rivalry
Roaming and territory mapping
Defense against predators
Defense of young
Nesting or housing
Parental caretaking
?Visual image and erotic arousal

- Principles of identification and complementation in the postnatal differentiation of gender identity/role; comparison with bilingualism
- Gender-dimorphic brain-mind schemas
- Precursor phases (haptic, oral, anal) of gender dimorphism in childhood
- Childhood sex-rehearsal play
- Sexuality in the so-called latency period
- Pubertal hormones affect thresholds, not dimorphism of eroticism
- Sex roles versus sex-coded roles
- Transpositions of masculine/feminine (Table 21-2)
- Transposition syndromes
- Homosexuality and bisexuality
- Transvestism and transsexualism

Topic 2.   Pair Bonding and its Dysfunctions.

- Movies: "Techniques of Foreplay" and "Positions and Techniques of Coitus" (shown simultaneously)
- Three phases of sexuality and eroticism: proception, acception, conception (Table 21-3)
- Proception: olfactory (pheromonal), visual, and tactual phyletic mechanisms

Table 21-2
Gender Identity/Role Transpositions

	Total	Partial	Arbitrary
Chronic	Transsexualism	Homosexualism	Sex-coded work and legal status
Episodic	Transvestism	Bisexualism	Sex-coded play, manners, and grooming

Table 21-3
Three Phases of Eroticism and Sexuality

	Activity	Organs	Disorders
Proception	Solicitation, attraction, courtship	Eyes, nose, skin	Gender transpositions, paraphilias of inclusion or displacement, apathy
Acception	Erection, lubrication, copulation	Mouth, genitals, anus	Hypophilias, hyperphilias
Conception	Pregnancy, delivery, childcare	Internal reproductive, mammary	Sterility, anovulation, miscarriage, nonlactation

- Visual imagery in perception, memory, and fantasy
- Visual imagery in sex dreams and in masturbatory and coital fantasies
- Visual erotica: satiation effect
- Visual erotica: male/female and age differences
- Casual versus long-term pair bonding; falling in love
- Love and sex, commitments and responsibilities
- Romantic fantasy projected onto a partner (the ink-blot effect); illusion and disillusion; paraphilic case examples
- Paraphilias (Table 21-4)
- Paraphilias and commercial pornography
- Paraphilic imagery illustrated in commercially distributed 8mm "porno" movies

Table 21-4
Inclusion or Displacement Paraphilias

Apotemnophilia (amputation)	Mysophilia (filth)
Acrotomophilia (amputee partner)	Narratophilia (erotic talk)
Coprophilia (feces)	Necrophilia (corpse)
Exhibitionism	Pedophilia (child)
Erotic Strangulation Suicide	Pictophilia (pictures)
Fetishism	Rape
Frotteurism (rubbing)	Sadism
Gerontophilia (elder)	Scoptophilia (watching coitus)
Hypnophilia (sleeping partner)	Telephone Scatologia (lewdness)
Kleptomania (stealing)	Troilism
Klismaphilia (enema)	Urophilia or Undinism (urine)
Lust Murder	Voyeurism or Peeping Tomism
Masochism	Zoophilia (animal)

Topic 3A.   Copulatory Function and Dysfunction.

- Movie: "Physiological Responses of the Sexually Stimulated Female in the Laboratory"
- From above the belt to below the belt: phobia and inhibition
- Aging effects
- Hypophilia/hyperphilia/paraphilia and the three phases of eroticism
- Hypophilias in both sexes (Table 21-5)
- Differential diagnosis of hypophilias: neurologic, vascular, functional inhibition
- Hypophilias: fight each other (passive aggression) with the sex organs
- Behind the hypophilia may lurk a paraphilia
- Dual sex therapy: treating the partnership
- Somesthetic versus ideogogic therapy
- Behavioral modification therapy
- Pubertal delay and failure
- Pubertas praecox
- Hyperphilias in both sexes: range and differential diagnosis
- Aphrodisiacs
- Movie: "Physiological Responses of the Sexually Stimulated Male in the Laboratory"

Topic 3B.   Developmental Juvenile and Adolescent Sex Education.

- Developmental etiology and prevention of dysfunction in childhood
- Early sex education and the physician
- Conceptual and pictorial sex education in childhood
- Nudity at home
- Witnessing coitus

Table 21-5
Hypophilias, Male & Female (Partial
or Complete)

Male	Female
Erotic apathy	Erotic apathy
Penile anesthesia	Vulval anesthesia
Anorgasmia	Anorgasmia
Erectile impotence	Vaginal dryness
Premature ejaculation	Vaginismus
Coital pain	Dyspareunia

Table 21-6
Four Traditions of Pair-Bonding

Origin	Type	First Breeding	Family Type
Mediterranean	Virgin Bride; double standard	After legal bonding	Nuclear
Nordic	Betrothal; equality of sexes	Before legal bonding	Nuclear
American Slave	Serial pair-bonding; expendable male	Independent of legal bonding	Grandparental
Polynesian	Premarital affairs; late-age patriarchy	Before legal bonding	Kinship

- Childhood sex rehearsal play
- Incest; child abuse
- "Porno" books and pictures in childhood
- Preadolescent sociology of sex: contraception, abortion, V.D., romantic mismatching
- Adolescent pair-bonding and intercourse
- Four American traditions of pair-bonding (Table 21-6)
- The sexual revolution and the tide of history

SUMMARY

The implicit contract between a medical student and a medical school is that medical knowledge will be transmitted so that the student will be made into a doctor. In human sexology, this process requires that the student become professionally nonjudgmental with his patients. To require or indoctrinate personal change other than to be professionally nonjudgmental is an intrusion on a student's personal privacy and values, unless it is separately contracted on the basis of informed consent. Some students fail to attain the sexological status of being professionally nonjudgmental, which automatically disqualifies them from any aspect of clinical medicine in which applied sexology is integral to the complete delivery of health care. Sexology is unique among medical specialties insofar as the basic unit is the couple, or the partnership, not the individual. Ideally, the content of a course in sexology covers the complete range and variety of sexual-erotic function and dysfunction from the point of view not of the laboratory results, nor of the organ system, but of the person as a whole as a sexual partner.

GENERAL BIBLIOGRAPHY

Required Reading

1. Avers CJ: Biology of Sex. New York, Wiley & Sons, 1974
2. Money J: Intersexual problems. Clin Obstet Gynecol 16:169–191, 1973 (R)*
3. Money J: Sex reassignment. Int J Psychiatry, 9:249–282, 1970 (R)*
4. Money J, Ehrhardt AA: Man and Woman, Boy and Girl: The differentiation and dimorphism of gender identity from conception to maturity. Baltimore, Johns Hopkins University Press, 1972
5. Money J, Primrose C: Sexual dimorphism and dissociation in the psychology of male transsexuals, in Green R, Money J (eds): Transsexualism and Sex Reassignment. Baltimore, Johns Hopkins University Press, 1969 (See interview schedules)

Reference Reading

1. Beach FA: Behavioral endocrinology: An emerging discipline. Am Sci 63:178–187, 1975 (R)*
2. Comfort A(ed): The Joy of Sex: A Gourmet Guide to Love Making. New York, Crown, 1973
3. Kaplan HS: The New Sex Therapy: Active Treatment of Sexual Dysfunctions. New York, Brunner/Mazel, 1974
4. Money J: The birth-control age. The Chronicle of Higher Education, 8(8):20, 1973 (R)*
5. Money J: Determinants of human sexual identity and behavior, in Sager CJ, Kaplan HS (eds): Progress in Group and Family Therapy. New York, Brunner/Mazel, 1972 (R)*
6. Money J: Sex Errors of the Body. Baltimore, The Johns Hopkins University Press, 1968

Films

1. *"Methods and Positions of Coitus,"* 1974. Naigles W, PhD, Producer; Clark LeM, MS, MD, Director. EDCOA Productions, 310 Cedar Lane, Teaneck, N.J. 07666
2. *"Methods and Positions of Foreplay,"* 1974. Naigles W, PhD, Producer; Clark LeM, MS, MD, Director. Unpublished.
3. *"Our Birth Film,"* 1974. Milner EM, Producer; Kliman T Writer/Director; Money J, PhD, Baramki T, MD, Professional Consultants. Milner-Fenwick, Inc., 3800 Liberty Heights Avenue, Baltimore, Md, 21215
4. *"Physiological Responses of the Sexually Stimulated Female in the Laboratory,"* 1974. Wagner G, Creator. Focus International, 505 West End Avenue, New York, NY 10024
5. *"Physiological Responses of the Sexually Stimulated Male in the Laboratory,"* 1975. Wagner G, Creator. Focus International, 505 West End Avenue, New York, NY 10024

R* = Reproduced in the Book of Readings given to students with their course outline.

Douglas Wallace

22
The University of California-San Francisco Program

DEVELOPMENT OF THE HUMAN SEXUALITY PROGRAM

The Human Sexuality Program began in December 1966 when the Dean of the School of Medicine, in response to a petition from second-year medical students, approved an experimental elective course titled "Sexual Problems in Medical Practice" for the 1967 spring academic year.

Following evaluations of subsequent elective courses in 1968 and 1969, the Curriculum Committee of the School of Medicine recommended that a required course in "Human Sexuality and Medical Practice" for preclinical medical students be established in 1970. Although the course was initially designed for medical students, nursing and pharmacy students were also enrolled. A number of students taking the course expressed interest in further work in sexual health education and in the treatment of sexual problems. Concurrently, individuals and groups in the community began to express similar interests.

In response to this growing volume of interest and demonstrated University and community need, detailed planning for the present Human Sexuality Program was started in the summer of 1971. Several assumptions guided this planning:

1. Human sexuality is an important and heretofore neglected area of health care and health care training.

251

2. Sexual functioning bears a reciprocal relationship to individual physical and mental health, family stability, and numerous other areas of social concern.
3. Current emphasis within the health care professions on treating the whole person and the rapidly expanding public demand for sexual health services create an immediate need at the undergraduate, graduate, and continuing education levels for professional education in sexual health care.
4. The study of human sexuality is a discipline in its own right; the treatment and prevention of sexual disorders and the development of new methods of treatment and prevention are activities best conducted in a bio-social setting which encompasses somatic, social, behavioral, cultural, and environmental factors.

Objectives of the program include the following:

1. The development of new and effective methods of education and training in the delivery of sexual health care for medical students, residents and interns;
2. the improvement of sexual health-care delivery services through the continuing education of physicians and other members of the health and helping professions;
3. the continued development of new, inexpensive yet effective methods of counseling persons suffering from common sex problems utilizing self-help, group, and educational procedures;
4. continued assistance to other educational institutions and community agencies who wish to develop appropriate training and service capabilities in human sexuality;
5. continued research efforts in the area of sexual functioning, the effects of physical illness on such functioning, and the importance of other dimensions such as touch and sex-role stereotyping.

Funding from several local foundations enabled the Program to begin operation as an entirely self-supporting, Organized Activity in the School of Medicine in June 1972, with the late Herbert E. Vandervoort, MD, as the Faculty Member in Charge. The Organized Activity status, in contrast with departmental status, provided the largest possible base and the greatest amount of freedom for the growth of an innovative program in the sensitive and emotion-laden area of human sexuality.

The period from 1972 to 1977 was one of dynamic growth and differentiation, with the addition of practicum training in sex counseling, a project in sex and disability, expanded research and evaluation capabilities, and increased educational offerings. The latter part of this period was marked by the development of an Academic Plan and a search for a departmental home. In late 1976, some four months after the premature death of Dr. Vandervoort, administrative responsibility for the Human Sexuality Program was assigned to the Department of Psychiatry. The program remained self-supporting, however.

During the five years from 1972 to 1977, the program has strived to achieve a balanced integration of treatment, education, training, research, and community service utilizing an interdisciplinary professional staff. It has sought to answer questions such as these: what is meant by the terms "sexuality" and "sexual health;" how can the medical sciences provide sexual health care; and what kinds of academic programs will have the greatest impact on the qualify of care available to consumers? While our experience to date represents a significant contribution to the existing body of theoretical and empirical knowledge of the field, it would be premature to attempt to supply definitive answers to these questions.

The systems perspective adopted by the program views sexual behavior as psychobiological phenomena occurring within a sociocultural context. This conceptualization encompasses a range of topics: interplay of sexual expression and individual physical and mental health, sexual behavior and marital family stability, sexual behavior and drug and alcohol abuse, psychosexual rehabilitation of the disabled, and sexual health as an integral component of total health.

The concept of sexual health is a relatively recent formulation. The program has followed the definition provided by the World Health Organization:

> Sexual health is the integration of the somatic, emotional, intellectual, and social aspects of sexual being, in ways that are positively enriching and that enhance personality, communication and love. . . . The concept of sexual health includes three basic elements: (1) a capacity to enjoy and control sexual and reproductive behavior in accordance with a social and personal ethic, (2) freedom from fear, shame, guilt, false beliefs, and other psychological factors inhibiting sexual response and impairing socio-sexual relationships, (3) freedom from organic disorders, diseases and deficiencies that interfere with sexual and reproductive functions.[1]

Sexual health care thus encompasses both preventive and remedial measures, and our program has taken the position that all health care personnel should be in a prime position to provide patients with emotional support, acceptance, information, and guidance conducive to sexual health. Conversely, the health professional who is uneasy or ill-informed may have a countertherapeutic effect or cause iatrogenic dysfunction. Since little attention has traditionally been paid to the training of physicians and other health care professionals in the provision of sexual health care, the quality and availability of sexual health care have been inadequate. The organization of the program and its activities are based on an assessment of the training needs in this area.

ORGANIZATION AND ACTIVITIES

The program is organized into several areas based upon principal function: Sex Counseling Unit, Education, Sex and Disability Unit, and Research. Each area performs a diverse set of activities, with the staff participating in the activities of their own and other areas as the need arises. A closer look at the activities of each area will demonstrate the relationship between the organization and activities of the program and its objectives.

Sex Counseling Unit

This element of the Human Sexuality Program offers sex counseling services to the community and provides clinical experience for its counseling trainees. These trainees include physicians, social workers, psychologists, and psychotherapists, all of whom have extensive experience in working with relationship and sexual problems.

The counseling service is designed primarily for persons who feel dissatisfaction with some element of their sexual functioning. There are no eligibility requirements, although each application is reviewed by the staff to decide whether the program is likely to meet the applicant's needs. Counseling services include the following:

Sex Counseling for Couples.   For most couples the program consists of approximately ten 50-minute weekly counseling sessions, usually with a male-female counseling team. At the counselor's discretion, sessions may be held more or less frequently. In these sessions, counselors discuss details of the couple's sexual relationship and help them to discover ways in which they can increase the level of sexual and emotional satisfaction in their relationship. Couples who enroll in the program are required to set aside five to seven hours a week for home assignments.

Sex Counseling for Men.   Counseling is available to men who do not have steady partners or whose partners are unable or unwilling to participate in counseling. The most common problems are inability to have or maintain erections, difficulty in delaying ejaculation as long as desired, inability to ejaculate, and loss of interest in sex. Individual counseling with either a male or a female therapist usually consists of a single one-hour session a week for as long as necessary to resolve the problem. Men's sex therapy groups, consisting of four to eight clients and a male and female leader, meet for a two-hour session each week for 10–12 weeks. The group explores new behaviors designed to deal with specific problems of its members. For some individuals, a combination of group and individual therapy is used.

Social Enhancement Courses. Men and women who want to develop skill and confidence in making contact and relating to others in ways that are consistent with their own values and feelings may attend a Social Enhancement Course, conducted by a male and female leader in two all-day sessions on consecutive Saturdays.

Sex Counseling for Women. Several programs are offered for women who have concerns about sex and achieving orgasm. For example, in the preorgasmic group, six women who have rarely or never experienced orgasm or who cannot consistently masturbate to orgasm meet twice weekly for ten sessions with two female therapists. Another group treats secondarily nonorgasmic women who wish to broaden their orgasmic ability, such as having orgasms with a partner. Women who are consistently orgasmic with manual masturbation are accepted into this group which meets once a week for ten sessions.

Gay Counseling. Persons identifying themselves as gay may be seen through the gay program with gay counselors (both male and female), or they may choose to be seen in the clinic without going through the gay program. Gay couples may also be seen together for counseling.

Educational Seminar. An educational seminar, featuring lectures and films, is held approximately once every five weeks under the leadership of the staff. The general public and all persons who request counseling services are invited. The seminar is designed primarily as a preliminary sexuality course for potential counseling clients. Following the seminar, these people are better able to decide whether or not to enter the counseling program.

The Sex Counseling Unit averages more than 7000 client visits a year. Services are provided by approximately 24 counseling trainees during a nine-month practicum training program in sex therapy conducted by the clinic staff. Supervised experience in a variety of formats with different types of clients and problems helps trainees to develop the skills that will be most useful to them in their future work. Prerequisites for practicum trainees are: (1) previous supervised counseling experience, (2) completion of two courses: "Introduction to Sex Counseling Principles" and "Health Aspects of Human Sexuality," and (3) a comfortable awareness of their own sexuality and that of others. The practicum experience requires a minimum commitment of 16–20 hours a week, which is divided into three hours of didactic instruction and case conference, three hours of supervision, six to nine hours with clients, two hours of administrative activities, and two to three hours of assigned reading or supervised research.

Each trainee negotiates a behavioral contract with his or her supervisor at the beginning of training, and the trainee's progress in meeting these goals is continually evaluated. Trainees who, in the judgment of their supervisors, need remedial training may be required to attend special courses at additional expense (either at the University of California or elsewhere) to develop the required skills. If the supervisor believes that a trainee's skills are so deficient that they cannot be remedied during the course of training, the trainee will be dropped from the program or asked to extend his or her commitment.

Those individuals who complete the program satisfactorily are eligible to apply for certification as a sex therapist by the American Association of Sex Educators, Counselors, and Therapists. The program does not currently offer a certificate or an academic degree, but Sex Counseling Unit hours may be used for credit toward California licenses as Psychologist; Marriage, Family and Child Counselor; or Clinical Social Worker.

Education

The educational activities of the program may be roughly divided into academic courses for registered students and continuing education courses for practicing health and helping professionals. Education staff are primarily responsible for the continuing education courses, but they also provide coordination and support for other courses.

Academic Activity. "Human Sexuality and Medical Practice" is a 20-hour required core course offered once each year to 155 second-year medical students. The interrelationships between social, behavioral, and clinical aspects of human sexuality are presented in lectures, audio-visual presentations, role-played demonstrations, panel discussions, and small group discussions. Since we believe that students must examine the potential influence of their personal sexual value systems and attendant emotions upon their professional activity, a portion of this course is devoted to sexual attitude reassessment. Although there is only one required course in human sexuality, many students become aware of a deficit in their sexual health care skills during their later clerkship years and subsequently enroll in more advanced elective courses.

One such elective course is the one-month block elective in human sexuality for medical students, nurses and nursing students, residents, and physicians in any field. The objectives of this elective are to explore a wide spectrum of human sexual behavior, to survey the effects of disease and disability on sexuality, to increase the students' abilities to talk with patients about sexual problems and options, to make students more comfortable with their own sexuality, and to enable students to study one topic in depth. The elective is designed as a general introduction, not as training in sex therapy techniques, and consists of seminars, field trips, reading, and the preparation of a project. Seminar topics include: sexual problems and counseling approaches in various medical and nursing specialties (family practice, hospital nursing and nurse practitioners, internal medicine, obstetrics and gynecology, pediatrics, psychiatry, urology); the anatomy, physiology, and endocrinology of sexual functioning; sex history-taking; common sexual dysfunctions and their treatment; male and female sexuality; gender roles and androgeny; sex in childhood, adolescence, and aging; sex and disability; and alternate sexual and marital life styles. Various educational and counseling techniques are discussed, including "fair-fight training" and the use of films to improve sexual functioning.

Students attend a weekly personal growth group, led by a co-therapy team, to increase their comfort with their understanding of their own sexuality. Students have an opportunity to learn about body work and massage, to learn and practice sexologic examinations, and to visit lesbian and gay bars and coffee houses in San Francisco. These seminars and activities are planned daily for two to six hours. In the remaining time students are expected to read, meet with resource persons, and work on a project of special interest culminating in an academic paper, an annotated bibliography, an educational pamphlet, or a paper on the evolution of their personal sexual perspectives.

Program staff participate in teaching a required course in human sexuality for pharmacy students and in several courses offered by the School of Nursing, as well as making presentations during grand rounds and at special lectures.

Continuing Education. Approximately 1000 practicing professionals attend continuing education courses each year. The 20-hour "Health Aspects of Human Sexuality" course is designed to help the professional to be more effective in assisting patients and clients with their sexual concerns by acquiring accurate information about human sexual response and behavior, a comfortable acceptance of his or her own sexual practice and values as well as those of others, and an awareness of sexuality in all phases of health and mental health care. This programmed educational process uses films, didactic presentations, discussion, and several small group meetings to accomplish its objectives.

"Introduction to Sex Counseling Principles" is a 50-hour course, given over two consecutive weekends, designed to increase the proficiency and sensitivity of practicing professionals in working with sexual aspects of human behavior. The course is not intended to qualify participants as fully trained sex therapists, but it does provide current information regarding the treatment of sexual problems and related areas of behavior, opportunities to increase comfort with collecting information from and imparting information to persons with sexual difficulties or concerns, practice in basic interviewing and counseling techniques as adapted to sexual issues, and methods for integrating the principles of sex counseling into all areas of health care and social welfare. The couples co-counseling method provides the basic structure for this course, as well as a context for exploring fundamental aspects of functional and dysfunctional sexual behavior. Other treatment approaches are also presented. The emphasis is on broad principles that can be adapted by the professional to a wide range of individuals or couples. Course content includes such topic areas as sexual physiology and anatomy, social scripting of sexuality, communication skills, stepwise progression toward sexual satisfaction, overview of sex therapy, shared and solo sensual experience, and the theory and practice of home assignments. Content information is presented through lectures, film, and role-played demonstrations; small groups provide a context for the practice of skills and the integration of feedback from group members.

Other continuing education courses on specific topics have been developed for more limited audiences. "Lesbian and Gay Men: Clinical and Cultural Perspectives" is a 20-hour course for professionals, patterned after the "Health Aspects of Human Sexuality" course but focused on the social, psychological, and medical concerns of individuals who describe themselves as lesbian, gay, or bisexual. An "Office Management of Sexual Problems" course is directed toward physicians who wish to improve their ability to discuss sexual material with patients; provide patients with information concerning sexual difficulties which might be associated with their medical condition, surgery, or medication; alleviate common sexual problems in the context of an office practice; and make appropriate referrals. A 16-hour "Women's Sexual Health Education Seminar" is designed to teach participants about sexuality and the part it plays in a woman's life, to assist them in making responsible decisions about their own sexuality, and to increase their self-confidence and satisfaction in sexual relationships. Course content includes information about male and female sexual response, masturbation, sex roles, myths, fantasy, and the importance of touch in sexual relating. Another special course on "Sex and Disability" will be discussed in the following section.

Sex and Disability Unit

This component of the Human Sexuality Program provides clinical services, training, and continuing education. The population served includes not only persons with physical disabilities and other medical conditions, but also their spouses, intimates, families, health care providers, and other interested persons. Counseling services are provided for disabled individuals and couples who are orthopedically or neurologically handicapped or who have a chronic health problem which affects their self-image and sexuality.

Unit staff conduct lectures and workshops for a variety of students and professionals. One program provides 12 months of didactic and supervised practicum experience designed to train both disabled and able-bodied persons who have significant contact with the disabled to provide sociosexual counseling and education related to sex and disability to disabled persons. Efforts are currently being made to provide training for special education teachers in new approaches to family-life education for disabled students. This program involves a sequential series of three workshops and is open to qualified special education teachers and faculty.

The unit staff also conducts a continuing education course for health and helping professionals which attempts to increase the participants' awareness of the fact that the physically disabled or disadvantaged are sexual beings, with many of the same concerns about their sexuality as the able-bodied, as well as some unique concerns. Information is provided regarding the implications which various developmental or trauma-induced physical disabilities have for sexual development and function. Audio-visual presentations and panel presentations by individuals who are themselves disabled play an important role in achieving course objectives of increased participant awareness. Evaluation efforts, which are discussed in the next section, have documented the positive influence on the average course participant.

Research and Evaluation

Activities have been concerned primarily with collection of empirical data on the effectiveness and efficiency of various treatment, training, and educational methods. One significant product of this effort was validation of group treatment methods for primary anorgasmic women. Another was demonstration of the effectiveness of the "Aspects of Human Sexuality" course for increasing the sexual awareness of practicing health professionals and subsequent improvements in the quality of sexual health care provided their patients.

Each educational offering is evaluated, using a battery of questionnaires designed to assess changes in attitudes and values, behavior, and knowledge. The model format requires a precourse measure; an immediate postcourse measure which focuses on the personal relevance and perceived adequacy of the course and its components; and a follow-up measure eight weeks after the course, a portion of which assesses the manner and the degree to which the course content is being incorporated into the individual's professional practice.

Basic research is currently being conducted in the areas of sex-role stereotyping and its effects on sexual functioning, and the effects of somatosensory deprivation during early childhood on subsequent adult sexual behavior. A computerized data base composed of therapy-related data from over 1000 clients is being evaluated for internal reliability. This data base will permit the testing of several hypotheses concerning dysfunction/treatment interactions, general therapeutic effectiveness of various treatment modalities, and the etiology of common sexual dysfunctions.

Media Production. In cooperation with the Communications Office for Research and Teaching, University of California, San Francisco, the Human Sexuality Program has produced two films relating to sex therapy techniques and issues. "Reaching Orgasm" demonstrates a six-step series of home assignments used in counseling preorgasmic women in the Sex Counseling Unit. In the film, "The Sexological Experience," a couple demonstrates one way of doing a sexological examination in their home. Open communication between the partners is emphasized throughout the experience. A handbook has been developed to accompany both films. The handbook presents common myths about sexual functioning, information regarding sexual anatomy, the sexual-response cycle, and methods of increasing sexual responsiveness. Used conjointly, the film demonstrates the major concepts, while the handbook presents a discussion of attitudes related to the concepts and provides guided practice using the concepts. The films and the handbooks have proven useful in the counseling of clients and in the training of new therapists. Additional topics being considered include sexuality throughout the life cycle, male sexual response, and sexuality and the mastectomy patient.

FUTURE DIRECTIONS

The Human Sexuality Program was developed in 1972 in response to the perceived needs of health professionals, who were being asked by their patients to provide sexual health care services. This need still exists; and it may exist to a larger degree than in 1972. As the field of sex therapy matures, and as the current narrow conceptualization of sexuality broadens to take in those interpersonal and intrapsychic dimensions which are inextricably bound to it, the intensity and diversity of the program's activities will change. One cannot expect to understand human sexuality within its appropriate bio-social context without synthesizing the data and approaches from a broad range of disciplines into a viable conceptual framework. The sexual function will remain incomprehensible until this fusion occurs; the Human Sexuality Program will endeavor to continue to contribute to this process.

REFERENCES

1. Education and Treatment in Human Sexuality: The Training of Health Professionals. World Health Organization Technical Report Series, No. 572, Geneva, 1975, p 6

Francois E. Alouf

23
The Northwestern University Medical School Program

Like many other human sexuality programs in the country,[1] the Northwestern University Medical School human sexuality course came into being as the result of a very close cooperation between interested medical students, multidisciplinary faculty members (gynecology, obstetrics, psychiatry, community medicine, psychology), and the medical school administration (dean and associate deans). Very early in the planning stage, most of the committee members agreed that to get a new course approved as a required part of the core curriculum by the curriculum committee of the medical school would necessitate a great deal of time and effort, and it was decided to offer the course as an elective. From the beginning, then, the course was established as an elective (for credit) experience. Since the course began in the spring of 1972 the course's objectives and format have been frequently modified based on several formal evaluations by the participants and the teaching faculty.

Objectives

Currently our *objectives* are the following:

1. To increase the student's awareness that:
   a. a wide variety of sexual problems exist
   b. many of these problems are presented to physicians.

263

2. For medical students to learn attitudinally that:
   a. sexuality and its expression is a fundamental part of one's total personality
   b. unless a physician begins to understand his or her own sexual values, beliefs, biases, and misconceptions, he or she will be unknowingly limited in his or her ability to provide optimal medical care
   c. a physician's judgment is frequently handicapped by personal taboos and hasty responses or over-reactions to sexual information and stimuli
   d. a physician needs more than his or her personal experiences and private opinions to help patients
   e. developing feelings of tolerance toward other people's values and sexual lifestyles is essential to becoming an empathetic listener, without which one is professionally handicapped
3. For medical students to learn cognitively:
   a. the changing role of maleness and femaleness in contemporary society
   b. the existence of a wide spectrum of human sexual behaviors and of many points of view in "controversial" sexual issues
   c. accurate physiology of human sexuality with which he or she can demythologize earlier societal and parental misinformation
   d. the fact that physical health and sexual health are interdependent and inseparable
   e. physiology and psychology of sexual dysfunction
   f. the relationship between various sexual patterns of behavior and transmission and prevention of venereal diseases
   g. the variety of birth control methods
4. For medical students to learn the therapeutic skills needed to:
   a. develop sufficient rapport so that their patients feel comfortable in seeking information, reassurance, and therapy about sexual expectations and problems
   b. decide whether they will include or exclude the management of sexual problems in their medical practice
   c. suspect, diagnose, and influence the outcome of their patients' sexual problems

Format

As educators, we recognize that teaching strategy and format are intricately linked to the course objectives. In our judgment, the students need a human sexuality curriculum that includes (1) an accurate transmission of information, (2) an opportunity to reassess one's own values and attitudes toward the wide range of human sexual behavior, and (3) the acquisition of therapeutic skills that would enable the student to better understand and influence the outcome of his or her patients' sexual difficulties.

Based on our experience of the last four years, it has become evident that the student's receptiveness to, and absorption and comprehension of sexual information often increases dramatically once he or she has developed a more accepting attitude toward what the student might have considered a taboo subject. Stimulated by the work of McIlvenna at the National Sex Forum, Vandervoort at the University of California (San Francisco) Medical School, and Chilgren at the University of Minnesota Medical School, we adopted with some modifications the Sexual Attitude Reassessment (SAR) Workshop format. Essentially the SAR process:

1. Aims at increasing the students' understanding of people's sexual attitudes and feelings that differ from their own.
2. Encourages self-acceptance as sexual and sensual beings with a right to select and direct one's relationships with others.
3. Facilitates in the students the development of a tolerant attitude toward people whose sexual values differ from their own.
4. Asserts that sex and sexuality are natural functions and are integral parts of ourselves.
5. Endorses the students' right to know about the range of human sexual behavior.
6. Endorses the individual's right to his or her own beliefs or convictions.
7. Encourages self-knowledge as a necessary base upon which sexual health and tolerance are built.

Vandervoort and McIlvenna[2] and Lief[3] have described in detail the essential components of a SAR workshop: desensitization, resensitization, integration, and implosion. Very briefly, in order to portray the wide range of sexual attitudes and behaviors that exist in our society the SAR utilizes films, slides, tapes, panel presentations, nonverbal exercises, and small group meetings. Through the use of graphic audio-visual sexual materials, the participants are immediately immersed into one to several hours of viewing explicit sex films, some of which are projected simultaneously. The films are presented in a planned sequence that first introduces commercially produced, "hard core" explicit erotic genital activity, illustrating the broad variety of human sexual activity (e.g., heterosexuality, homosexuality, bisexuality, masturbation, oral–genital sex, anal sex, group sex, sex with animals). This sequence is intended to "desensitize" the participants and render them less over-reactive to explicit sexual stimuli. This phase is followed by the "resensitization" and endorsement sequence, wherein films mostly produced by the National Sex Forum, and specifically designed to represent "relational" sexual activity between caring partners, are shown. Again the purpose of this segment of the SAR is to stimulate the participants' thinking and feeling processes.

The films are followed by small group discussions of eight to ten participants, led by facilitators who have already experienced the SAR process and have attained a comfortable level of dealing with their own sexuality. These groups are not designed to be "encounter" or "therapy" sessions. The aim of the small group meetings is to encourage the individual members to discuss their feelings, attitudes, and reactions to the films in an atmosphere of openness and objectivity. Such a process seems to augment the participants' opportunity to learn more about themselves and the other members in the group, and at the same time contributes greatly to the demythologization and the demystification of one's feelings about sexuality. Trust exercises and body massages, also part of the SAR process, are used to augment the participants' awareness of their own bodies through learning about the meaning of touch (e.g., sensual versus sexual, comforting versus aggressive, reassuring versus rejecting) and to learn the significance of nonverbal behavior.

A panel on "alternate life-styles" is also included. Panelists and participants have the opportunity to interact and experience each other as "real people." The particular choice of life-styles usually represented are: celibacy, monogamy, open marriage, bi-sexuality, group marriage, swinging, and homosexuality. An important part of the SAR also features a presentation on sexual scripting and sexual cultural myths of men and women in contemporary society.

These presentations are followed by the same-sex small group meetings at which men and women, in their separate groups, are able to discuss many of their feelings and attitudes about their respective role-scripting. It is in these meetings that both men and women most often begin to share concrete information about (1) themselves and their socialization into sexual beings, (2) their feelings concerning their sexual responses, (3) the variety of sexual responses that they may have experienced over the years and how these may have evolved, (4) the myths, fantasies, fears, and inhibitions surrounding masturbation and how they may have dealt with them, (5) the myths and fantasies surrounding such areas as orgasmic release, simultaneous orgasms, "faking orgasms," oral genital activity, penile and vaginal sizes, sex during menstruation, and anal sex, (6) the necessity to get in touch with one's own sexuality and to begin accepting responsibility for one's own sexual responses, (7) communicating with oneself and with one's partner(s) one's own sexual needs, concerns, fantasies, and in some cases, desire to enrich the range of one's sexual and emotional life.

After the same-sex group meeting is over, all participants assemble in one large group. By using the "fish bowl" method, all the men (or women) at first sit in the inner circle with the participants of the opposite sex on the outside circle, "listening in" on the same-sex group's reporting. After a while the listeners change places with the reporting members, whose turn is now to listen in. Once both groups have reported their feelings and reactions, both groups are then encouraged to interact freely by commenting on what they have heard and by asking questions of each other. In our experience the "fish bowl" process has proven itself to be one of the most significant and effective segments of information transmission during the SAR process. It has a very important demythologizing value. In addition to the small group experience that the participants are involved in during the SAR, the "fish bowl" format provides them with another opportunity to "check out" and often disconfirm many of their misconceptions, prejudices, and biases concerning sexuality.

The SAR process with the group discussion, films, body awareness exercises, and panels is an intense 16-hour weekend experience that has become identified as "implosion."[3] The SAR workshops are held four times a year, and where applicable the participants are encouraged to register with their "significant other."

We mentioned earlier that the students need accurate information, a tolerant attitude toward the wide range of human sexual behaviors, and skills that would enable them to influence the outcome of their patients' sexual problems. So, in addition to the SAR, the Northwestern University program in human sexuality has three other components: (1) didactic, (2) small group leader training, and (3) sex therapy skills development.

Didactic. A human-sexuality lectures series consisting of 12-13 two-hour lectures is held once a week in the evening, generally during the winter quarter. The topics vary from year to year. Most recently the subjects covered were: sex and medical illness; sexual dysfunction; sex and aging; physiology of the sexual response in men and women; sexual identity development in children, adolescents, and adults; myths and reality of male and female sexuality; cultural differences in sexuality and reproduction; the medical, social, and legal aspects of rape; open sexuality; and primary relationships. In addition to the lectures, a human sexuality syllabus, updated yearly, has been developed and is made available to those students who may be taking an elective in human sexuality. The syllabus consists of seven sections, with reprints from the literature covering the following: (1) psychophysiology of human sexual response, (2) the sex hormones and gender identity, (3) mammalian sexual behavior, (4) contraception and venereal disease, (5) aspects of female and male sexuality, (6) social aspects of human sexuality, and (7) sexual dysfunctions.

Small-group Leader Training. Students who have already participated in at least one SAR workshop, and are interested in expanding their skills in that area, are encouraged to participate in the training program for SAR leaders. In addition to the SAR workshop, the other prerequisites are successful completion of the Behavioral Sciences Courses I and II (part of the core curriculum for freshman and sophomore medical students). Both courses emphasize, among other subjects, interviewing skill and interpersonal dynamics. Training methods for group leaders include role-playing, nonverbal exercises, discussion groups, and a variety of group leading techniques. New leaders are then paired with more experienced co-leaders during their first workshop assignment. At the conclusion of the first day of each SAR workshop, all the group leaders meet and process the day's interactions. Following the workshop, the participants evaluate (anonymously) the two-day experience and also their group leaders. Those evaluations are discussed with the leaders.

Sex Therapy Skills Development. Students interested in learning short-term sex therapy are offered training in that area once they successfully complete the Behavioral Science I and II courses, attend at least one SAR workshop, participate in the SAR small-group discussion leaders' training program, and have one or more co-leading experiences in the SAR. These graduated steps are helpful in assessing the student's motivation, interest, sensitivity, psychological-mindedness, and capacity to learn and apply sex therapy techniques.

The sex therapy skills development program has a didactic and a clinical component. In addition to attending the human sexuality lecture series, the student is encouraged to become thoroughly familiar with the human sexuality syllabus and other literature relevant to the treatment of sexual dysfunctions. The Human Sexuality Clinic is not as yet an independent program, and patients with sexual dysfunctions are essentially handled on a referral basis through the general outpatient clinic of the Institute of Psychiatry of the Northwestern Memorial Hospital, which is the clinical base for the Department of Psychiatry of the Northwestern University Medical School. Once a patient or a couple has been accepted for sex therapy, the student trainees (a male and a female) are assigned a senior faculty member with special expertise in the area of sexual therapy as a treatment supervisor.

EVALUATION

Attempts have been made to measure changes in students' attitudes resulting from the sex education courses. The Sex Knowledge and Attitudes Test (SKAT) developed by Lief and Reed has been used extensively.[4] Pretest and posttest studies have demonstrated that changes in students' attitudes and feelings do occur. The changes are mostly in the direction of an increased tolerance toward different points of view, as well as an increase in the acceptance of other people's sexual choices, orientation, and life-styles.

Our own evaluations confirm those findings. Of the 160 medical students who completed the evaluation form for the last four SAR workshops, the following responses were given to questions using a five-point Likert scale:

85.7 percent felt that they had increased their knowledge of their own sexual attitudes and behavior

84 percent felt that they had increased their knowledge of the sexual behavior and attitudes of others

84 percent felt more comfortable with their own attitudes and values

70 percent felt less threatened by sexual attitudes and values that were different from their own

68 percent felt less pressured to conform to attitudes and values that were different from their own

80.1 percent felt they had an increased awareness of their own bodies

84 percent felt more able to distinguish between the sexual and the sensual

82.3 percent felt they had increased their understanding of the personal, social, and cultural meaning of sex-role scripting

80 percent felt they had increased their understanding of the meaning of touching

80 percent felt the workshop had made them more comfortable in discussing sexual issues with their patients

Golden and Liston have expressed misgivings about the extent and duration of the reported changes.[5] They point out that variables such as whether the course is elective or required, is chosen by the student for personal or career reasons, as well as the format and the biases of the instructors, all contribute to contamination of the results reported. Recently, Mandel administered the SKAT to 500 undergraduate students at Northwestern University (Evanston Campus) in an attempt to determine if any significant differences existed "between students who attend voluntary human sexuality courses and those who do not."[6] Upon completion of the SKAT, all the students who took the test were invited to participate in a one-day human sexuality workshop. Fifty-seven students took advantage of the offer.

Mandel's preliminary findings indicate that the "workshop participants knew more about sex, had more liberal attitudes, felt more adjusted sexually than their peers" than those who chose not to attend the workshops. Obviously these findings raise an important question. Should all medical students be required to participate in a human sexuality program, or should such a program continue to be an elective? If such a program is primarily attracting those students who "need it" the least, what about the other students who will also be consulted by patients having sexual adjustment problems?

SUMMARY

Through a series of graduated learning experiences, the Human Sexuality program at Northwestern University Medical School, offers the medical students an opportunity to become more cognizant of their own sexual attitudes and values, and to increase their competence at developing rapport with their patients, so that the patients can feel more comfortable in seeking information, reassurance, and therapy for their sexual difficulties. The program also aims at enabling tomorrow's physician to become more sensitive to the feelings and expectations of his or her patients, and more skilled at helping them clarify for themselves their sexual needs and the ways by which these needs can be met. We think that such a clarification process enhances the patients' potential for maintaining through their lives growth-promoting relationships that foster sexual and emotional health. The teaching format combines the attitudinal approach (through the SAR workshops), the didactic approach (through lectures and assigned readings), and the clinical approach (through a supervised, short-term sex therapy program).

REFERENCES

1. Alouf FE, Tyler EA: Sex education. U.S. medical students, in Laury GV (ed): Médecine et Hygiène, Journal Suisse d'Informations Médicales, 35, 1977, Genève, Suisse
2. Vandervoort HE, McIlvenna T: Sexually explicit media in medical school curricula, in Green R (ed): Human Sexuality: A Health Practitioner's Text. Baltimore, Williams & Wilkins, 1975

3. Lief HI: Obstacles to the ideal and complete sex education of the medical student and physician, in Zubin J, Money J (eds): Contemporary Sexual Behavior. Baltimore, Johns Hopkins University Press, 1973

4. Lief, HI, Reed, DM: Sex knowledge and attitude test (SKAT). University of Pennsylvania School of Medicine, 1970

5. Golden JS, Liston EH: Medical sex education; The world of illusion and the practical realities. J Med Educ 47:761–771, 1972

6. Mandel JB: The sexual attitude reassessment, the workshop participant and attitude change. Presented at the International Congress of Sexology, Montreal, 1976

Domeena C. Renshaw

24
The Loyola Program

WHY?

Why a Sex Clinic and an Elective Training Program at a Jesuit University Medical School in metropolitan Chicago? Simply because of a real need in 1972. We were receiving sex dysfunction referrals from the gynecology and urology departments (the psychiatry corridor is sandwiched between these two neighbors). At Intake Meeting, the psychiatry residents would present the cases evaluated, make a simple diagnostic statement (e.g., premature ejaculation), and when I would ask what the disposition had been, they would shrug and say "Nothing, I sent him home." When asked why, they would state that they did not know what to do with the patient. It was at once apparent to me as a faculty educator that in order to know what to do, they needed to be taught.

Having read the Masters and Johnson work in this field, I set about designing a program for the realities of this medical school. I approached the chairman of gynecology, who was interested and supportive, as was the chairman of urology. Both agreed that if an elective program could be designed, they would offer it to their residents. My chairman of psychiatry was equally supportive. Second-year psychiatry residents were enthusiastic, and there was an immediate cluster of two volunteer teams for our first elective.

HOW?

I am sure the rapid take-off of this program is due to the fact that no money was requested, no committees were sought out. The Sex Clinic was simply an additional service to be rendered by the regular Psychiatric Outpatient Clinic. The psychiatric social worker who handled intake was pleased, since she had numbers of couples inquiring. I knew of one expensive local resource, a private psychiatrist at an urban hospital. There were many costly so-called sex clinics of unknown quality in the Chicago area to which we declined to refer.

My personal dilemma was how to obtain referrals of suitable cases for the trainees without exaggerating our potential or being flooded with patients. I sent a mimeographed notice to all Loyola medical staff. This resulted in referral of an exhibitionist and a woman having an affair! We then gave out a one-paragraph news item to urban papers, "Loyola Sex Clinic Opens." Referrals have not stopped since then.

Our pioneer planning group (a male and female second-year psychiatric resident, the intake social worker, and myself) met twice and agreed that some initial didactic input was essential before the clinical experience. I knew we could not adopt the 14-day schedule of the Masters and Johnson program as described in their writings, due to medical school realities. A half-day-a-week elective program for ten weeks was designed with three weeks of didactic and seven weeks of clinical contact.[1]

It was a fumbling beginning. In my own anxiety, we designed into the first clinical week what we now do in three weeks! The allotted time of four hours for the session seemed excessive for doing a sexual history by a dual-sex team of the patient couple, but, of course, was hardly sufficient. I participated personally as co-therapist in the first two semesters to be aware of both difficulties and potential of the program, which I felt had to be structured rather carefully to allow for the predictable transience of resident assignments. In July 1972, I did not think of using this experience as an elective for medical students; that was to come two years later, and they have been splendid!

DIDACTIC PROGRAM

Three didactic workshops are scheduled on Fridays from 1–6 PM for all trainees, regardless of what day of the week they will be seeing their assigned couple.

Workshop I. Potential male–female teams are introduced to each other, asked to sit together through the three-week didactic sessions to get to know each other before they work together as a clinical team. Using 35mm slides and films, the male and female human sexual response-cycle is carefully described and contrasted. Then the many factors that inhibit and stimulate sexuality are outlined, and the speculative neurophysiological pathways are discussed. The input of all the distant senses, such as vision, taste, smell, touch, and hearing are carefully illustrated with clinical anecdotes as to how these might enhance or inhibit sexual responses in patients. The effect of memory, positive and negative, is similarly linked to clinical vignettes to emphasize the need for a detailed early sexual history (childhood, teens, into the current life of the patient). Imagination (fantasy) may be a positive factor, "I am going to succeed" or the opposite, "I will fail again (e.g., to have an orgasm or to hold my erection)." Would-be therapists therefore must ask about fantasy before, during, and after sex, in order to understand the patient.

Although there are differences in each semester's trainee group, questions, comments, and suggestions are vigorous. Team members in the workshop are asked to get in touch with their own responses of anxiety or arousal to the audio-visual material. Privacy is respected. Some will share feelings; others may do so a week later or not at all. Some role-playing is attempted at the end of the first workshop (e.g., a team meets their couple for the first time and introduces themselves and the program).

Workshop II. This is an introduction to cross-cultural sexuality, where slides from art and sculpture through the centuries depict all varieties of explicit sexual behavior from ancient Egyptians to primitive Peruvians, Africans, and current Danish and United States sexual activities. It is stressed that sexual customs differ, as does language and artwork style. A cross-racial film is also shown. I mention to the group that it is easier to deal with portrayed sexuality (whether it is homosexuality, bestiality, or regular heterosexual, traditional coitus) while looking at ancient drawings or pottery (distant in time and place) than looking at someone similar to ourselves, with whom we can more closely (but also with discomfort) identify. Some trainee members may share personal discomfort, while others may angrily challenge why they need to be exposed to "this range" of sexual behavior when, for instance, homosexual couples were not likely to be seen by them. (Loyola Sex Clinic only treats married couples, being part of a Catholic University.) This dialogue is a useful medium to point out that while trainees need not condone sexual behavior of others, they must understand and accept it and be able to listen to whatever the patient might present. Not uncommonly, patients who come with sexual problems have questioned their own sexual identity, thinking "if I cannot make it with my female partner, maybe I'm homosexual" or vice versa for a female. Optimal care is compromised if further disclosure is rapidly sealed off when the patient realizes that the therapist is upset at the material disclosed.[2,3]

The dynamics of interpersonal exchange and techniques of relationship therapy are discussed, with emphasis to avoid one-to-one therapy within the foursome of the treatment format. At times, one partner who does not have a sexual symptom adopts a posture of "let us three fix her or him." This must be changed from the first session by emphasizing that *the relationship will be the patient* and there is no uninvolved member.

Also, in workshop two, a simulated team and couple role-play history-taking. The Clinic has used a structured eight-page history sheet, starting with familiar medical and social data, then on to questions about early sex behavior, incest, rape, preferences for different sexual activities, fantasy, and related topics. Other teams "fish-bowl" the volunteer role-players, freely interrupt and correct, or add to the role-players' exchange. Teams thus become more comfortable with the thought of what they will face in the coming weeks. Also the role-players often portray so resistant a couple that any real couple will be easy after this!

Workshop III.   Patient couples are assigned to each team. Intake sheets are distributed with names of patients and their problems as defined from their initial phone interview. This arouses a high level of anxiety as the reality of the following week becomes clear. The experiential activity of the three five-hour workshops has gone a long way toward building a sense of warmth and closeness in the group. Although the groups have been as large as 40 trainees, this has not been a deterrent to interaction, and very few trainees have not been able to speak up and participate. If a particularly shy member is noted, I will draw them into the role-playing, and they have done well. They have been honest enough to admit to their own anxieties in coming into the sex field, and this has endeared them to other members, who will share their own particular struggles before attempting the Sex Clinic training. One psychiatry resident admitted he had anxiously seen three "skin flicks" before rotating, because he felt he might then be better able to brace himself for the materials to be seen.

A substantial workshop package is given to teams in the first week for study and discussion. The required minimum reading material for would-be trainees is Bellevue and Richter's *Understanding Human Sexuality*. Masters and Johnson's volumes are used for reference, and teams are expected to read about the particular symptoms of the couple they will be seeing.

Specific suggested treatment techniques for each of the presented sex symptoms are then discussed. Role-playing is again used for anticipated clinical interactions, including the sexological examination. A large Raggedy Andy doll is used, and a penis and vagina innovated. The need is thus emphasized of doing a good and thorough educational sexological examination in the presence of both members of the dual-sex team and both members of the patient couple. This segment usually causes great hilarity. The whole "fish-bowl group" joins in and hazes the anxious role-players, while the simulated couple have not hesitated to give team members a hard time.

Then the "Fantastic Voyage into Self" (a look at the individual's self-esteem and total body) is also role-played, as well as the "Marcel Marceau" (non-verbal session), when couples are asked to interact on given cues without words, only with body language.

The workshops end with a reminder for trainees that for seven weeks thay *are* Loyola to the couples. Dress code, behavior, and ethical code must take this into account. Respect for the value system of the patient is primary.

CLINICAL METHOD

Up to five patient couples are seen by five teams once a week for seven weeks for 4–5-hour sessions (including supervision). The first and second sessions, history-taking and the physicals, are the longest.

Clinical Week 1.   Each couple is met by their dual-sex team and supervisors, and introduced. Couples are told that they will be seen by their primary therapists, and that a supervisor may drop in from time to time (for trouble-shooting). The teams begin with a roundtable foursome for a contract statement, outlining the methods to be used, and clarifying any questions that the couples may have. The male therapist/male patient and female therapist/female patient start on the history. After about 90 minutes, there is a 20-minute supervisory break to recapitulate and extract essential life patterns. Therapists cross-over for a further hour of history (male therapist/female patient and female therapist/male patient).

Then the five couples and ten therapists convene in a conference room. The supervisor welcomes all again, reassures the couples, and briefly runs over some general issues: (1) treating the coupleship as the patient, (2) making time for the home exercises (½-hour per day), (3) exploring and learning the sexual self, (4) discussing sexual feelings and preferences at home, (5) no intercourse during week-one, (6) explaining the relaxing nondemanding sensual foreplay suggested for week-one, and (7) generalizing specific concerns that emerged in a particular history (e.g., small penis, sexual aversion).

The couples are not introduced to each other. The anonymity maintains a sex education format. These group sessions seem to be therapeutic, reducing the sense of being "unique." Older couples are in disbelief that younger couples today have problems ("We thought that there was a sexual revolution and they've made it"), while younger couples have said, "We thought the older people would already have worked it out." The team members specifically observe their couple's reactions for later discussion.

Little colored pipe-cleaner dolls (made to show breasts and a penis) are used to show clearly suggested positions for home loveplay. Couples are encouraged to plan an erotic surprise for each other, rather than complain that the "homework is mechanical or forced." Couples have a stretch break.

Final supervisory suggestions for each team's roundtable depend on the couple's history. For example: "Recapitulate that both had unhappy childhoods. Maybe they could discuss this more at home this week. Also, in the past, both have had difficulty saying what they liked or disliked about their sexual life. Tell them to be open this week, particularly during the sensate focus exchange . . ."

Clinical Week 2. All patients have a thorough physical examination and an educational sexological examination done with both team members and the spouse in the room. A gynecologist is in consultative attendance for each session and may be called in. Then all the couples and teams meet in the conference room for a didactic session (with audiovisuals) about sexual anatomy and physiology, which they have just seen on themselves. Factors which may interfere with sexual function are outlined. The film "Female Sexual Response" is shown to all. Team members watch their couple's interaction to discuss afterward in the roundtable. Usually the assignments at home will still be "no genital and breast contact this week."

Clinical Week 3. Roundtable with the couple to hear their week's activities at home and compare their written sheets. After supervision, one spouse goes with the team into a separate room for the Fantastic Voyage into Self. The patient stands before a mirror and tells what he or she likes/dislikes/wants to change about the body. Then the patient is asked to take a "pretend trip as little me" into "big me" and give feedback to the therapists of "what you see and feel" about every internal organ and aspect of the body.

This exercise may sound trite when read, but it has been an extremely valuable projective test (almost a body Rorschach!) and may help to get in touch with self. It has often been difficult for the patient, but can be therapeutic. A patient with low self-esteem may be assisted by reassurance, suggestions, or simply recognition of realistic assets.

The partner, meanwhile, is completing the Minnesota Multiphasic Personality Inventory, which is used more as a time filler and possible research tool, rather than for any striking value. Yet, patients are invariably intrigued by this long test and want to know "what did it say?" They are told in generalities during week-five or -six.

Clinical Week 4. A roundtable discussion of the past week notes concordance or discordance. *Not* bringing in the homework sheets is an important aspect of understanding the couple's functioning. There are times when an uninvolved partner will not bring in his or her homework sheet until perhaps the fifth week, when they really become involved in the program for the first time. Every aspect is discussed openly in therapy, with an emphasis that the team, as well as the couple, learn to use "I-language" rather than "you-language," which blames rather than takes full responsibility for personal reactions. For example, "I feel, John, that you are uninvolved. Could you complete your sheet to say how you feel about Linda's reactions this week?" rather than "you never bring in homework sheets."

The non-verbal "Marcel Marceau" session is done. Cues are given by the team to the couple: "Show John how you felt about his bringing you roses." "Show Linda how you would like her to get ready for bed." "Say goodbye forever" is often highly emotional, particularly for couples threatening divorce.

Clinical Week 5. Roundtable discussion of home exercises is followed by a general session of couples and teams in the conference room. Such issues as making time, use of "I-language," and emphasis on the relationship as patient may be discussed. Then, the film "Squeeze Technique" is shown to all couples, even those who do not have premature ejaculation. It portrays female-on-top coitus (excellent for nearly all sexual dysfunctions, also an alternative position for others). Moreover, the film is erotic, yet acceptable with its scientific dialogue. The Gorm-Wagner "Female Sexual Response" is reshown, since the first time couples see it, by their own admission, most see very little of the content. The "Squeeze Technique" film is shown once more. Thus all the couples will have seen each film twice. Some couples have even asked to see them yet again, admitting to being "shocked and at first almost seeing nothing."

We learn constantly from the couples, and the biased sample of troubled couples who seek out our Sexual Dysfunction Clinic need this degree of permission to view explicit sexual material. Often, this is the first time in their lives. The presence and permission of the partner and team is also therapeutic.

Clinical Weeks 6 and 7. These weeks are spent talking, integrating, and terminating sessions. Fears and feelings about separation from the Clinic are discussed. We emphasize "no therapy is good therapy," namely, if we have done a good job of directing them toward each other in a healing relationship, most will not need the Sex Clinic at the end of the time. However, for some couples, alternatives for follow-up are offered, and this greatly reduces the anxiety about termination. Loyola Clinic is a permanent resource should couples have problems at a later time.

The option of coming back after about nine or ten weeks for a one hour follow-up has been popular. This extends the "work" of couples, knowing they will come back to report on what they have done since the seven weeks of Clinic. Many couples call to say that they are fine and have done well and do not exercise the optional follow-up, but some do come back to reinforce their gains or to stop from slipping back into old avoidance patterns.

SUPERVISION

Supervision can make or break a program. Someone on a Sex Clinic Training Program must take responsibility for facilitation and permanence, especially when so many part-timers share in the actual clinical work. On the first visit, all patient couples should be introduced to the supervisor in addition to their therapists. They should know that their case will be discussed on each visit, that a supervisor may join a session (for interpretation, clarification, reinforcement, or congratulation).

Experienced therapists (some trainees were postgraduates in their sixties) benefit from time-out to confer, share, have peer exchange, as well as input from a detached colleague.

Inexperienced therapists benefit from condensing material, gathered in such bulk. The supervisor assists them to understand the interactional dynamics that they have reported, and suggests areas requiring further questioning for the co-therapist, when they switch over. This heightens each therapist's clinical awareness and skill. Main points and individual patterns are extracted. A great supervisory and memory aid has been a simple 8x11-inch card, divided into a "his" and "hers" for each couple (see Table 24-1). Important highlights are thus recorded for critical linkage

Table 24-1

Married _____ years	Therapists: _____
Children _____	Jim Blake
_____ called Clinic	Joan Smith
	Tuesday nights 2-5-77

JONES

Educ.	Age	John	Linda	Age	Educ.	Phone
Job	Relig.		Relig.		Job	B.C.

1. Sexual Sx: Duration	1. Sexual Sx: Duration

2. Freq. Intercourse
   Freq. Masturbation
	2. Freq. Intercourse
	   Freq. Masturbation

3. Main Problem	3. Main Problem
4. Previous Help	4. Previous Help
5. Medications	5. Medications
6. Alcohol	6. Alcohol
7. Illness	7. Illness

8. Dad: age/job/rels/role today
   Mom: age/job/rels/role today
   Sibs: age/job/rels/role today
	8. Dad: age/job/rel/role today
	   Mom: age/job/rels/role today
	   Sibs: age/job/rels/role today

9. Previous marriage/s:
   ex-wife age/job/rel/role today
   why divorced
	9. Previous marriage/s:
	   ex-hus. age/job/rel/role today
	   why divorced

10. Affair (details as 9)	10. Affair (details as 9)

11. This courtship:
   What attracted?
   What problems now?
	11. This courtship:
	   What attracted?
	   What problems now?

12. Early sex experiences
   Incest: First I/C
	12. Early sex experiences
	   Incest: First I/C

13. Sex fantasy	13. Sex fantasy

Following weeks:
2nd week: homework:
                 Physical (Linda):
                 Physical (John):
3rd week: homework:
                 Fantastic Voyage (Linda):
                 Fantastic Voyage (John):

Result:
  Sexual Sx: 4th week: homework:
  John _____   Marcel Marceau (Linda):
  Linda _____   Marcel Marceau (John):
Comments: 5th week: homework:
                 reactions:
             6th week: homework:
Follow-up Appointment: reactions:
_____   7th week: homework:
                 reactions:

from week to week. Supervisor flexibility is ensured (to keep the histories straight when sharing supervision or a therapy session). The supervisor's astute feedback is educative, and openness in supervision should match openness in therapy. Often supervision becomes an important way of allowing husband-wife therapy teams to understand and grow in their own interactions.

Through the careful structure of this training program, the supervisory process itself may be taught, so that a pool of experienced sex educators may slowly be built.

TRAINEES

Up to February 1978 there have been 422 new trainees. Of these, 121 have reelected to work with further couples. Often these have been full-time Loyola staff social workers, who now form a fine resource as "therapist pool."

Each dual-sex team consists of at least one physician or medical student, who is responsible for the physical examination and initial mental status examination with diagnosis of the patient couple. Progress notes are a shared responsibility.

Residents in psychiatry, gynecology, urology, and family practice have rotated, with excellent departmental collaboration. Residents from other local (and distant) medical schools have also trained, as have postgraduates from family practice, pediatrics, gynecology, and psychiatry. Some have come from out of state or abroad.

Medical students were "allowed" to train in the third year of the Sex Clinic, after I overcame my own anxiety about how they would cope. They have done exceptionally well. To date, 135 medical students (124 from Loyola, 3 from South Africa, 8 from local medical schools) have gone through the program. Fifteen student wives have rotated as co-therapists.

Other disciplines who have trained have been mostly social workers, social work students, nurses, psychologists, counselors, medical assistants, and ministers. A total of 32 spouses rotated; their occupations have included lawyer, economist, teacher, and housewife. All have done well.

For all trainees, the "entry anxiety" of the first clinical week is extremely high. Often they are ashen and tremulous when they go out with me to meet their couples. Slowly, by the first supervisory session, both color in their cheeks and confidence in themselves have returned.

For non-physicians and non-nurses, being present in the physical and sexological examination has been anticipated with much anxiety. All have survived! They have recorded data and held the mirror. According to their reports, this defense of "being busy" greatly assisted them to cope with the experience. Couples benefit from the dual-sex model, and there is marked enhancement of therapist bonding plus patient-therapist trust after the sexological examination.

Follow-up of trainees is a goal of the program, but one that is extraordinarily difficult. Medical students are predictably transient, as are residents. Postgraduates have been easiest to follow.

There is a waiting list of non-Loyola candidates for training.

THE COUPLES

Couples with sexual dysfunction phone our Intake Psychiatric Social Worker, who has been with the program since its inception in 1972. Only married couples are accepted for the training program. Single persons with sex problems are routinely assigned to psychiatry residents who have already rotated through the Sex Clinic.

The symptom, duration of marriage, and some basic information is obtained by phone. This is followed by a form letter, describing the training program, its seven weeks of involvement, the fee ($350 package for seven weeks). The waiting list is unfortunately long (200 couples), in spite of the fact that we refer many couples to our trainees in the area. Some couples wait from ten months to two years.

To date (February 1978), of 268 couples who have been evaluated for treatment, only two couples did not show. Fourteen of these couples discontinued at week-one, which really is the true screening day. Four discontinued at their own request, two because they refused to have a physical (one had had treatment for uterine carcinoma three years ago, another had a lobotomy for lung cancer, both without follow-up).

We requested that seven couples "go back on the waiting list" for ethical reasons. One partner had a current secret affair. To continue a pretense of sex therapy and enter into a "conspiracy of secrecy" would have been destructive. Without exception, time together was a big problem, so without breaking confidentiality, we take the blame. I say that the Clinic has a very simple program, where success is highly dependent on the couple doing daily exercises at home, otherwise it cannot work. Therefore, we will place them again on the waiting list, until their schedules improve and they can participate.

Profile of the Couples

Physical and psychiatric problems have not been deterrents. One paraplegic, numerous diabetics, postcoronary, and hypertensive patients have been treated. There have been 13 black couples, two Mexicans, a New Zealand student couple, and four immigrant European couples. Religions have covered the spectrum: Catholic, Protestant, Jewish, Moslem, "none." Twelve were unconsummated marriages, one of seven years' duration. Three patients were chronic schizophrenics, another a manic-depressive, some were extremely anxious, and three were clinically depressed. When indicated, medication was used during the course of the sex therapy.[4,5]

We have had as patients in the trainee Clinic 6 physicians, 5 dentists, 16 lawyers. After initial "therapist credential checks," all except three participated and improved.

Of the 254 couples treated (508 persons), 46 percent showed sexual dysfunction in both partners (often not clearly defined at telephone intake). Presenting symptoms were the following:

Male		Female	
76	secondary impotence	109	secondary orgasmic dysfunction
14	secondary impotence	60	primary orgasmic dysfunction
	(Post-premature ejaculation)	8	dyspareunia
75	premature ejaculation	9	primary orgasmic dysfunction +
7	primary impotence		dyspareunia + vaginismus
4	retarded ejaculation	4	vaginismus
21	no interest in sex	30	no interest in sex

Results of therapy are in process of computation, and a five-year follow-up is in process. Impressions of immediate results at the end of seven weeks are (for symptom reversal): premature ejaculation and secondary orgasmic dysfunction, about 98 percent; secondary impotence and primary orgasmic dysfunction, about 80 percent. All of the vaginismus and dyspareunia cases reversed. Lack of sexual interest were most difficult, yielding about 56 percent improvement.

PROGRAM DIFFICULTIES

Difficulties have centered mainly on realities of time and space. The popularity of the program with Loyola residents and medical students has created demands that place time pressures on me to supervise more and larger groups. My priorities have shifted in favor of making time for this task, since it has proven to be so rich a learning experience for trainees and so helpful to patients. Combining service and medical education is ideal.

Space has been a major difficulty, which we have solved by holding night clinics (5-10 PM) when outpatient offices are available. This time is optimum for working couples and most trainees. Some trainees (urology, gynecology, family practice) are unable to manipulate call schedules, so Friday, 1-6 PM is their only option. This presents a space crisis (two rooms per team needed for the first four weeks). It is a case of beg, borrow, and invade! We have on occasion used the linen closet on a Friday afternoon! The couples have been amazingly understanding.

Had we waited and planned for optimal conditions, we might still be waiting to start the program. Equipment is minimal: portable five-dollar framed 48-inch mirrors, one audiotape, a few 35mm slides, and two 16mm films suffice.

The predictable turnover of new and transient trainees might have been a major difficulty if the program had not been carefully structured to allow for this. Trainee worksheets clearly outline what happens when. Permanent faculty are available for intersession messages and for post-Clinic pick-up. So far, even though we now have 20 teams and 20 couples per semester, we have been able to manage, with the intake social worker supervisor taking responsibility until therapists can be linked up with their couples.

Screening non-Loyola applicants has been of concern, since I have not yet seen a negative letter of recommendation. The 350-dollar training fee has perhaps deterred most of the many sensation-seekers who apply. My priority, of course, is Loyola medical education. Therefore, the trainee waiting list gets longer as there are more Loyolans who elect to train.

My personal time limitations are the greatest current growth deterrent. There is no grant or other budget support to hire faculty specifically for the Sex Program.

Antisex groups have rumbled, mostly in 1972, and occasionally, like an extinct volcano, through the years. This has not been a major problem, since work of quality, quietly done, proves its own worth. Also, the President of Loyola University has been supportive at times when antisex groups have directly threatened to demonstrate. Extra security was placed on duty, and the groups did not appear.

I have invited medical colleagues and others who were curious or negativistic to attend the workshops and the supervisory sessions. This rapidly allays fears about imagined unknowns.

ADVANTAGES OF A TRAINING CLINIC

The fact that Loyola is a Jesuit institution has been a great advantage to the Sex Clinic, since the stature of the medical school enhanced trust and attraction of couples to the Loyola Program. Quality and morality are known to be priorities, so anxious couples may feel safer from exploitation. Also, being a *physician* Sex Clinic ensures ethical standards in a field already beleaguered with sensationalism and "anything goes."

For trainees, this program follows the traditional medical model of didactic teaching followed by supervised clinical experience. Knowledge and skill are developed in sequence, which influences the attitude of trainees to all of their future patients. Therefore, training medical students seems optimal to build open minds and interpersonal skills to care for their total patients. Residents, without exception, remark that they wish they had had this training earlier. None of our trainees will practice exclusively as sex therapists, but they will be physicians comfortable to evaluate and assist patients with sex problems. For all trainees, the collaborative training exposes them to the complexity of the interactional dynamics underlying sexual symptoms. The careful structure of the program allows layer after layer of these interactions to be revealed and dealt with.

The long five-hour sessions allow for getting to know the couples (and trainees) thoroughly. The intense involvement of the dual-sex team with their couple builds a healing therapeutic relationship.

For the couples, the Physician Training program has allowed for low-cost sex therapy, without discrimination against those with physical or psychiatric problems. Blue collar workers have been treated alongside millionaires in the program. Perhaps an index of patient satisfaction is the fact that about 24 couples have been willing to discuss their treatment with the news media. Some have gone on national television to tell other couples of their experience.

When indicated, the Program has referred six scrupulous patients to a priest, rabbi, or minister, with relief to those who went. Two more persons declined referral, admitting they were not ready to relinquish their *mis*interpretation of the dogma of their faith.

A real advantage of having the resource of trained full-time therapists available in and around Loyola has been to refer the approximately 10 percent of couples who require back-up psychotherapy after the seven weeks of sex therapy.

For physician colleagues, the Loyola Sex Program provides recognition of the value of sexual medicine. For the first time, the Sex Clinic serves as a diagnostic trial for cases of impotence arbitrarily presumed to be organic (therefore irreversible). Consequently, we can now challenge some medical myths, especially about diabetic impotence.[6] The cross-discipline six-year collaboration has enriched all of the involved specialties in a real way.

The research potential of the Loyola Program is considerable, but still rudimentary. Time, staff, and funds will be needed to expand this aspect. Changes in dyadic relationships, and how these changes affect sexual function, are complex but require study. Some sexual rating scales are being tested now at the Clinic, since unless we can "measure" dysfunction, how can we establish "cure?" Subjectivity is a problem in definition and in professional communication. Methodology must be carefully considered to ensure usefulness of what research is being done.

The trainees and changes in their attitudinal knowledge and skills are also under scrutiny. Self-evaluations (baseline and termination), a short test, and supervisory evaluations are used at present.

As in all of scholarship, the more we know in sexual medicine, the more we realize how little we know and how much there is yet to learn.

REFERENCES

1. Renshaw DC: Physician sexuality training program unique elective at Loyola. Chicago Med 77:868–870, 1974
2. Renshaw DC: Physician and sex therapy. S Afr Med J 50:1092–1095, 1976
3. Renshaw DC: Sex therapy in the 1970s. Psychiatr Opin 12:6–11, 1975
4. Renshaw DC: Sexual dysfunction in depression, in Kiev A (ed): Psychosomatic Manifestations of Depression. Amsterdam, Excerpta Medica, 1974, p 86–105
5. Renshaw DC: Answers to questions: Psychotropics in treatment of sexual dysfunctions. Med Aspects Hum Sexuality 11:6–9, 1977
6. Renshaw DC: Impotence in diabetes mellitus. Compr Therapy 2:47–50, 1976

Richard Green

25
Curriculum Training in Human Sexuality at the State University of New York at Stony Brook

CURRICULUM

The human sexuality training program at the State University of New York at Stony Brook is offered to undergraduates, medical students, physicians training for a medical specialty, graduate specialist physicians, and postdoctoral students in the social and behavioral sciences.

Undergraduate Level. Undergraduate courses, conducted primarily through the Department of Psychology, cover typical and atypical patterns of sexuality. Undergraduate psychology students who wish to pursue a course of independent study may apply for up to six hours credit during a semester. They are assigned to a faculty member who provides tutorial research training and develops a working relationship with the student. Some members of the human sexuality faculty hold joint appointments in the Department of Psychiatry and Behavioral Science and in the Department of Psychology.

Medical Students. A 24-hour segment on human sexuality is required for all sophomore medical students as part of the psycho-biology teaching system. Topics include typical and atypical patterns of psychosexual development, the role played by hormones both pre- and postnatally in sexual and sex-typed behaviors, medical disease and human sexuality, diagnosis and brief intervention for the treatment of sexual dysfunction, and, of particular significance, how to take a sexual history within the context of a general medical history.

Sexual history-taking is the focus of an educational research project designed to assess the most effective methods of teaching medical students. Three techniques are currently being tested and analyzed: (1) the medical student takes a sexual history from an actress who portrays a patient and the sexual history is videotaped; the student may then view the tape and receive feedback on the quality of the interview from members of the training staff; (2) students play the roles of both patient and therapist, using videotape and feedback; (3) students view a videotape of faculty members conducting a sexual history.

In the evaluation phase, students again interview a mock patient while being videotaped. Raters who are unaware of the teaching approach to which the student was exposed rate the interview on several parameters. We hope this study will generate data which will identify the most efficient techniques of teaching sexual history-taking to a general medical-student population. As part of their training, students also have the opportunity to view these final taped interviews with a faculty member.

Psychiatric Residents. In the psychiatric residency training curriculum, the same topics are covered each year at increasingly advanced levels. These topics include: sexual history-taking, treatment of the various sexual dysfunctions in males and females, common medical and psychiatric misconceptions about sexuality, diagnosis and treatment of atypical patterns of adult sexuality, childhood sexual disorders, cross-cultural aspects of human sexuality, sexuality in the aged, and the interface between sexuality and medical diseases. Residents also have the opportunity to participate in individual supervised research with members of the training faculty.

Postgraduate Education. Human sexuality is part of the continuing education program for physicians. Our most recent series of postgraduate seminars included treatment of the sexual dysfunctions, focusing on primary and second impotence and premature ejaculation in the male, primary and secondary nonorgasrnia in the female, and dyspareunia in the female. Emphasis has been on brief behavioral intervention, with a minor focus on physiological and surgical approaches.

Postdoctoral Fellowship. Our most ambitious program is a postdoctoral training program, designed for professionals who will remain in academic science, specializing in research and treatment in human sexuality. Each year this program supports nine fellows who come from such diverse disciplines as sociology, anthropology, clinical psychology, developmental psychology, physiological psychology, psychiatry, and gynecology. The program is designed as a two year program, with flexibility allowing a one to three year range.

Primary components of the first-year curriculum are several seminars, each held approximately two hours a week for six months, and tutorial research training. Seminar topics include research training in evaluation of clinical outcome studies in human sexual behavior, psychosexual differentiation, evaluation of manuscripts for possible publication in scholarly journals, critical evaluation of published articles, the role of sex hormones and other chemicals in human sexuality, biomedical instruments used to measure sexual behaviors, and the interface between medical syndromes and sexual behavior.

The tutorial research training component engages the fellow in an ongoing research project. Current projects involve atypical and typical patterns of sex-role development in children, clinical outcome of sexual dysfunction treatment, physiological and psychological parameters of sexual function, the interface between gynecologic disease and sexual dysfunction, and the evaluation and treatment of rape victims. The postdoctoral fellow functions at a level intermediate between that of principal investigator and research assistant, and often serves as project coordinator or director. During the first year, the fellow is expected to develop an individualized research program for the second year of training. The program may be a modification of a component of the first-year research project or a different project falling within the general areas outlined above. In the second-year seminars, fellows describe their ongoing research studies for group critique, outline various research models involved in studying human sexuality, and discuss effective preparation of research-grant applications to maximize opportunity for approval.

Audio-visual Production. We have produced color videotapes and 16mm color film materials which illustrate the treatment of sexual disorders, sexual history-taking, physical examination involving the sexual organs, and clinical interviews with individuals representing varieties of atypical sexual life-styles. This audio-visual library serves as a complement to lecture presentations and is also available for individual training.

Guest Lecturers. Scholars from many countries have visited our training program, and we have taken advantage of their unique skills by inviting them to present guest seminars. These seminars are open to all faculty, trainees, and research associates.

SUMMARY

The human sexuality training program at the State University of New York at Stony Brook, which is now three years old, has developed into a multifaceted, multilevel, interdisciplinary program designed to train scholars, general health care professionals, and specialists in sexual health care delivery.

William L. Maurice

26
Sex Education for Residents: The University of British Columbia Program

RESIDENCY SEX EDUCATION—THE RATIONALE

In the continuum of medical education, the principal beneficiaries of the inclusion of sexual issues in the curriculum have so far been students at the undergraduate level. It is apparent from detailed descriptions of a variety of model undergraduate programs, that cognitive and affective elements receive considerably greater attention than the teaching of practical skills.[1] Technology and ideology represent two explanations for this differential emphasis. The logistics of teaching sex history-taking and counseling skills to large classes of students are rather formidable. In addition, many feel that on ideological grounds, cognitive and attitude changes constitute prerequisites for the application of clinical skills. Given this educational orientation, it would not be surprising to find that students emerging from typical undergraduate programs would likely be somewhat limited in their capacity to apply clinically what they have learned in medical school. Indeed our experiences with senior residents in psychiatry and obstetrics/gynecology have not only confirmed this impression, but also have led us unalterably to the conclusion that *in the absence of a specific skill-training program, they are quite unable to carefully, purposefully, systematically, and comfortably elicit sex-related information from a patient.* The continuing clinical inadequacy of medical school graduates in dealing with sexual issues is one of the most persuasive arguments in favor of establishing discrete sex education programs at the residency level of medical education. Clinical ability must surely be the ultimate criterion of the need for a specific educational effort at this level and, likewise, the standard by which such a program should be judged. We are thus engaged in a remedial effort to help our residents deal with what we regard as an educational deficit.

There are other reasons for proposing a more concentrated sex education effort at the residency level. Firstly, in the pyramid of medical education, residents have traditionally functioned as surrogate supervisors for undergraduate students during the many hours when faculty are not present. Residents thus play a pivotal teaching role in the clinical years of the undergraduate program. Since clinical skills in medicine are gained largely by imitation, instructor attitudes and practices are crucial elements in influencing student behavior. It is unrealistic to expect undergraduates to deal with sexual concerns unless the rationale for doing so is understood, accepted, supported, and *practiced* by at least some supervisors in the system. If this premise is accepted, it then becomes self-evident that efforts directed at enhancing the sex education of residents may profoundly influence other students for whom the resident serves as an example. (It is worth emphasizing as well that the influence of residents not only extends downward to undergraduates, but also upward to faculty.)

Secondly, apart from the significance of the resident as an undergraduate teacher, direct benefits to the resident's patients are not inconsequential in defining the purpose of a specific sex education program at this level. Sexual problems are found in relative abundance in the practices of psychiatrists, obstetrician/gynecologists, urologists, and family doctors.[2] Those physicians in particular must therefore regard their skills as incomplete if they are unable to properly deal with a sexual complaint. It is especially regrettable to find these skills lacking in psychiatrists, since their special expertise in interviewing and psychotherapy make them potentially invaluable community resources in the treatment of sexual difficulties.

RESIDENCY SEX EDUCATION—THE EXPERIENTIAL MODEL

It may seem unnecessary to suggest that special educational experiences may profoundly influence one's professional direction. My own experience as a senior psychiatric resident indeed played a determining role, not only in developing a career interest in sexual issues, but also in shaping a philosophy and approach to professional sex education. During my first year of residency training, I can recall having confessed to the Professor my discomfort surrounding discussions of sexual matters with patients. His response can be vaguely recalled as one of insubstantial reassurance. The net result was my approaching the end of residency training as I began: unlettered in sexual matters and unschooled in the process of gathering sex-related information from patients. During the final year of training, a virtual metamorphosis took place, *not* however through lectures, books, small group discussions, or explicit movies. Rather, the change took place in the context of an elective research project in an established clinic specializing in the treatment of sexual dysfunctions. The project involved interviewing patients beginning treatment, and its purpose was to determine the extent of any association between sexual dysfunctions and psychiatric illness.[3] As part of the data-gathering process, audiotape recordings of treatment sessions (which were a routine facet of the treatment process) were reviewed. As the project evolved, the fringe benefits provided by the opportunity of listening to the tapes proved of greater significance than the extent of patient psychopathology. Exposure to the tapes represented a watershed in my own capacity to deal with sexual concerns. This device at once provided not only *permission* to enter what had previously seemed a charged field, but also a *rationale* and *method* for doing so. It provided a model for history-taking and treatment skills, and a vehicle for affective and cognitive change. It was itself both "desensitizing" and "resensitizing." In an unintrusive and inoffensive way, it illustrated the purpose of attitude shift, that is, for the interviewer to be capable of demonstrating an accepting and nonjudgmental posture. From the perspective of cognitive change, the tapes represented a virtual audio textbook as the panorama of sexual events were described by the participants.

The point of departure in the process described was the learning of a new skill. Knowledge and attitude change seemed to follow, rather than precede, skill change. Although this may not be in accord with the ideology of some sex educators, this observation should not be altogether surprising to seasoned sex therapists. The imposition of the behavioral task of sensate focus exercises in sex therapy begins a chain of events that in turn results in a new level of patient self-understanding, and an enhanced awareness, appreciation, and sensitivity toward what is sexual. These insights in turn permit and encourage other behavioral changes, and so the cycle continues. If such a process is of proven value for sexually dysfunctional patients, it is reasonable to assume that an analogous sex education model could be constructed and effectively applied to (presumably less disordered) health care professionals.

This "experiential" model has, in fact, been tested on a series of senior residents in psychiatry and obstetrics/gynecology. Our experience with this group has led us to the following conclusions: (1) that regardless of formal undergraduate educational inexperience, resident sex education can begin with the process of learning to take a sexual history; (2) that this method unambiguously provides the resident with the capacity to be useful to patients; (3) that professional competence can be directly tested in such a system, rather than be inferred; (4) that the process of talking with patients about sexual experiences usually results in a greater appreciation of the variety of human sexual activity, and that this in turn allows for a greater degree of professional self-understanding, tolerance, and flexibility; (5) that the most effective instrument for penetrating the barrier of professional inhibition is the experience of talking with patients seeking help because of their sexual problems, and therefore prepared to reveal intimate details of their sexual activities; and (6) that the development of confidence and comfort in talking with patients about their sexual experiences itself provokes a sense of professional curiosity, and that this secondarily provides a stimulus for cognitive change.

PRINCIPLES FOR LEARNING SEX HISTORY-TAKING

It is part of medical education rhetoric to suggest that clinical skills are learned "by doing." Learning to "do" has often meant immersion (sometimes submersion) in a clinical situation with little in the way of prior skill-training. The baptism-by-fire medical internship is still a familiar memory to many. The price paid by patients in such a system has rarely been calculated. In the area of sexual difficulties, the results of professional inadequacy are often readily apparent. Every sex therapist no doubt has a catalogue of stories documenting the unfortunate consequences of inadequate care in the hands of otherwise fully-trained and well-intentioned professionals. Applied to the treatment of sexual disorders, this version of "learning by doing" is unreasonable and potentially destructive. Specific clinical skills in history-taking and treatment must be acquired in a manner which protects the patient.

The first principle in designing such a system is that it must begin with repeated and direct observation of the trainee's interviews by skilled supervisors. Residents usually have mixed feelings about being directly observed. Initially there is a feeling of reassurance in not having to assume complete responsibility for something unfamiliar and uncomfortable. However, this soon gives way to a feeling of unease which may have several origins. Firstly, the resident may experience embarrassment at inadvertently revealing personal thoughts and feelings through the process of asking questions. This of course, becomes "grist for the mill," in that it provides a supreme opportunity to deal simultaneously with attitudinal and cognitive elements as well as interviewing techniques. Secondly, some residents may feel such a degree of supervision to be unnecessary. Many professionals misunderstand the process of learning to treat sexual disorders as simply learning a treatment technique. The complexities involved in acquiring the information on which to base decisions about treatment are often vastly underestimated. That is, professionals (especially those who regard themselves as "liberal-minded") tend to overrate their history-taking and therapeutic skills in this area, much the same as sexually dysfunctional couples beginning treatment sometimes protest to doubting therapists how excellent their "communication" is on sexual matters. For both groups, recognition of their limitations is often only apparent in retrospect. To the extent that exaggerated views of a resident's capacity results in resistance to direct supervision, this must be explained and interpreted by the supervisor.

The second principle is that history-taking and therapeutic skills are easier to teach and learn when dealing with one patient than with two (i.e., a couple). Student involvement with couples should be delayed until confidence and comfort have developed in managing single patients. Our clinical training experience with residents began with an attempt at pairing them with experienced therapists in the assessment and treatment of couples. The intricacies of the foursome were overwhelming for the novice. Interviewing a couple not only involved acquiring two histories, but also entailed simultaneously dealing with more general aspects of the couple relationship. One result for the resident was that of repeatedly "bailing out" by handing the interview back to the experienced therapist. Another outcome (especially for psychiatry residents) was a premature shift in the interview from the unfamiliar and discomfiting sexual agenda, to the more familiar theme of relationship conflicts.

Dealing with the solo patient is a much more familiar situation for the resident since it is the model practiced from the beginning of medical training. Since many sexual dysfunction clinics emphasize treatment of the couple, opportunities to see patients alone may be few. The advantages to a novice, however, are many. Most importantly, the agenda can usually be more easily confined to one of dissecting the person's specific sexual concerns, and there is less chance of inappropriately deflecting the discussion to other matters.

TECHNIQUES FOR LEARNING SEX HISTORY-TAKING

The teaching of clinical skills can thus be conceptualized into two stages: The first is learning history-taking and elementary counseling skills in the context of dealing with the solo patient. The second is the assessment and treatment of couple-related sexual difficulties.

The first stage can be subdivided into four steps:

1. Together with a supervisor, the resident listens to or observes a series of taped assessment interviews of individual men and women seeking help for sexual problems. As an introductory experience, this provides a picture of the syndromes commonly seen in a sexual dysfunction clinic, a review of the questions asked to clarify the nature of the complaint, and the techniques of asking questions and dealing with responses. This step provides the model and makes clear what is expected.

2. With model in hand, the student attempts to apply it to a live clinical situation using simulated patients, both men and women. This technique has recently been described in teaching sex history-taking to medical students.[4] "Programming" the simulated patient is not difficult. If standardized, this device provides a useful pre–post evaluation instrument for testing clinical skills. More importantly, using a simulated patient allows for "sins of omission and commission" on the part of the resident without causing damage to the patient and guilt to the student. It uniquely provides for immediate supervisor and "patient" feedback, and provides yet another forum for dealing with attitudinal and cognitive variables.

3. The resident and supervisor (together as co-participants), interview a series of individual men and women with sexual concerns. The experience for the resident evolves from one of observation to one of gradually taking more responsibility as confidence and capability permit. Such assessment interviews inescapably involve some level of therapeutic intervention even if simply in the form of reassurance, encouragement, or disseminating information. To the extent that this requires experience and confidence, such counseling skills almost invariably lag behind the development of the resident's history-taking ability. The supervisor cannot responsibly withdraw until the resident has shown competence in both facets of the interview.

4. The resident conducts the assessment of the patient alone and the audiotaped interview is reviewed with the supervisor. The timing of the move to the fourth step varies from one resident to another. While the presence of an experienced co-participant is initially reassuring to the resident, the supervisor's presence may eventually become an inhibiting influence. The resident may continue to defer to his more knowledgeable and seasoned colleague beyond the point where this is necessary or reasonable. Full confidence for the resident only occurs when patients are managed successfully without direct help.

The second stage in teaching clinical skills involves a recapitulation of the first, but in dealing with couples rather than individuals. The same four steps can be used: (1) listening to or observing taped interviews, (2) simulated couple interviews, (3) co-participating with a supervisor in direct patient contact, and (4) assessing and treating couples alone with indirect supervision.

The entire eight-step process can be viewed as a continuum, although overlap is obviously possible and perhaps even desirable. The level of experience acquired would depend on the resident's educational objectives. Minimal expectations for all residents should include: (1) comfort in discussing a broad range of sexual issues with both men and women, topics that would include developmental sexual experiences and more recent sexual activities; (2) the capability of asking questions which properly clarify common sexual complaints; (3) the ability to counsel patients with sexual concerns on the level of appropriately giving reassurance, encouragement, and advice; and (4) awareness of one's own professional capabilities and limitations so as to know when to refer.

For residents in specialties other than psychiatry, these minimal objectives are both attainable and sufficient. They can be accomplished within the first stage of training described, that is, in confining most of the resident's clinical experience to individual patients rather than couples. These objectives are sufficient in that they provide the resident with a wide range of diagnostic skills, but with more limited therapeutic proficiency. Training objectives for psychiatry residents should go beyond the minimal objectives outlined. As a medically-based discipline dealing with the vicissitudes of human behavior, psychiatry (unlike other specialties) can have a special place in the evaluation and treatment of those with sexual disorders. The intense emphasis in psychiatry on interviewing and psychotherapeutic skills, including interpersonal treatment techniques, provides an extensive foundation upon which the psychiatry resident can build experience with sexually-troubled patients. Thus residents in psychiatry should have experience with all eight steps in the training scheme described. Sex therapy with couples in particular can also provide a special opportunity to learn some of the many facets of marital therapy, and in addition, the resident can gain a better perspective on the mutual influences of psychiatric disorders and sexual dysfunctions.

The notion of emphasizing the non-psychiatric resident's educational experience with individual patients unfortunately conflicts with the prevailing ideology and approach to the treatment of sexual dysfunctions in which the focus is on the couple. Although apparently inconsistent, our experience suggests that it is nevertheless defensible for the following reasons:

1. As the discipline of sex therapy has matured, it has become apparent that the solution to some sexual problems does not necessarily involve treating the couple. The prime example is the use of masturba-

tion as a treatment device for women who have previously been anorgasmic.

2. Notwithstanding the rhetoric of medical practice which emphasizes the family (as in "family physician"), most physician-patient encounters involve *one* person as the patient. However regrettable this situation may sometimes be, it appears unlikely to change dramatically in the immediate future. To the extent that this observation is accurate, it would seem unnecessary to expect the nonpsychiatric resident to develop the more complicated clinical expertise of dealing with couples. Indeed, our own experience indicates that even when familiar with this modality of patient care, the resident's opportunity to practice clinically at this level will likely go unexploited.

3. Sex education courses represent a new development for residency-training programs. Modest proposals in terms of objectives and time (a valuable commodity in any postgraduate program) have a greater chance of acceptance and success. Overambitious efforts at training in this area may, firstly, represent a challenge to the priorities of the particular residency program, and secondly, if unsuccessful, jeopardize the attainment of what have been previously described as minimal goals. Modest objectives for a resident group do not exclude a more intensive and extensive experience for an individual with a special interest or aptitude.

SUMMARY

Despite the great progress made in establishing sex education programs at the undergraduate level, it is our impression that graduating medical students are unable to apply clinically what they have learned. The relative neglect of residency sex education programs is historically understandable, but nevertheless regrettable for at least two reasons: (1) residents are not available as "role models" to reinforce and continue the undergraduate program on a clinical level; and (2) residents in some specialties (obstetrics and gynecology, urology, psychiatry, and family practice) will encounter a disproportionately great number of patients with sexual difficulties and thus will find their ability to deal with these issues wanting. Our training experience with residents suggests that: (1) a resident sex education program can *begin* with the process of learning sex history-taking and elementary counseling skills, (2) whatever attitudinal changes are required of the resident do not necessarily have to precede the clinical experience but rather can occur in tandem or as a result of it, and (3) dealing with sexually distressed people is professionally disinhibiting, results in a greater degree of professional insight and tolerance, and itself provokes a sense of professional curiosity which then serves as a stimulus for cognitive change.

Residents in different specialties have different requirements. All residents should be capable of comfortably eliciting sex-related information from a patient, integrating information in the form of a diagnostic statement, and counseling individuals on the level of giving information, advice, reassurance, and encouragement. Psychiatry residents should build on their knowledge of human behavior and their clinical base of interviewing and interpersonal therapeutic skills by learning to diagnose and treat sexual disorders both with individual patients and in the context of the couple relationship. The latter experience can also provide an opportunity to learn aspects of marital therapy, as well as the mutual influences of psychiatric disorders and sexual dysfunctions.

REFERENCES

1. Lief HI, Karlen A, (eds): Sex Education in Medicine. New York, Halsted Press, 1976
2. Burnap DW, Golden JS: Sexual problems in medical practice. J Med Educ 42:673–680, 1967
3. Maurice WL, Guze SB: Sexual dysfunction and associated psychiatric disorders. Compr Psychiatry 11:539–543, 1970
4. Engel IM, Resnick PJ, Levine SB: The use of programmed patients and videotape in teaching medical students to take a sexual history. J Med Educ 51:425–427, 1976

Norman Rosenzweig
F. Paul Pearsall

27
The Sexuality Curriculum at Sinai Hospital of Detroit

The Department of Psychiatry at Sinai Hospital of Detroit has offered educational programs in human sexuality since September of 1972. As relatively late arrivals on the scene of sex education for health-care professionals, we were in a position to learn from the experience of others who had pioneered in this field. Some of these persons have contributed their valuable time to this book. The following description of the Sinai program is organized to allow the reader to trace the steps we followed in establishing our program, to examine how we articulated that program with the development of a clinical training and treatment program, and to see how we have adapted our program to better meet what we have perceived to be the changing needs of our student and patient population.

PLANNING AND PREPARATION

The authors of this chapter began their involvement in the pedagogical dimension of the field of human sexuality in the early 1960s. Both of us were involved with the teaching and supervision of students from the undergraduate level to medical and graduate school levels. We had both acknowledged early in our work what Calderone describes in her chapter as the "intersecting cycles and repetitions of patterns in sex attitudes and behavior," and were well aware that the topic of human sexuality could not be approached in the same manner as other curricula. We have attempted to maintain a historical perspective as we have structured our curriculum.

As each of the authors in this book has emphasized, we knew that health-care professionals could no longer pretend to help persons with their sexual development without first coming to grips with their own sexuality and any mythologized, judgmental orientation they may hold. As Lief stresses in his chapter, the temptation to impose one's own value system on the patient can only be avoided when the professional has been able to place his or her own sexuality in a realistic perspective both personally and professionally.

We decided early on to focus on the attitudinal dimension of the curriculum before working toward the enhancement of interventive skills. When we began our curriculum design in the "AMJ" period (the years following the publication of the Masters and Johnson volumes on human sexual response and human sexual inadequacy), there was already a proliferation of "sex therapists" rushing to help people with their sexuality, while neglecting the one dimension that separates the professional from the layperson—the possibility of offering "educated help."

We began by acknowledging our own need to look at our own sexual value systems as well as the more academic concerns of curriculum design. We saw the opportunity to do both and to draw from the ideas of others by attending the Summer Program in Human Sexuality offered by the Institute for Sex Research at Indiana University. From that excellent experience, we borrowed aspects of the Kinsey approach to sexuality curriculum, amended some of their ideas and those of other participants, and learned, as they themselves have learned over the years of their own self-evaluation, several things not to do.

We also collected materials from other programs operating throughout the country, and talked directly with program coordinators. One of the major purposes of this book is to facilitate this preparation process by providing a background reflecting the thinking of many of the programs now in progress, from which the reader may more readily develop his or her own program ideas and strategies.

Communication with Administrative Bodies

After we had clarified our thinking and reaffirmed our belief that the attitudinal dimension of the curriculum would be our initial focus, meetings with hospital administration were held. We did not want various committees to be in a post hoc position of approving or disapproving programs, but rather wanted them to be involved from the outset in planning the program. We hoped that such an approach would allow the administration to function from a position of knowledge and participation, anticipating rather than reacting to any potential problems they might encounter.

Our experience with the administration at Sinai Hospital of Detroit was in keeping with the optimism described in the chapter by Vasconcellos and Wallace and, as they state in their work, probably related to open, clear communication and specific definition of terms, purpose, method, and responsibility.

Staffing

As we met repeatedly and for long hours discussing the formation of our program, we knew that we could not and should not serve as the total faculty of the program. As Lief warns in his chapter, one of the most serious difficulties with a sexuality curriculum is managing to institutionalize the program and to separate it from the personalities of individual faculty and program designers. We had already seen examples of programs which initially succeeded due to the enthusiastic participation of the original faculty, but which later faltered due in part to the absence or subsequent lack of involvement of the original faculty.

We decided to offer our program to our own psychiatry staff as a starting point, with the hope that this would "teach the teachers," generate future small group facilitators, and "test" our program on an audience with whom we could maintain contact, receive direct evaluation and criticism, and minimize the impact of any of our early mistakes through person-to-person discussion.

As Bjorksten and Aronoff point out in their chapters, matching information to be presented to teacher and teacher-style is an important task. We felt that the broader the base of faculty from which to choose, the more success we would have in articulating our program with the various cognitive styles of the students. Even in our first program, we attempted to divide topics not only by interest and competence, but also by comfort and style. While this is a highly subjective process, the attempt seems worth the effort.

The decision to start small and start with our own group and staff was most productive in terms of constructive feedback, as well as in raising staff interest and involvement in the program. It also resulted in the participation of members of various disciplines, including various teaching and facilitator styles. This was to pay off later when we attempted to offer programs to various student groups, such as students from the physician's assistant program, parent groups, and hospital house staff.

The Lesson Plan

Other contributors to this book have offered outlines and materials from their programs. Our general approach was to present a series of topical segments, each consisting of brief didactic lectures, accompanied by explicit audio-visual materials, followed by small group discussions, with the strongest emphasis on the latter. As we received the contributions for this book, we noted the consistency with which the opportunity for small-group discussion and attitude examination was highlighted by the majority of authors.

Our first task was to decide how much lecture should be balanced with how much film, and how much group discussion. Flatter's chapter on small-group process is drawn from our experience with over 400 participants in our programs. He stresses our emphasis on well-trained, experienced, supervised, and sensitive group facilitators. We feel that the small-group experience is the core of the curriculum, but we also know that unsequenced, disconnected, directionless, or poorly led groups can be at best a waste of time, and at worst potentially destructive for facilitator and student alike.

We have devoted considerable time in training our facilitators and in evaluating their skills from program to program. Facilitators meet together between segments during our programs for mutual support, identification of potential problems and favorable outcomes, and the pooling of their mutual experience to suggest techniques to one another.

At this point, we feel compelled to share a bias we have regarding the conduct of the small-group experience. There are programs which overtly or covertly encourage intimate physical contact as a part of the small-group agenda. It is our feeling that such a practice is unproductive and potentially counterproductive to the program goal of examination of sexual attitudes and feelings. To assume that "sexual experimentation" in this context is effective in attitude reassessment is to think it possible to separate intimate sexuality from the whole of the person's emotional being. We feel this is not possible and that experimentation of this type can unbalance effective systems that cannot be put back into balance in an academically based program. Indeed, we have suggested availability of clinical referral for students who experience difficulty with the program itself. Intimate personal experimentation or attempting to extend the range of sexual experience should be done, in our bias, at the election of the individual, external to the educational program itself.

Our next concern in the lesson plan was films. As we have stated, whenever we have neglected our own advice and shortened group time in favor of lecture or film, evaluations have reflected participant dissatisfaction with this decision. However, without appropriate stimulus from films and lectures, the groups seem to lack purpose and cohesiveness. Briggs' chapter deals with issues related to the use of audio-visual materials, and we share her opinion on the importance of the role of the technician. Indeed, the team approach to the entire program is most important, and the technician is certainly a key member of the team.

The lectures were our third concern. Certainly, we did not consider ourselves sex experts, but we did feel that "demythologizing" was one important objective. It is also given emphasis among the several objectives identified by Alouf and the other authors who have shared their programs in this book. We initially thought that the didactic material could serve as a "safety valve" for those students who chose not to become immediately involved emotionally in the group experience. We anticipated that such persons would temporarily immerse themselves in "facts and data." Of course, we were wrong in this assumption, for those who did not become involved in the groups tended to be equally uninvolved in the didactic aspects of the program.

The intent of the lectures was to structure the focus of each segment, to provide transition points, and to serve as a modality for the presentation of data. Handouts were distributed for all lectures, consisting of detailed bibliographies, related charts, and supportive material which the student could use for later reference. This material helped to emphasize to the student that he or she need not attempt to assimilate all of the factual data during the workshop, thereby furthering our goal of preparing the student rather than truly teaching the subject matter. The material distributed also seemed to serve as a "transitional object" for some of the participants, who carried the package of material with them through dinners and during coffee breaks.

We rehearsed and re-rehearsed the lectures, cross-checking one another's facts and style of presentation. We were particularly careful to spot any hint of agism, sexism, or other judgmental or insensitive orientation to subject matter. Several "dry-runs" were held to check timing and relevance of films. Such planning and rehearsal is time well spent in reducing disruptions caused by faulty projectors, redundancies in lectures, repeats of jokes, or poor program-fit that may lead to diversion of major program goals.

As indicated earlier, another distraction from the goals of the educational program is a type of regression by some participants who criticized the smallest details from the color of the name badge to cold carrots at dinner. While such criticism cannot be avoided, it helps if teaching staff and group facilitators are aware of the nature of such criticism and make every effort to minimize the frequency of small problems. It also helps if staff are able to maintain their sensitivity and responsiveness to criticism while keeping in mind that criticism is unavoidable and due in part to not only our mistakes and misjudgments as faculty but also to the threatening nature of sexuality curriculum.

Sequencing of the program involved consideration of several options. The chapters by Stayton, Cole, Bjorksten, and Gebhard identify key components of a sexuality curriculum. Placing these in a lesson plan was a difficult task. One approach would be to follow a developmental course from conception through adulthood to variations in human sexuality, including such specialized topics as sex and the physically impaired, and the paraphilias. Another would move from a cultural, nomothetic approach to a more personalized, idiographic focus. Our decision was to attempt to follow a sequence from what seemed safer and less anxiety-provoking material at the start, gradually moving to more threatening material. Both films and lectures followed this plan, progressing from a more factual, societal focus to more subjective, personal issues, such as sexual relationship options, gender identity, and personal-professional role relationships.

A problem with our early programs was our attempt to do too much for too many too quickly. We have learned over time to present a small amount of material accurately, hoping that the subjective and attitudinal aspect of the experience would set the stage for more effective processing of data by students at a later date.

Our early attempts at curriculum design did not focus at all on treatment techniques. We learned to include more on this subject as time went on, but did so in a manner that promoted student evaluation of their attitudes and feelings regarding sexual distress, rather than focusing on skills or technique. It was our bias that treatment skills were best learned following the experience of the initial program, and through observation and supervision.

Finally, our lesson plan dealt with the issue of timing. Options included an intensive workshop format, daily course work, weekly seminars, and other variations on these themes. We anticipated, and have since verified a "student life-cycle" which is experienced in the sexuality program. There is movement through an initial period of anxiety, against which the student erects various defenses, with the student finally moving to a strong need for closure and preparation for "reentry" into personal and student-professional roles. The intensive weekend format served our purposes, allowing a complete focus on the program and freedom from other duties during that time.

We also decided to divide the program into two phases. The introductory program was followed several weeks later by an advanced workshop. We did this to allow time for the participants to react and deal personally with the program. The impact of the sexuality curriculum seems delayed, with a possible "refractory period" or "numbness" as the student reenters his or her life space.

One entire student group was invited back to Sinai one year following their participation in the workshop. They reported similar experiences, but also stated that the workshops had tended to initiate a growth process that continued long after the program was over. When students returned for the advanced workshop six weeks following their basic workshop experience, their starting point was far ahead of the point they had left off earlier. The two-phase model seems to foster this type of personal development.

We made every effort to stick to time schedules so that films started on time. Lectures were timed closely, meal times held as scheduled, and discussion groups conducted on schedule. We found it helpful to schedule all meals and coffee breaks for the entire group together. We have noted that several kinds of grouping form in this intensive type of experience, including the discussion groups, spontaneous subgroups, and the total group of students. Being aware of these levels of group formation and dealing with the several levels in the program design is helpful in preventing individual or subgroup isolation, scapegoating, or other such phenomena. To help with this, we have scheduled a final session with all faculty and facilitators present so that a "closure" discussion may be held. While this approach may seem unwieldly, our experience has been most favorable with this "total-group closure" approach.

EVALUATION

The chapter by Miller and Williams on assessment of sexuality programs reflects our own position regarding this aspect of sexuality curriculum development. We began by using the Sex Knowledge and Attitude Test (SKAT) developed at the Marriage Council of Philadelphia by Harold Lief. We divided the test into pre- and postprogram-administration format, and later added our own assessment instrument. We have continued to modify our assessment technique and will report on these efforts in the near future.

Because of our own involvement and investment in our program, we invited an evaluator from another program to assess our project. Dr. William Stayton served as a participant-observer and made several helpful suggestions. As an example, Dr. Stayton sensed that we were sending a double message: on the one hand we claimed that our program was not designed to teach treatment techniques, yet lecture examples and illustrative materials often related to clinical material. He felt that this aroused confusion which tended to distract the students from the goal of attitude reassessment. We have since made many efforts to be more clear in purpose. The suggestions by Dr. Stayton and the "outside view" that he offered were extremely valuable, and we suggest that other programs employ this form of assessment as they begin their curriculum.

STUDENT GROUP

After our work with our own department, we opened our program to health-care professionals, at first from the local area, and later from throughout the country. It is valuable to have prior knowledge of the background of the students. We have also found it helpful to encourage participation in the program by significant partners of the students. Partners are placed in different discussion groups, but mutual attendance seems to decrease the difficulty of the "reentry phenomenon."

We have found it helpful to alter our films and lectures from program to program, group to group. This not only helps us maintain our sanity by reducing the boredom quotient, but also takes into account the different entry points of each student group. The first rule for all group facilitators is protection of each of the group members from pressure or any form of coercion. We feel that the sex educator is still at risk if he or she neglects the uniqueness of each individual or is not aware of what Calderone refers to in her chapter as "the inevitable conservative and often unreasoned backlash" to sexuality education.

At Sinai, for example, there was much corridor gossip about our weekend workshops, and we sensed that staff curiosity could lead to unwarranted criticism. We dealt with this situation by offering a special program to hospital staff, including all employee levels. This strategy has helped diminish jokes and talk about "a sex clinic over there in psychiatry." Once hospital personnel have gone through the program themselves, they seem to value the experience and speak most highly of their time with the program.

CLINICAL TRAINING

As stated, it has not been the purpose of our curriculum to train therapists. We offer internships, fellowships, and other programs for that purpose. We have attempted to promote a reexamination by the professional of his or her own attitudes, so that the professional will be better able to acquire the skills necessary for effective, informed intervention.

As our curriculum developed, it did so along with the development of our treatment program. The Problems of Daily Living Clinic is a section within the Department of Psychiatry at Sinai Hospital of Detroit which offers short-term treatment for various difficulties which persons experience in coping with transitional life crises.

The intent of this program has been to offer a truly "preventive" psychiatric service with clearly contracted treatment goals. A multidisciplinary staff offers treatment in the area of crises occurring during the life-cycle, ranging from premarital adjustment through family therapy to death and dying programs. One aspect of the treatment program includes help with sexual distress. In the clinic, such distress is defined as a breakdown in the intimate sending and receiving systems between persons. This program has grown through the last five years and is now in the process of publishing the results of a treatment program of over 100 couples.

Psychiatric residents, psychology and social work interns, medical students, residents in family medicine, and other professionals have been trained in the Clinic. Here, the student begins with the sexuality curriculum outlined in this chapter. Then the student is given the opportunity not to become a "sex therapist," but rather to acquire the skills to work sensitively, nonjudgmentally, and effectively with various aspects of sexual adjustment. All students view several cases on videotape with a supervisor present, observe ongoing cases with a supervisor, take part in an ongoing weekly seminar, attend courses in human sexuality with a more didactic focus, and are later assigned to work with a senior therapist in team treatment. Finally, the student works with another student as a team.

Full-time students are also involved in the research programs within the Clinic and serve as lecturers and group facilitators at sexuality programs. They terminate their experience with a final case presentation. This amounts to approximately 1000 hours of directly supervised work in such skills as history-taking, case preparation and feedback, behavioral prescriptions, and follow-up. Students have evaluated this experience most highly and continue to feel that the attitudinal program was the most important aspect of the experience.

SUMMARY AND CONCLUSION

This concluding chapter has attempted to integrate and illustrate several points made throughout this book. We are indebted to all of the authors who have given their time to promote this important field. It is hoped that this chapter and this book will help the reader to a more productive journey in the development of a sexuality curriculum; for certainly such an effort is much more a journey than a final destination. The field of human sexuality may well be one avenue for drawing the profession together in mutual educational and clinical efforts. If we can do so cautiously but with constant effort to improve through innovation, scientifically but never without humanness and sensitivity, then we as professionals may be better able to travel with our patients, rather than around or at them.

PART VI

Appendixes

Ronald J. Bantis

Audio-Visual Aids in the Sexuality Curriculum

Audio-visual aids have often proved to be excellent learning tools for educating professionals. However, before planning to use audio-visual aids for workshops, lectures, seminars, or therapy, one must ask these questions:

1. What type of audio-visual aids do I want?
2. Where do I get them?
3. What is the cost and availability?
4. What equipment do I need?
5. Can I manage this equipment or should someone else do it?

These are crucial questions that must be answered well in advance of the presentation.

It has been my experience that all audio-visual materials should be prescreened. A film, as described in a catalog, may sound ideal for a particular purpose, but when it arrives, you may find it contains contradictory data or that it has an obnoxious soundtrack. If you do not discover these facts until the day of your presentation, your whole program may suffer. I have found it necessary on certain occasions to edit-out scenes and completely re-do film sound tracks so that the final product will illustrate various concepts without distracting or confusing the audience. An overall review of audio-visual materials to be utilized is a good rule to practice.

In Appendix A, I have listed several audio-visual materials, many of which are commonly used in sexuality workshops, seminars, and clinical situations. The list contains films used in the Problems of Daily Living Clinic, the National Sex Forum, and other programs. More detailed information and additional films may be obtained by contacting the distributors listed in Appendix D.

Be sure to allow enough time for shipping and receiving films, tapes, slides, and other materials. After your order has been confirmed, call the distributor to be sure that everything will still be available at the requested time.

Audio-visual materials are offered in a variety of formats. The most common are:

slides	$\begin{cases} \text{35mm (2 x 2) slides} \\ 3\frac{1}{4} \text{ x } 4'' \text{ (lantern) slides} \\ \text{35mm (filmstrip) slides} \end{cases}$
motion picture	$\begin{cases} \text{standard – regular 8 – motion picture} \\ \text{super 8 – motion picture} \\ \text{16mm – motion picture} \end{cases}$
videotape	$\begin{cases} 1'' \text{ videotape (reel)} \\ \frac{1}{2}'' \text{ videotape (reel)} \\ \frac{3}{4}'' \text{ videotape (V-matic cassette)} \\ \frac{1}{2}'' \text{ videotape (Betamax cassette)} \end{cases}$
audiotape	$\begin{cases} \frac{1}{4} \text{ audiotape (reel)} \\ \text{audiotape (cassettes)} \end{cases}$

Some materials are only available in certain formats, so be sure to specify which format suits your needs.

Once the decision has been made to use audio-visual materials, the next question is: "Who will run the equipment?" At this point, one should evaluate whether he or she can technically handle such equipment. Most equipment is relatively simple to operate, and a brief lesson by a qualified technician may suffice. One must know how to set up, thread, and focus projectors. A projection bulb may burn out, so it is also a good rule to have spare bulbs for all projectors being used and know how to replace them quickly. Where it is important to maintain a high level of professionalism throughout a presentation, one might consider having a projectionist-technician to assist in all technical aspects of the program.

Audio-visual aids can be very useful in the education of professionals, but without the proper presentation and technical ability, an otherwise good presentation can be turned into an unprofessional and totally negative learning experience.

Name of Film and Available Formats	Brief Summary	Usage	Availability
Sex Education			
Sex and the Professional 25 min/Color S 16mm/S8	A film about health-care professionals and their attitudes toward sexuality.	Used mostly for workshops and orientation seminars.	Texture Films
Sexological Examination 28 min/Color S 16mm/Video	A woman therapist instructs a couple in self-examination so that they come to understand their own and each other's body and pleasure.	Also used for workshops and seminars.	Multi-Media
Physiological Responses of the Sexually Stimulated Male in the Laboratory 16 min/Color S 16mm	Demonstrates the full sexual response-cycle, utilizing Masters & Johnson terminology and concepts.	Occasionally used clinically. Excellent for workshops and seminars.	Focus International
Physiological Responses of the Sexually Stimulated Female in the Laboratory 16 min/Color S 16mm	Demonstrates the full sexual response-cycle, illustrating external genitalia in pre- intra- and postorgasmic stages.	Same as above.	Focus International
Erogenist 11 min/Color S 16mm/S8/Video	A woman receives a full body massage with body lotion, then is manually stimulated to orgasm without intercourse.	Frequently used clinically and for workshops and seminars. Excellent for showing touching and closeness.	Multi-Media

Name of Film and Available Formats	Brief Summary	Usage	Availability
Give to Get 11 min/Color S 16mm/S8/Video	Demonstrates a mutual full-body massage with kissing and breast caressing, then moving to intercourse on a waterbed.	Frequently used clinically and for workshops and seminars. Soundtrack leaves something to be desired.	Multi-Media
Squeeze Technique 10 min/Color S 16mm/S8/Video	Demonstrates the technique introduced by James Seamans in "Premature Ejaculation." Some errors in narration.	Used clinically for treatment of premature ejaculation and occasionally for seminars.	Multi-Media
About Sex 15 min/Color S 16mm	A discussion about sex with young people dealing with myths, birth control, feelings, led by Angel Martinez.	Used for workshops, seminars, and lectures. Very interesting for young people.	Texture Films
Fullness 13 min/Color S 16mm	A young couple share their relationship and sexuality during the woman's eighth month of pregnancy.	Used clinically, for workshops and seminars.	Multi-Media
Hope is Not a Method 16 min/Color S 16mm	Presents information about conception and birth control.	Used for workshops, seminars, and lectures.	Perennial Education
Sexual Response Cycle Color/35mm Slides	A series of color slides illustrating male and female sexual response.	Frequently used clinically and for workshops, lectures, and seminars.	Multi-Media

Title	Description	Notes	Distributor
Both/And 15 min/Color S 16mm	A group of nude people discuss their bisexual experiences and backgrounds; interspersed are scenes of group sexuality activity and images of the group members.	Used for workshops and seminars.	Multi-Media

Masturbation

Title	Description	Notes	Distributor
Male Masturbation 5 min/Color S 16mm	A young man masturbates himself while lying on a couch.	Frequently used clinically and for workshops, lectures, and seminars. This one moves quickly.	Focus International
Feeling Good 25 min/Color S 16mm/Video	Men discuss their boyhood experiences and feelings today about self-sexuality; interwoven are images of two men's masturbating patterns.	Used for workshops and specific clinical situations.	Multi-Media
Margo 11 min/Color S 16 mm/Video	A young, heavy-set woman bathes and then oils her body. She then stimulates her genitalia to a moving orgasm.	Frequently used clinically and for workshops and seminars.	Multi-Media
Joy in Her Pleasure 11 min/Color S 16mm/Video	A mature couple share a pleasurable masturbatory experience. She guides him to manually stimulate her to several audible orgasms.	Used clinically and for workshops and seminars. Has a very good sound-track.	Multi-Media

Name of Film and Available Formats	Brief Summary	Usage	Availability
Homosexuality			
Vir Amat 15 min/Color S 16mm/S8/Video	A film about two men enjoying each other sexually and nonsexually.	Used frequently for workshops, lectures, and seminars. Occasionally used clinically.	Multi-Media
A Gay View/Male 17 min/Color S 16mm/Video	Three gay men intensely and personally discuss their first sexual attitudes and experiences.	Used for workshops, seminars. and specific clinical situations.	Multi-Media
Holding 15 min/Color S 16mm/S8/Video	Shows a loving lesbian relationship; both enjoying oral-genital activity and self enjoyment.	Used frequently for workshops, lectures and seminars. Occasionally used clinically.	Multi-Media
Lavender 35 min/B&W 16mm	Two young women relating in a variety of nonsexual ways. A narration explains their feelings toward loving and lesbianism.	Used frequently for workshops, lectures, and seminars.	Perennial Education
In Winterlight 18 min/Color S 16mm	Two women share their sexuality in a tender and loving manner; they use their hands and a vibrator to enjoy and pleasure; one reaches a marked orgasm.	Can be used for workshops and seminars. Occasionally used for specific clinical situations.	Multi-Media

CBS — Homosexuals 35 min/B&W 16mm	A film produced by CBS for television about how society sees the homosexual, as well as how homosexuals see themselves.	Used mostly for workshops and seminars. An excellent film on how things were a decade ago.	Carousel Films, Inc.
Heterosexuality			
Unfolding 17 min/B&W 16mm/S8/Video	Double and triple exposures blend together ocean, hills, sun, man, and woman into a dream-like universal awareness.	Used clinically and for workshops and seminars. A good introductory film. We changed the soundtrack to Wagner's "Siegfried Idyl."	Multi-Media
Rich & Judy 12 min/Color 16mm/S8/Video	A young couple engages in some outdoor activities, including some sexual pleasuring, foreplay, oral-genital activity, coitus.	Most frequently used clinically as well as for workshops, lectures, and seminars. A gentle introductory film.	Multi-Media
Ripple of Time 24 min/Color S 16mm/Video	A mature couple of ages 50 and 63 leisurely discuss their sexuality and engage in an active lovemaking episode.	Frequently used clinically and for workshops and seminars. Excellent for showing the value of sexuality to older persons.	Multi-Media
Close-Up 20 min/Color S 16mm	A young couple engage in lengthy foreplay, afterwards moving to an active, audible coitus.	Used clinically and for workshops and seminars. An excellent free-form film.	EdCoa Productions

321

Name of Film and Available Formats	Brief Summary	Usage	Availability
Free 12 min/Color S S8/Video	An active Black couple walk out into the country. They undress and have a fun-filled sexually stimulating afternoon.	Frequently used clinically and for workshops and seminars. A warm feeling film.	Multi-Media
Sun Brushed 14 min/Color S 16mm/Video	A young couple make love on an outdoor deck.	Can be used for workshops, seminars, and clinically.	Multi-Media
Humor & Mood Alteration			
Birds, Bees & Storks 5 min/Color S 16mm	A cartoon, narrated by Peter Sellers, with a father having a talk with his son about sex.	Frequently used for workshops, lectures, and seminars. A good ice-breaker.	Contemporary Films
Love Toad 5 min/Color S 16 mm	A funny animation of two colorful bean-bag toads having mutual animated oral-genital sex and intercourse.	Frequently used clinically and in workshops, lectures, and seminars. A funny film.	Multi-Media
A Quickie 5 min/B&W 16mm	A couple hastily perform a quick sex act in a small room.	Frequently used clinically, and for workshops, seminars, and lectures. Fast moving and amusing.	Multi-Media

Title	Description	Notes	Producer
Bodies 5 min/Color S 16mm	A cast of many people undress and show their physiques to the camera.	Used for workshops, lectures, and seminars. Fast and humorous.	EdCoa Productions
World Erotica 160 Color 35mm Slides	An outstanding collection of erotic art drawn from a variety of cultures and time periods.	Used for workshops, lectures, and seminars. An excellent mood-setter.	Multi-Media
Genesis 34 Color 35mm Slides	Cartoonist Dan O'Neill illustrates a humorous look at the creation of man and his penis and all the taboos he imposes on his sexuality.	Excellent for workshops, lectures, and seminars.	Multi-Media

Disability

Title	Description	Notes	Producer
Just What Can You Do 23 min/Color S 16mm/Video	A discussion led by Dr. Theodore Cole with a panel of spinal cord-injured persons about their sexuality.	Mostly used for workshops, lectures and seminars. Occasionally used clinically.	Multi-Media
Touching 16 min/Color S 16mm/Video	The man in this film is a paraplegic with a C-6 spinal cord injury. The couple in their 30s are in constant contact throughout the film; a high emphasis on oral sexuality.	Same as above.	Multi-Media
If Ever Two Were One 14 min/Color S 16mm/Video	This film shows a paraplegic man and his partner, both in their 30s, engaging in a sensous, slow-paced love-making episode.	Planned as a companion film to *Touching*; excellent for workshops, seminars, and lectures.	Multi-Media

Name of Film and Available Formats	Brief Summary	Usage	Availability
Possibilities 12 min/Color S 16mm	A warm sensitive film showing a male quadriplegic's sexual relationship; several positions are demonstrated.	Used clinically and for workshops, lectures, and seminars.	Multi-Media
Don't Tell The Cripples About Sex 39 min 16mm/Video	Two men and two women with cerebral palsy discuss their sexual experiences and self-images with Dr. Ted Cole in this two-part film.	An excellent film for workshops, lectures, and seminars.	Multi-Media
Give It a Try 33 min/Color S 16mm	A quadriplegic man who is recently home from the hospital makes an attempt to reestablish his relationship with his able-bodied wife.	Used clinically and for workshops.	Multi-Media
A Bridge to Disability 15 min/Color S 16mm	After a car accident and hospitalization, a young man learns that he may never walk again. This identity crisis is discussed.	Used clinically and for workshops.	Multi-Media

Title	Description	Usage	Format
Artists' Fantasy 15 min/Color S 16mm	This film is about a young man confined to a wheelchair by cerebral palsy. He shares his feelings about sex and body image, along with his fantasies revealed in his drawings.	Used for workshops and lectures.	Multi-Media
Bringing It Up 17 min/Color S 16mm	Dr. Ted Cole models the kinds of questions and issues that are raised when a spinal cord-injured person starts asking about his sexual future. James Boen shares the feelings and concerns he had when he was injured several years ago.	Used clinically and for workshops and lectures.	Multi-Media

APPENDIX B

Books: Sexuality and Physical Impairment

All books listed below are available through Multi-Media Resource Center.

1. *Sexuality and the Spinal-Cord Injured Woman,* Sue Bregman
2. *Sexual Options for Paraplegics and Quadriplegics,* Thomas O. Mooney, Theodore M. Cole, M.D., and Richard Chilgren, M.D. Boston, Little Brown and Company. 1975.
3. *The Sensuous Wheeler: Sexual Adjustment for the Spinal-Cord Injured,* Barry Rabin, Ph.D.

APPENDIX C

Video Tape: Program on Disability

3/4″ Cassette. All video tapes run 30–40 minutes.

1. *Orientation to the Sexuality of Physical Disability.* Several basic assumptions and objectives to disability sex education and treatment programs are discussed.
2. *Anatomy and Physiology of the Sexual Response Cycle.* With the help of schematic artwork and photographs, a man and woman describe the anatomy of the adult sex organs and their functions during sexual arousal.
3. *Medical and Institutional Aspects.* A physician presents an illustrated classification of disabilities that includes both children and adults who have been disabled suddenly or progressively.
4. *Body Image, Disability and Sexuality.* A panel of physically disabled men and women discuss some thoughts and feelings about their bodies. They contrast the difference between being disabled at an early age as opposed to later on in life.
5. *Sexual Counseling of Physically Disabled Adults.* Four rehabilitation professionals explain how they conduct an initial interview and how they deal with people who have different life-styles. They also discuss how their own personalities and attitudes affect what they do and how they do it.
6. *Sexuality and Disability Adjustment.* A physician, a psychologist, and a disabled man and woman discuss the relationship of sexuality to other aspects of adjustment.

7. *Sexual Variations*. Several aspects of the range of sexual behavior, including transvestism, exhibitionism, transsexuality, and homosexuality are presented to dispel myths and to increase understanding.

APPENDIX D

Suppliers of Audio-Visual Materials

Carousel Films, Inc., 1501 Broadway, Suite 1503, New York, New York 10036.

Contemporary Films, McGraw-Hill, 330 W. 42nd Street, New York, NY 10036.

EdCoa Productions, 310 Cedar Lane, Teaneck, New Jersey 07666.

Focus International, Inc., 505 West End Ave., New York, New York 10024.

Multi-Media Resource Center, 1525 Franklin Street, San Francisco, California 94109.

Perennial Education, Inc., P.O. Box 236, 1825 Willow Road, Northfield, Illinois 60093.

Texture Films, Inc., 1600 Broadway, New York, New York 10019.

Index